AMERICAN
CONSTITUTIONAL CUSTOM:
A Forgotten Factor In The Founding

AMERICAN CONSTITUTIONAL CUSTOM:

A Forgotten Factor In The Founding

By

BURLEIGH CUSHING RODICK

PHILOSOPHICAL LIBRARY
NEW YORK

To the Memory of
S. M. S.
Artist — Administrator — Scholar

"The charm of guessing ancient motives from the records of ancient deeds fascinated me. There is much in the pursuit to appeal to a gambler." D. G. Hogarth: Accidents of an Anti-quary's Life, Macmillan, London, 1910, p. 2.

"The American constitution is no exception to the rule that everything which has power to win the obedience and respect of men must have its roots deep in the past and that the more slowly every institution has grown, so much the more endur-ing it is likely to prove. There is little in the Constitution that is absolutely new. There is much that is as old as Magna Carta." James Bryce: The American Commonwealth. Two volumes, Macmillan, New York, 1910, Volume I, p. 28.

"The myth that the fathers modelled the American Constitu-tion on the British instrument dies hard . . . So positively native to the American soil is the Constitution of the United States that it is surely an American institution if there is any such thing." Wilfred E. Binkley and Malcolm C. Moos: A Grammar of American Politics, New York, Alfred A. Knopf, 1949, p. 39.

FOREWORD

This is a thoughtful book for thoughtful readers. It is also a pioneering work in a historical analysis and interpretation in a field which lies closely beside the most familiar pattern of American history, but which has not been sufficiently surveyed by those whose interest has been concentrated upon the outcome of the work of the Founding Fathers of the Constitution rather than upon the influences drawn from the political heritage, which has so largely determined the direction of their thought and activities.

The American Revolution was no exception to the rule of all revolutionary movements in that the ideals which it treasured most and for which it fought with deepest conviction, were old, familiar principles of justice and freedom, ignored or abused by the government in power but cherished and given new life by the compelling individualism of colonial society. The Revolution began as a movement to recover the "rights of Englishmen;" its creative task was to weave these into a new pattern, that of the "rights of Americans." This task was so absorbing, involving the great and almost untried experiment of federal union and the diverse interests of a population flung out over a wide continent, that the forward-looking creators of American polity progressively lost sight of the old world rehearsal of their great drama of democracy, in the long history that stretched from Magna Carta to the struggle against Stuart tyranny in the seventeenth century. Yet, as these pages amply prove, the protests and the rebellion against King George III and his ministers were justified by the same reasoning as had found voice in Coke's championing of the common law and Locke's theories of constitutional government.

These are familiar facts. But what is not familiar, and furnishes the charm of exploration in this volume, is the analysis of the American political heritage in its own home-land, distinguishing the political claims of the seventeenth century puritans and the new, wealthy commercial class from the self-centered Whigs of the eighteenth century. Which of these, how far and whence, entered into the colonial scene?

In the effort to answer questions like these, the author of this book has devoted years of intensive study. His achievement, offered with the modesty of a scholar who is aware of the essential limitations of all pioneering, will be gratefully appreciated by those who wish to see this great experiment in democratic government given its proper place in the elusive but vital history of freedom.

JAMES T. SHOTWELL

CONTENTS

CONTENTS

PREFATORY NOTE

These antiquarian notes are so brief and fragmentary that the writer is by no means certain that he should print them; yet he has spent so many years of labor in their preparation that he is tempted to put them in book form while he is still alive and able to see them through the press. The documentary material dealing with this period is so vast that no person could hope to exhaust it in his lifetime. Since he has left so many of the sources unexplored, the writer feels that he should not call this a work of research. He has, however, expended so much thought and labor upon the project that he hopes it may have some slight value as an interpretative study.

The evidence seems to reveal the fact that we had an Anglo-American constitutional and cultural heritage. Such indeed was the view of some of the earlier writers. In recent years there has sometimes been a tendency to treat such a viewpoint as a "myth" by emphasizing the purely indigenous factors of our constitutional growth. Yet surely our bill of rights as well as certain other phases of our American constitutional system have had their earlier English counterparts. At the same time the writer feels that he has recognized the growth of certain constitutional customs that were more or less the product of our American political climate. He hopes that the tone and temper of his work will indicate that he has sought humbly for the truth and is not a special pleader. In tracing political and social forces there is always the danger that one may be guilty of the error in logic known as *post hoc ergo propter hoc*. One should always ask the extent to which similar situations have been the product of similar forces and state his conclusions with caution and moderation. By rigorous condensation and excision we have reduced three hundred years of constitutional custom to less

than two hundred pages of text. Custom naturally contains
a recurring element so that a certain amount of repetition
has been inevitable. This was especially true of our revolutionary period and its aftermath when the customs of freedom and authority alternated with persistent regularity. Yet
we have tried briefly to indicate the particular conditions that
marked the onset of each custom, its actual impact and resi-
dual effects. The custom made for continuity; its factual
framework for modification.

This writer naturally owes a great debt to the specialists
who have explored the general field. He feels especially indebted to *McLaughlin's Constitutional History of the United
States* and his *Foundations of American Constitutionalism.*
He did not read these two volumes till he had completed the
first draft of his work and the fact that he arrived at similar
conclusions by working independently may help to strengthen
their validity. His debt to *Hockett's Constitutional History of
the United States* and *M. Conyers Read's The Constitution
Reconsidered,* is scarcely less great. Professor Hockett has well
emphasized the element of continuity in our constitutional
growth. The volume edited by Professor Read was eclectic in
its viewpoint, yet this writer owes much to its rare insights.
He also hopes that he has assimilated his sources and developed
a synthesis that is not wholly devoid of value. This, however,
is for the reader to decide.

He also owes a great debt to his former teachers of history
and political science in the graduate schools at Harvard and
Columbia. Two of them are now numbered among those
other living whom we call the dead: — Frederick Jackson
Turner of Harvard, who gave the writer an enduring sense
of the habits and customs of the American frontier; and
Judge John Bassett Moore of Columbia, who emphasized the
importance of habit, custom and tradition in his brilliant presentation of international law and diplomacy. We also wish
to acknowledge our debt to the thousands of students who
have attended our classes in the great municipal colleges of
New York City during the past quarter of a century. In the

give and take of socialized class discussions these students have exemplified the virtues of a free and rugged democracy in action: a democracy that is strong and vital because it is firmly rooted in the past and has much in common with the great democratic movements of all ages; Wyclif and his Lollards, Cromwell and John Lilburne of the Commonwealth, Sam Adams and his men of the Boston town meeting.

We must also add our voice to that vast chorus in praise of the officials at the New York Public Library. If these notes have any value it is due in no small measure to the kindness, patience and wisdom of Mr. Lewis M. Stark, Chief of the Rare Book Division; Mr. Gerald D. McDonald, Chief of the American History Division; Mr. Sylvester L. Vigilante, head of the American History Room, and his Associates, Mr. Ivor Avellino, and Miss Shirley Barker.

Our colleague, Miss Margaret Gustaferro, with her highly specialized knowledge of American constitutional law, rendered vital aid at a critical period. We owe a still greater debt to the distinguished scholar and publicist who has written the Foreword to this work. He displayed his great kindness by reading the entire manuscript, while his rich store of scholarship and wisdom has saved us from many a slip. All the errors and imperfections that remain should be charged against the writer.

These notes may have no value yet we venture to suggest that the cause they serve is beyond price: the love of art and letters for their own sake. This is a fact that the world may some day learn, although one who shrinks from all absolutes is perhaps permitted to entertain a modest doubt. Meanwhile those who love these things must serve them as best they may for the saving of their own souls. Perhaps this was the thought George Gissing had in mind when he wrote in his *Ryecroft*: "The zeal for learning is never out of date; the example — were there no more — burns before one as a sacred fire, forever unquenchable."

It may seem a bit presumptuous for a teacher in day and evening classes in one of New York's "subway colleges" and whose "study" has so often been a subway car, to enter a general field where so many distinguished scholars have spent a lifetime of labor. Yet to quote again from *Ryecroft,* which is one of our favorite bedside books, we think we know how he felt when he wrote: —

"How many a time, after long labour on some piece of writing, brought at length to its conclusion, have I laid down the pen with a sigh of thankfulness. The work was full of faults, but I had wrought sincerely, had done what time and circumstance and my own nature permitted."

BURLEIGH CUSHING RODICK

INTRODUCTION

"For there are always some who passionately seek to hold
fast to the past; there are always others who passionately seek
to snatch at what they imagine to be the future. But the wise
man, standing midway between both parties and sympathiz-
ing with each, knows that we are ever in the stage of transition. The present is in every age merely the shifting point
at which past and future meet, and we can have no quarrel
with either. There can be no world without traditions; neither can there be any life without movement. As Heraclitus
knew at the outset of modern philosophy, we cannot bathe
twice in the same stream, though, as we know today, the
stream still flows in an unending circle. There is never a
moment when the new dawn is not breaking over the earth,
and never a moment when the sunset ceases to die. It is
well to greet serenely even the first glimmer of the dawn
when we see it, not hastening towards it with undue speed,
nor leaving the sunset without gratitude for the dying light
that once was dawn." Havelock Ellis: Studies in the Psychology of Sex. Volume VI, Sex in Relation to Society, F. A.
Davis Company, Philadelphia, 1927, pp. 641-642.

"He who looks at the constitution of individuals accustomed to eat any sort of meat or drink or do any work which
they could get, may see that they are at first disordered, but
afterwards as time goes on, their bodies grow adapted to them,
and they learn to know and like variety, and have good
health and enjoyment of life. . . A similar principle we may
imagine to hold good about the minds of men and the nature of their souls. For when they have been brought up on
certain laws, which by some Divine Providence have remained unchanged during long ages, so that no one has any
memory or tradition of their ever having been otherwise than
they are, then everyone is afraid and ashamed to change that

which is established. . ." The Dialogues of Plato. Translated by B. Jowett. Five vols. Second edition. Oxford, Clarendon Press. 1875. Vol. 5. The Law, p. 367.

The individual as a political person in the modern state is subject to a great extent to the influence of habit, custom and tradition. He stands between two forces striving for the mastery: the forces of political continuity and the forces of political change. Neither is able to gain a complete victory but a political balance is struck which is represented by the actual course of political events. This actual course is an intermingling of the two elements; the old as represented by the traditional forces; and the new, which is made inevitable by the fact that the present is always able to make headway against the past to such an extent that its various elements can never be reassembled in the precise order in which they once occurred. The political present is always firmly rooted in the political past; the stream of political thought and action is a blending of the past and the present in which there is always an element of the old in the new and the new in the old.[1]

There are many reasons why this should be so. We are the product of numerous forces which have been shaped and guided by the laws of continuity. We are influenced by our biological heritage and human nature, while it is doubtless subject to modification and change, would in actual practice seem to be a force that evolves but slowly. We are born to a complex social heritage that includes a state of society with various laws, customs, institutions and habits of thought that have their roots firmly grounded in the past. We are also conditioned by our geography and physical environment. Thus while man may at times prefer change and is at all times conditioned by it, he is also shaped by these relatively static elements.

If we examine this problem more closely we shall see that it contains an objective and subjective element. Man is influenced by the forces of custom and he also seeks to control them. Physical and natural features play a vital part in the creation of habit, custom and tradition; and while successive generations of men may at times be able to modify them, it would seem that in the endless struggle between man and nature, man is both the victor and the vanquished. The situation may be a bit different when it involves a contest between man and man, that is, the struggle among different groups of men who are engaged in recreating and re-interpreting the past. In each generation there are leaders and groups seeking to influence their fellow-men by appeals to habit, custom and tradition. The "past" is always ransacked by those persons and groups who would use it to influence the "present" and the "future." The motives may range all the way from the objective student and scholar who wishes merely to re-create the past in order that he may understand it, to those who have no interest in the "actual" past for its own sake; who conjure up a "past" that never had any actual existence and make appeals to this figment of their own imagining for the sake of what they hope may promote some personal, partisan or group advantage. Scholars may evoke the past for its own sake; others for special purposes of their own. It therefore follows that the "past" is always with us in at least a dual sense. There is the objective deterministic past which has actually shaped the present in the sense that everything which exists is the inevitable result of a long series of antecedent circumstances and an unbroken chain of historic causation.[2] There is also the "mythical" past which man has created as the result of his conscious or unconscious or "subconscious" misconceptions, imaginings and emotions. One may be as "real" as the other in the sense that "myth" may play as great a part in shaping the course of events as "fact." The chief distinction would seem to lie in this: — in the first case the custom has been received and man has been unable or unwilling to alter it, or the alteration has been a slow and gradual process extending over a comparatively long period of time; while in the case of the "myth created past" man has consciously or unconsciously endeavored to rearrange his heritage. He has been an "artist" in the selection of his "facts." Old customs have been fragmented and new customs created in a comparatively short space of time. In the first case man has been more or less the creature of his past; in the second case he has endeavored to recreate it and control it in such a way that it may be his servant and do his bidding in the re-shaping of the world in accordance with his own desires. Perhaps this involves little more than saying that man has always endeavored to re-create his past even though in doing so he has acted from varying motives and has achieved widely divergent results.

This conclusion also raises a great many vital problems: the conditions that make for victory or defeat in the struggle between man and his environment; the circumstances under which "change" is more likely to be achieved and the rate and tempo of that change. The problems involved in "man-made" customs are even more numerous: the groups mainly responsible for changing conditions; the motives and objects involved; the conditions that promote or retard the rate and direction of change; the effect of special and extraordinary conditions; the effect upon the persons and groups involved and upon our constitutional and political structure; the effect upon our intercourse with other nations.

So far as the present writer has been able to discover, no complete and comprehensive account of American political tradition has as yet been written. Such a study would be invaluable yet it would also involve the weighing and evaluating of a vast amount of material in areas where our techniques of measurement are as yet far from perfect. This is especially true of habit and custom in its relation to the electorate and public opinion and propaganda. With the limited time and space at his command, the present writer is unable to make such an extended study. It is, however, his purpose to present a brief general survey of habit, custom and tradition as it developed in early American politics with the hope that it may encourage later investigators to engage in actual pioneering within the field.

CHAPTER I

ECONOMIC AND SOCIAL FORCES

"All the institutions . . . which are now venerated as most ancient were once new . . . and what is this day supported by precedents will hereafter become a precedent." Tacitus: Annals, D. A. Talboys, Oxford, 1839, Book XI, Sec. 24, pp. 226-227.

"The impermanence of custom is a truism. Belief in the rapidity of change of custom is exaggerated, however, because it is precisely the comparatively slight divergences from what is socially established that arouse attention. A comparison of American life today with the life of a medieval English town would in the larger perspective of cultural anthropology, illustrate rather the relative permanence of culture than its tendency to change." Edward Sapir—Article on *Custom,* in Encyclopedia of the Social Sciences, The Macmillan Company, New York, 1942, Vols. III-IV—pp. 659-662.

An examination of the influence of habit, custom and tradition in early American politics must of necessity require a brief glance at the European background. America was a child of the European renaissance and the commercial revolution. Europe was able to impress the political thought of its day upon colonial America to the extent that it was applicable to American conditions and encountered no check in the form of political thought that was more indigenous to the American soil. This is attested by the fact that there is scarcely a single important feature of our American political system that does not bear the imprint of an earlier European tradition.[1]

From continental and English sources we inherited the idea of natural law and the social contract.[2] Christopher

Saint German, in his famous work entitled *Doctor* and *Student,* had declared that in England the natural law was called the law of reason.[3] Yet the term natural law survived in the chancellor's court and achieved some of its greatest triumphs in the English revolutions of the seventeenth century when it was employed by Sir Edward Coke in Calvin's case;[4] used repeatedly by "Free Born" John Lilburne, the great republican leader in the Cromwellian revolution;[5] and expanded by the republican and parliamentary writers as they based their ideas of the social contract largely upon the theory of an earlier natural law and state of nature. These concepts were vital factors in the European revolutions of the seventeenth and eighteenth centuries[6] and part of our political inheritance as a European colony. The American revolutionary leaders argued that the ideas of natural law and the social contract applied with especial force to American conditions.[7] They rebelled, as had their English ancestors, upon the alleged ground that there had been a violation of the social contract and drew their arguments from the same writers: Milton, Sidney, Harrington and Locke. Milton pleaded for the largest possible amount of individual liberty,[8] popular sovereignty and the separation of church and state.[9] Sidney emphasized the idea of the social contract as an agreement by which the people reserved certain powers for themselves with the understanding that the entire instrument might be revoked if the ruler failed to promote the general welfare.[10] The influence of these ideas may be seen in the philosophy of the American revolution and the Declaration of Independence; the concept of delegated and reserved powers, a written bill of rights, documentary constitutions and their formal amendment.

Harrington in his *Oceana* placed especial stress upon the principle that political power tends to follow the distribution of wealth.[11] He advocated a senate of natural aristocrats, a representative council and an executive agency, a secret ballot, indirect election, rotation in office and compulsory state education. His views definitely influenced the political thinking of John Adams, George Mason, and the founding fathers during the course of the revolution and the federal convention; and may have had an earlier influence in the creation of the constitutions of Carolina, Pennsylvania and New Jersey.[12] These concepts of a state of nature, natural law, social contract and the right of revolution were finally elaborated by John Locke and it was to him that the founding fathers were so deeply indebted.[13]

Closely associated with the European political tradition is the religious factor. When the first English settlements were established in America the separation of church and state had not been achieved in Europe, so that the American colonists were prone to follow the European tradition and establish state churches. Roger Williams was the first founder of an American colony definitely to depart from this tradition; yet in so doing he was following another and more radical religious custom that he had learned at the University of Cambridge. Europe had seen the rise of a democratic religious philosophy among the churchmen of the late middle ages. Extending throughout western Europe, the movement had embraced the names of Thomas Aquinas,[14] Marsilius of Padua,[15] John Huss in Bohemia[16] and John Wyclif[17] in England. Wyclif and Huss had suffered persecution and death. Their teachings had led to popular revolts. These, too, were crushed. Yet their spirit of dissent still lingered among the tillers of the soil and the trading and commercial classes of the towns.[18]

This democratic tradition also continued within the church in the form of the conciliar movement under the leadership of such men as John Gerson,[19] chancellor of the University of Paris, and Cardinal Nicholas of Cues.[20] These men endeavored to expand the ideas of natural law and the social contract[21] and reorganize the church along more democratic lines. The movement continued until the Reformation, of which it was, in a sense, the precursor. With the coming of Luther and the great national revolt among the German people, the church felt the need of establishing a united front against its enemies, with the result that the counter-reformation and the Council of Trent temporarily put an end to the liberal movement within the church itself. Yet it established a liberal tradition in the political-religious affairs of western Europe in the early national period that foreshadowed the development of a conflict between theocracy and a more liberal form of government in church and state. This struggle was also inherited by America with the result that a similar contest developed in the English colonies except in Rhode Island where the liberal tradition was adopted from the outset.

The most vital phase of this political-religious tradition that Europe bequeathed to America was embodied in the power of Calvinism. It was, so to speak, a culmination of the various forces of dissent that we have enumerated. So far as Europe was concerned it may be said to have inaugurated a relatively new order of affairs; yet, as we have indicated its roots were deep in the older traditions of European dissent. We are, however, chiefly concerned with the fact that Calvinism was well established in Europe before the founding of the first English colonies in America. It was a pervasive force that seems temporarily to have tinged the character of the New England theocracy and the Presbyterian Scots and Scotch Irish of the American colonial frontier, even though in the long run it was forced to yield to religious fragmentation and secular individualism.[22]

The American colonists also inherited certain economic traditions that have vitally influenced the growth of American politics. High on the list should be cited the English common law[23] with its traditional respect for the ownership of land. This represented law and order, stability, the maintenance of the status quo, the respect for things as they were.[24] It was a basic source of political power because the American colonies inherited the English custom of making the ownership of land, even more than the exercise of a religious test, the requirement for colonial suffrage.[25] This was especially true in the charters of the proprietary colonies which represented an attempt to continue many of the habits and customs of English feudalism in the American wilderness. Thus William Penn, as lord proprietor of the three lower counties on the Delaware, was also the political sovereign and owner of the soil.[26]

Another European tradition with vast political implications is to be found in the commercial revolution and the rise of English mercantilism.[27] America was so definitely the child of the commercial revolution that our political and social heritage bears unmistakable marks of its origin. The English chartered companies which evolved from the English medieval boroughs and guilds[28] were given such large grants of land in America, together with the right to exercise such sovereign powers as coinage, taxation, defense, the regulation of trade and private property, that under the circumstances—the distance from the mother country and the difficulties of communication—the political independence of these lands would seem to have been inevitable.[29] Thus the germ of American political nationalism was contained in the habits and customs of the English medieval boroughs and guilds that were later extended to the English trading corporations and through them carried to the English colonies in America.[30]

The early national state that emerged from English feudalism naturally retained numerous marks of its origin. The king of England still considered the state as his fief—it was, so to speak, his estate—and he was the sole landed proprietor.[31] Yet the growth of the merchant guilds and the companies chartered for foreign trade also forced a modification of this feudal concept. The English chartered companies became so powerful in the seventeenth century that they exerted an increasing influence in parliament; while in the English civil war they furnished a large proportion of the men and money that overthrew the king. These events gradually compelled the adoption of a different conception of sovereignty and a different theory of the state. In the trading corporation one exerted an influence in proportion to the number of shares of stock that he controlled in the organization. The effect of this powerful economic factor soon became evident in the affairs of state. There was a marked tendency for the new national leaders to acquire interests in the great chartered companies. One has but to call the roll of the councillors of Queen Elizabeth, the Stuarts and the Restoration to see how often they were the founders of great trading companies. Under their direction there was a definite tendency for the state to become permeated with the spirit of a great trading corporation in which one exerted power and influence in proportion to the amount of money he had invested in commercial England as a great trading venture. In feudal days one's position in society was largely determined by his holdings in land; in the new commercial age by his holdings in these overseas ventures. Yet again, there was nothing wholly new in this: political philosophers since the days of Aristotle had emphasized the stake in society idea; that there was a marked tendency for the wealth of the community to exercise a large measure of its political power.

Here, therefore, was an important European tradition carried to colonial America with the first trading companies; an element of economic determinism foreshadowing the fact that the great constitutional struggles of colonial America and the United States were to be interwoven with the relations between the state and great propertied interests. At the time of the establishment of the London and Plymouth Companies a bitter contest developed in England between the older landed groups and the newer commercial interests for the control of the government. It ended with the triumph of the commercial groups. The seeds of the same struggle were carried to colonial America with similar results. The late eighteenth century saw the slow but gradual ascendency of commercial wealth over landed interests; an event that foreshadowed the still greater triumphs of corporate wealth in the United States of the next century.

There was a strong effort on the part of the New England colonial leaders in the seventeenth century to continue the autocratic and theocratic traditions of medieval Europe with the magistrate acting as vice-regent for the king in his capacity as head of a theocratic church. A man like John Winthrop closely resembled an English magistrate of the seventeenth century with the autocratic leanings of his caste, as he endeavored to continue these old-world traditions in the American wilderness. His contempt for democratic forms of government is well-known. In an oft-quoted passage he declared that:—". . . A Democratie is, among most civill nations, accounted the meanest and worst of all forms of government and therefore in writers, it is branded with the Reproachful Epithets as Belfora muttoru capitu, a monster, etc. Historyes doe recorde, that it hath been alwayees of least continuance and fullest of trouble."[32] These Puritan leaders—John Winthrop, Master John Cotton, the Mather dynasty and Jonathan Edwards in the next century labored diligently, if ultimately in vain, to continue these oligarchic traditions of the old world in the new. It was an effort to continue the tradition of the autocratic state that Calvin had established at Geneva, that Cromwell, perhaps partly against his will, had established in England; a system that Calvinism had always endeavored to establish when it was in a position to do so.

Yet English Puritanism also bore within itself the seeds of certain liberal European traditions and transmitted them to colonial America. Calvinism itself, in announcing the priesthood of all believers and in professing to hold that church and state were separate societies, contributed towards continuing the liberal European tradition despite the rigidity of its creed and its philosophical orthodoxy. By a paradox that has never been fully explained, religious toleration was developed within an ecclesiastical organization which had been dedicated to religious conformity. It seems to have become infected with the radical political and religious thought of seventeenth century England to such an extent that it developed democratic ideas of free association, social compact and local self government. These, in turn, became the germ cells of our American "democratic" theory.[33] The spirit of English individualism in the seventeenth century thus tended to make Calvinism a liberalizing force.

This conflict between the conservatism of Calvinism that

was derived from the continental Europe of the sixteenth century and the radical political philosophy of England in the seventeenth century soon became apparent both in England and America. During the civil war there arose a fierce struggle in England between the Calvinistic Presbyterians and the Independents for the control of the government. The English colonies in America also inherited a similar contest between radical and conservative elements. As early as 1645 Winthrop observed that there were two distinct groups in his colony. He declared that: ". . . two of the magistrates and many of the deputies were of the opinion that the magistrates exercised too much power, and that the people's liberty was greatly in danger; other of the deputies, being about half, and all the rest of the magistrates were of a different judgment and that authority was very much slighted, which, if not timely remedied, would endanger the commonwealth and bring us to a mere democracy."[34]

This divergence became even clearer in the minds of the American colonists with the beginning of their great revolutionary struggle against the mother country in the eighteenth century. The leaders of the revolutionary movement realized that radical political views could not be aided by a conservative theology with the result that the older and more formal Calvinism tended to disappear. Perhaps it would be more correct to suggest that it was transformed into various units of social energy by the liberalism implicit in the spirit of English independency and the new American environment. This indeed may be little more than saying that it doubtless contributed towards the customary growth of our colonial and early national life in terms of our concepts of individual political, economic, social and religious liberty balanced by vestigial remains of sumptuary authority.

CHAPTER II

THE ANGLO-AMERICAN
CONSTITUTIONAL TRADITION (1620-1776)

"With the world of intellectual production, as with that of organic generation, nature makes no sudden starts. *Natura nihil facit per saltum*; and in the history of philosophy there are no absolute beginnings. Fix where we may the origin of this or that doctrine or idea. . . the specialist will still be able to find us some earlier anticipation of that doctrine, that mental tendency." Walter Pater: Plato and Platonism, MacMillan And Co., London, 1922, p. 5.

"Habit is thus the enormous fly-wheel of society, its most precious conservative agent. It alone is what keeps us all within the bounds of ordinance." William James: Psychology. Henry Holt and Company, New York, 1915, Chapter 10, p. 143.

The years from 1620 to 1689 represented a period in which the English government evolved certain general constitutional principles for the rule of its colonial possessions in America. They were the product of an extended constitutional evolution in England and were destined to create long continuing traditions in the American colonies and in the government of the United States.

A brief examination of these constitutional principles would seem to reveal their general concern with balance of power politics, colonialism and imperial trade. These motives were largely explicit in the grant of royal charters,[1] although it was not until somewhat later that the government endeavored to take a more direct initiative in aiding these projects.[2] As the trading classes grew more powerful the pressure upon the government for direct action in these matters gained a

9

corresponding impetus[3] until it culminated in the middle class government of Cromwell[4] and his Western Design, which represented a more or less comprehensive plan to drive the Spanish from the Caribbean and establish English dependencies in that area.[5] The movement partially failed although it led to the capture of Jamaica.[6] It is perhaps even more important to suggest that it began the custom of a more definite interest in and direction of British colonization on the part of the crown.[7]

Nor did this Anglo-American interest in the "Western Design" cease with the achievement of American independence. The custom of concern with the British West Indies became a matter of concurrent interest on the part of both Britain and the United States. The American government continued the custom during the administrations of Washington and Adams by making repeated efforts to induce Britain to open these ports to American trade and commerce. Such later developments as the Monroe Doctrine,[8] the Clayton-Bulwer treaty,[9] American filibustering,[10] the Spanish-American war,[11] the Panama Canal,[12] and the various American interventions demonstrate the continuing custom of the "Western Design" in Anglo-American policy. Cromwell endeavored without success to induce certain Puritan settlers of New England to migrate to Jamaica in order to counteract its "popish" population.[13] This custom had its later counterpart along our western and southern frontiers as British and early American governments encouraged land companies and settlers to occupy these areas and counterbalance the influence of the "popish" Spanish, French and their Indian allies.

Even before the government of Cromwell, a committee of the Privy Council in 1633, under the chairmanship of Archbishop Laud had been appointed to investigate the general problem of colonial migration as a phase of national policy.[14] Laud seems to have feared that the Puritan migration would strengthen non-conformity in the English possessions overseas. Other leaders for the crown felt that England was losing valuable groups of gentry, artisans and manual workers and that the country was suffering a loss of its gold and silver and movable goods.[15] This early thinking along mercantilistic lines marked the beginning of a customary policy[16] that continued as long as the American colonies remained a part of the British empire; it had its continuing counterpart when the early American national government under the dominance of the eastern seaboard endeavored to impose restrictions upon the expanding life of the American frontier in such matters as representation, taxation, internal improvements, military defense and statehood.[17] The power of the Laud commission was based upon the royal prerogative which was declining in the face of the growing independence of the colonies and the increasing ascendency of parliament.[18] The "executive power" of the American government under the Articles of Confederation was also unable to keep the inhabitants of the northwest frontier under governmental control and it was compelled to recognize the fact of their growing independence by the grant of the Ordinance of 1787.

As an illustration of the British attempt to continue the medieval constitutionalism of the homeland in the American wilderness, we may cite the example of the proprietary grants. It seems to have been the aim of Sir Fernando Gorges to establish in New England a government that closely resembled the medieval palatinate of Durham,[19] with a governor general, a council consisting of the New England patentees and such medieval ex-officio members as "a bishop, chancellor, treasurer, marshal, admiral, master of the ordinance and the like," together with a "court of parliament" consisting of members representing the territory, called at the will of the governor to act as a law making body. The territorial grand divisions were counties, baronies and hundreds, as in medieval England; while the English medieval system of local government was to be maintained by the sub-division of the territories into manors and the establishment of manorial courts. Provision was also made for the establishment of incorporated towns as in the commercial England of the day, with each town sending a delegate to sit in the assembly.[20]

Similar ideas abounded in the proprietary patent to Maryland under Calvert[21] and in John Locke's constitution for the Carolinas,[22] thus showing that a considerable proportion of the English nobility and gentry seem to have been obsessed with the idea that the constitutional customs of medieval England could be transferred to the American wilderness and continued in operation without any serious modification or change.[23] Strange as this idea may seem in retrospect, it had a measure of customary and constitutional warrant in the minds of the proprietary governors in the sense that they doubtless felt that certain conditions in America resembled those in England that had led to the creations of the counties palatinate on the Scottish and Welsh borders. · In both cases they seem to have felt that the distance from the home government, the presence of warlike enemies and the general condition of anarchy and disorder required the grant of exceptional executive powers to insure them against the risks of failure.[24]

It may be urged that these constitutional customs of medieval England failed to find a permanent foothold in the American wilderness. Yet the failure was in no sense due to any lack of persistent effort on the part of these proprietors; while many of these anomalous customs took a temporary root in the American soil and existed as noxious weeds tending to check the growth of indigenous American constitutional customs.[25] Many large estates carved from these proprietary grants along the Atlantic seaboard were not fragmented into small holdings until the Revolutionary era was well advanced.[26] The Gorges grant delayed the growth of local self-government in the province of Maine; while the inhabitants of Pennsylvania and Maryland were long cursed with dues and taxes of a semi-feudal nature.[27] We have also seen that it was the plan of Shaftesbury and the Whigs to continue the custom of the English palatinate in the constitution for the Carolinas[28] that was largely drafted by John Locke. It ostensibly endeavored to impose the customs of an English class society upon the American wilderness;[29] and while the attempt met with a qualified failure and never developed precisely as planned, the rise and growth of the plantation system in the Carolinas saw the re-creation of a semi-feudalistic society[30] and the evolution of class distinctions not wholly unlike the earlier customs of the English palatinate. In both situations we see the presence of large landed proprietors influenced by conditions of danger and the needs for defense and organizing along the lines of a semi-feudalistic oligarchy. This patriarchal system of government continued in the southern part of the United States until after the Civil War and traces of it still exist. In this limited sense, therefore, it may be said that English feudalism has been a continuing custom in the political and social evolution of the United States. Lord Fairfax and his enormous land holdings had vast influence in forming the early political customs of Virginia and the political views of Washington, George Mason and John Marshall;[31] and while leaders of the type of Patrick Henry introduced liberal reforms during the revolutionary era, and Jefferson succeeded in abolishing primogeniture and disestablishing the state church, it is perhaps no accident that Virginia has a continuing aristocratic tradition that has not yet wholly disappeared.

The problem of the proprietary grant represented merely one phase of the English constitutional attitude towards the government of the American colonies. The weight of authority seems to point to the conclusion that England's long-range constitutional view was that sovereign power over British territory in North America was vested in the crown;[32] that it by no means divested itself of this sovereign right by the grant of colonial charters;[33] that the colonies so created still owed it allegiance[34] and were subject to royal acts and proclamations, the royal disallowance of laws,[35] executive vetoes by colonial governors,[36] judicial review by the English courts,[37] and the acts, orders and decrees of parliament.[38] Parliamentary regulation of overseas possessions developed during the reign of Elizabeth,[39] and while they temporarily grew less with the attempt of James I to extend the royal prerogative, the Commons continued to assert its privilege in this legislative area. Thus in 1621 a bill was introduced in the Commons to defeat the monopolistic right of the New England Company to Atlantic coast fishing;[40] and while the Secretary of State denied the right of parliament "to make any laws here for those countries which are not as yet annexed to the Crown," parliament continued to assert its right to "make laws here for Virginia."[41] During the Civil War parliament succeeded to the royal power and claimed the right to legislate without royal consent. This was confirmed by the act of 19 May 1649, which established the Commonwealth and declared that "the people of England and of all the dominions and territories thereunto belonging, are and shall be and are hereby constituted, made, established, and confirmed to be a commonwealth and Free State; and shall from henceforth be governed as a Commonwealth and Free State by the supreme authority of this nation, the representatives of the people in Parliament and by such as they shall appoint and constitute as officers and ministers under them for the good of the people, and that without any king or House of Lords."[42] This act foreshadowed the American doctrine of popular sovereignty as expressed in the documentary constitutions of the first American state governments,[43] the preamble of the national documentary constitution of 1787, as well as the English Statute of Westminster passed in 1931.[44] The doctrine of parliamentary supremacy was reaffirmed by the Navigation Act of 1651,[45] by a series of Navigation Acts during the Restoration and in the great Navigation Act of 1696.[46] It may be said, therefore, that the general right of parliament to legislate for the dominions was established as a custom and principle of English constitutional law; and while the colonies raised the cry of immunity from direct taxation at the time of the American Revolution, this "rationalized" interpretation was based largely upon the older customary theories of contract and consent. Briefly to anticipate the evolution of this taxing power, we may say that it was transferred to the American Congress as a result of the

Document of 1787 and survived in the general right of Congress to exercise its delegated powers in national legislation for the people of the United States. It is true that during the period under discussion both the king and parliament largely abstained from direct interference in American colonial affairs; this abstention, however, was doubtless due in great measure to the distance from the mother country, the difficulties of communication, preoccupation with domestic and foreign problems and general negligence.[47] It would certainly be incorrect to say that it represented a carefully planned and calculated policy. Never at any time did crown or parliament admit that by their policy of abstention they had relinquished their sovereign rights. English political leaders were in general agreement in regard to the supremacy of crown and parliament over the British dominions in North America; even the English Whigs who were opposed to the exercise of some of these prerogatives in the period prior to the outbreak of the American Revolution, did not so much question the legality of these established customs as the expediency of their exercise. This concept of ultimate imperial sovereignty in the hands of crown and parliament was a principle that suffered slight variation from the time of the founding of the first English settlements in America until the formal separation from the mother country as a result of the American Revolution. A relatively unimportant exception to this principle may perhaps be found in the case of the Pilgrims. They had received no grant of corporate right from the king and based their Mayflower Compact and their right of self-government upon the principle of mutual agreement and the social compact.[48] This government may have been of doubtful legal validity, although it has been suggested that it may have been based in part upon an old custom of the sea by which passengers might form a government for themselves during the course of a sea voyage.[49] Presumably such a government would end with the voyage itself and should have been succeeded by a grant of government from the crown.[50] Since this was not the case, the colony seems to have based its local self-government upon the general theory of the social compact. Thus while the Pilgrims did not follow the general custom of allegiance to the crown under a formal grant, they seem to have based their right of local self-government upon the customary English law which permitted groups possessing a certain consciousness of kind to unite in voluntary associations.[51]

The appointment of a royal commission to investigate the affairs of Massachusetts Bay foreshadowed the coming of Edward Randolph and the establishment of the Dominion of New England.[52] Thus England resumed its custom of centralization which it claimed never to have abandoned and it was continued with varying degrees of stringency until the outbreak of the Revolution. There was ample constitutional custom for centralization combined with the anomalous customs of administrative discretion and laxity in enforcement. It might perhaps be suggested that the comparative success in the policy of centralization was a factor that finally united the colonies in its opposition. In so doing, however, they also claimed that they were defending the sound constitutional customs of natural right and social contract. In the meantime the Dominion of New England had demonstrated England's intention to make effective its customary constitutional theory of centralized responsibility of the British dominions to the crown;[53] while the custom thus affirmed developed into a broader and more uniform attempt at centralized imperial control with the accession of William of Orange in 1689.

We have suggested some of the customary duties of American colonials. What were their customary rights? They always insisted that they had the same rights they would have possessed had they remained in England. Just what did they mean by this? The answer becomes a bit clearer if we recall the constitutional revolution achieved by the great English defender of the "common law" Sir Edward Coke in the earlier part of the seventeenth century. The question is still highly controversial yet the weight of authority seems to indicate that he spear-headed the attack of the Puritans and the rising commercial classes in a dynamic revision of English constitutional law and the administration of justice. Seizing upon "Magna Carta" as his major weapon, he took this semi-feudalistic and relatively static document[54] and revitalized it until it became the "watchword of English liberty." If this is an overstatement of the situation let us hasten to add that all the authorities seem to agree that he quickened the tempo of its evolution. He first endeavored to use the courts to overcome the acts of a packed parliament. In Bonham's case and in Calvin's case, both decided in 1610,[55] he declared that acts clearly contrary to the constitution, right reason and the law of nature, were void. Failing in this attempt to defeat the royal prerogative, he joined the revolutionary leaders in getting control of parliament and was largely instrumental in shaping the Petition of Right of 1628.

This period also coincided with the founding of the first English colonies in America and the great Puritan migration. The American colonists were well aware of Coke's great constitutional struggle against the Stuart tyranny. They tended in a sense to constitute the left wing of his revolutionary army and demanded that the principles of "Magna Carta" be embodied in their charters. The words "Magna Carta" became a generic term in colonial America to describe the constitutional and personal liberties which they insisted they had inherited from England. The term was repeatedly employed by the colonial legislatures and the colonial courts and culminated in our American bill of rights.[56]

Yet even this great constitutional and functional revolution was not devoid of certain customary and relatively static elements. Despite the work of Sir Edward Coke, or perhaps because of it, there were relatively few changes in the English administration of justice until the nineteenth century was well advanced. A similar situation developed in America where many states still retain elements of the English legal system that have long been abolished in the mother country. Coke and his colonial compeers insisted that they were not constitutional revolutionists but were restoring the "ancient liberties" of an older England that had existed before the Tudor and Stuart despotisms. Coke also insisted that his conception of Magna Carta and the common law rested upon "right reason" and the "law of nature" which was immutable and unchangeable. Finally and most important of all, we see beneath the surface of constitutional change a stubborn element of custom and continuity that most writers on Anglo-American law and the Anglo-American administration of justice have tended to minimize or disregard altogether. Coke's commercial elites had triumphed over the landed elites yet in their actual ability to win their rights before the courts, most Englishmen had achieved little more than exchange one set of masters for another. A similar situation existed in colonial America where artisans, landless persons, indentured servants, Indians and negro slaves were sometimes protected by the courts as an act of grace or humanity but less often as a matter of customary right.[57] The bill of rights that evolved in the British empire of the seventeenth century consisted largely of a set of "parchment rights" as far as most of its inhabitants were concerned simply because they lacked the means to avail themselves of the rights guaranteed by this great charter of English "liberties." Briefly to digress, we might add that this problem of equal and exact justice to all still confounds the Anglo-American judicial system. The expense of litigation is so great in civil suits that the stronger party has a definite advantage in presentation and appeals; while in criminal cases the defendant who is economically powerful is in a much better position to defend himself. Such palliatives as private legal aid and public defender systems have barely scratched the surface of the problem. Britain doubtless has one of the best judicial systems in the world. Yet as late as 1945 an English judge could still say: "It is as if a person who wished to buy a cheap car were told that he could only have a Rolls or a Daimler. He would at once admit that the Rolls or the Daimler was the best of cars, but he would say that he could not afford it. So with our present system of litigation."[58]

In addition to claiming the general constitutional rights guaranteed by Magna Carta, the American colonists emphasized certain special constitutional principles which they maintained they had inherited from England. They held that the grant of a colonial charter partook of the nature of a social contract that could not be abrogated by the party making the grant because to do so would violate the principle of natural right which they claimed was a part of the British constitution.[59] Certain colonial leaders also maintained that it was a sound principle of the British constitution that rights and privileges long enjoyed tended to become imprescriptible. In their emphasis upon the social contract they were undoubtedly indebted to Locke,[60] who had in turn been influenced by the medieval schoolmen of the English and Continental church.[61] Blackstone in his Commentaries was also later to emphasize the idea that the doctrine of imprescriptible rights was one of the most ancient and revered principles of the English constitutional system.

A special word should perhaps be added in regard to the evolution of the idea of the social contract and its effects upon the growth of the English constitutional system. The theory as developed by Locke was employed by the English Whigs to limit the power of the Stuart kings,[62] justify the glorious revolution of 1688,[63] and sanction the supremacy of a parliament in which they were dominant.[64] It is perhaps significant that the group which had employed the social contract as an argument against royal absolutism, failed to employ it against themselves and the growth of parliamentary centralization under their own oligarchic control. This is an illustration of still older political custom to the effect that political struggles are quite as much contests for power as for principles and that former inequities may continue to exist under thinly disguised semantics. The change in constitutional custom as a result of the glorious revolution was in certain areas more theoretical than real. The habit of exploiting the so-called "lower orders" at home and the American colonials overseas still continued. The revolution merely meant that they had suffered a change of exploiters and that the new exploiter was parliament acting as an agent of the mercantilists rather than the king acting for the older medieval groups.[65] Another continuation of the custom may be seen in the fact that the middle class leaders of the American Revolution used the same argument of the social compact against parliament and the London merchants that the English middle class leaders of parliament had employed against the king and the older landed classes in the revolution of 1688.[66] Thus the habit of identifying the interests of one's "class" with that of the "general" welfare proved to be a continuing and continuous custom.

Another principle of the English constitution that became a vital factor in the evolution of the American constitutional system was one that developed from the grant of charters to the early English guilds. These charters were later adapted and expanded to meet the needs of companies engaged in trading overseas[67] and derived their powers from the crown.[68] The guild, the chartered company, the chartered colony and the early American states contained statements of the various enumerated powers that they might exercise as governing bodies.[69] Thus the enumerated powers of the English trading guild furnished the customary basis for the evolution that led to the idea of enumerated powers in our American constitutional system.[70] One may even say that the functional organization of the English guilds and trading companies contained the germs of our later American political functionalism.[71] Thus the Virginia Company had as its executive a "treasurer" and a group of assistants, a general court and a body of stockholders.[72] The treasurer and the assistants became the prototype of the president and board of directors of the modern business organization, which in turn foreshadowed the American executive and his cabinet or council; while the general court presaged the American legislature, and the stockholders the electorate.[73]

Practically all the ideas and principles employed by the English middle class leaders in their interpretation of the English constitution during their struggles with the Stuart kings, were later employed by the American middle class leaders in their struggles against king and parliament. These constitutional principles represented a complex intermingling of juristic and political traditions. We see the continental customs of natural right and natural law[74] evolving into the English juristic concepts of right reason and the English common law.[75] Yet, on the other hand, we also see the juristic concept of the social contract[76] developing such political connotative customs as check and balance,[77] separation of powers,[78] delegated and reserved powers,[79] limited powers,[80] and even an adumbration of British and American federalism with its concept of a territorial division of powers and its concomitant principles of local home rule,[81] the doctrine of unconstitutionality,[82] the inviolability of custom and imprescriptible rights.[83] These principles of English constitutionalism represent a more or less unbroken Anglo-American constitutional tradition in the sense that subject to certain modification and change, they have woven themselves into the fabric of our American constitutional system. The English constitutional principles of check and balance and separation have continued in the form of American political functionalism in which the American executive has become the heir of the English crown and the American legislature the heir of parliament; while the English judicial system and the English vice-admiralty and maritime jurisdiction[84] has been inherited by the American federal courts.[85] The right of the American courts to exercise judicial review may also be traced in part to the power exercised by the Board of Trade[86] and the Privy Council[87] in overruling American colonial laws and decisions as well as the judicial decisions of Sir Edward Coke in Bonham's case and Calvin's case,[88] when, as we have seen, he declared that an act of parliament clearly contrary to "nature" and "reason" was void. Since the Privy Council had the right to interpret colonial charters, the American colonies early developed the idea of limited government in relation to imperial government and law. This, in turn, contains one of the germs of American federalism since the power of the states is limited by the powers which they have delegated to the national government; while the Supreme Court continues the custom of the Privy Council in the sense that it settles jurisdictional disputes between the national government and the states, even as the Privy Council settled jurisdictional disputes between the imperial government and the colonies.[89]

Simultaneously with the growth of this incipient or inchoate federal idea within the empire is the fact that the English colonies in America early developed the concept of federalism among themselves. The most important act of voluntary union among the colonies in the seventeenth century was the New England Confederation of 1643,[90] which consisted of the colonies of Massachusetts, Plymouth, Connecticut and New Haven. Each colony appointed two commissioners to deal with war and peace, the raising of men and money in proportion to population, the promotion of justice and the rendition of fugitives and criminals.[91] The vote of six commissioners of the eight was required to execute the powers of the board;[92] and while Rhode Island was denied membership,[93] and the provision for the grant of men and money on the basis of population proved to be a serious weakness, it is perhaps well to recall that this was a written document with enumerated and distributed powers that foreshadowed the document of 1787.[94] Such a project as the Albany plan of union also represented an attempt to establish the lines of constitutional and functional demarcation within the empire;[95] and while the movement failed of success at that time, its central idea of functional and territorial division of powers was elaborated and adopted by the federal convention at Philadelphia.[96] It might even be said that an inchoate system of functional division in the administration of government had already developed within the empire prior to the American Revolution in the sense that parliament legislated in the field of imperial affairs, which included imperial commerce, interterritorial relations, Indian affairs, foreign relations and war; while each colony possessed more or less freedom in legislation and administration in such local matters as domestic relations, the laws governing master and servant and guardian and ward; the general field of probate law and the inheritance of estates; civil and criminal law and such aspects of the police power as the health, safety and education of the people.[97] Broadly speaking, these customs continued under the federal constitution with Congress succeeding parliament in the field of general legislation and the regulation of interstate and foreign commerce;[98] while the states and local government continued to possess those local laws and customs that they had already exercised as colonies and local areas within the empire.[99] It is true that the principle of territorial federalism failed to prevent the American Revolution and the dismemberment of the empire; yet this, in turn foreshadowed a continuing struggle for an internal balance of power among the various geographical sections that composed the United States. It constituted a vital phase of our constitutional development in the earlier days of the republic and failed again to maintain an internal constitutional stability when it culminated in the American Civil War.[100]

CHAPTER III

THE AMERICAN
ADMINISTRATIVE TRADITION (1689-1829)

"For, in truth, custom is a violent and treacherous school-
mistress. She, by little and little, slily and unperceived, slips
in the foot of her authority, but having by this gentle and
humble beginning, with the benefit of time, fixed and established it, she then unmasks a furious and tyrannic counten-
ance, against which we have no more the courage or the
power so much as to lift up our eyes." Essays of Montaigne.
Translated by Charles Cotton. Edited by William Carew
Hazlitt. Five volumes, London, 1923. Privately printed for
the Narvarre Society. Vol. I, Chap. XXII, p. 123.

The period from 1713 to 1753 has sometimes been called
the era of comparative "neglect" in which England permitted
its colonies on the mainland of North America to govern
themselves largely as they wished. To the extent that this
was true it helped to establish a custom of local self-government within the colonies that was so thoroughly entrenched
by 1753 that Britain's efforts at centralized control thereafter,
ended in failure and the establishment of American independence.[1] This period of colonization in America was also a
time when English leaders displayed considerable ingenuity
in creating and manipulating the balance of power in their
relations with the Spanish, Dutch, French, and the states of
the Holy Roman Empire.[2] It was an important factor in
England's ability to defend itself at home and establish colonial dominions in America, Asia and Africa against its com-
peting rivals.[3]

This period of comparative neglect of the English colonies
in America was due in no small measure to the fact that it

24

was a period in English constitutional history when there existed a virtual impasse between the executive and legislative branches of the English government in the exercise of the functions of colonial administration. The executive, as represented by the crown, was unable to function effectively through royal proclamations, orders in council, or such executive departments as the Treasury or the Admiralty; parliament refused to cooperate with men, money or supplies; and the courts of law refused to recognize royal and executive orders, proclamations, instructions and royal commissions as grounds for actions pleadable at law.[4] This naturally led the English colonies in America to encroach upon the power of the royal governors[5] and strengthened the custom of American self-government. It is again important to recall that the English Whigs had inherited the principles of check and balance and separation of powers from John Locke[6] and the revolution of 1688. Blackstone later defended these principles in his Commentaries in a statement that was widely quoted:—"In all tyrannical governments, the supreme magistracy, or the right both of *making* and *enforcing* the laws is vested in one and the same man, or one and the same body of men; and wherever these two powers are united together, there can be no public liberty."[7] The influence of Blackstone upon American thought in general[8] and American lawyers in particular in the period preceding the American Revolution was certainly not inconsiderable.[9] Despite the fact that other forces were involved, the element of custom in transmitting check and balance and separation from the English to the American constitutional system was a factor of importance.

It is largely a truism to say that England's loss of its American colonies was due in no small measure to its failure in the field of public administration;[10] yet a brief glance at England's effort in this field will perhaps be worth while if it will enable us to see its influence upon the origin and early evolution of public administration in our own constitutional system. The English constitutional custom of check and balance

and separation of powers may have been in part responsible
for the fact that the English planters and merchants were
not infrequently unable to reach an agreement with the members of parliament in the formulation and operation of mercantilistic policies.[11] The habit and custom of English individualism in matters of public policy[12] may also have been
in part responsible for the fact that the mercantilists were
not always in agreement among themselves in regard to the
legislative and administrative policies that would best promote their own interests, even though they had developed the
custom of thinking primarily of their own concerns and sec-
ondarily of the interests of the empire in general and of the
American colonists in particular. The fact that the colonists
suffered as little as they did was due in no small measure to
the poor administration and lax enforcement of these trade
laws:[13] a custom that was established at their inception and
prevailed with sporadic attempts at enforcement throughout
the period.[14] With the coming of William of Orange and
the outbreak of the war with France, England began a more
determined effort to establish and administer a stronger colonial policy. English leaders were influenced to take this step
by the needs of imperial defense,[15] the failure or inability of
the colonies to cooperate for their mutual protection, and the
fact that imperial and colonial trade was hampered by numerous acts of piracy[16] and a wide-scale evasion of the various
trade laws.[17] This led to the passage of a series of imperial
acts, the chief of which were the Navigation Act of 1696,[18]
the creation of the Board of Trade,[19] efforts to increase the
power of the customs service,[20] the establishment of the vice-
admiralty courts for the hearing of customs cases;[21] and the
issuance of strict instructions to the colonial governors in
which they were enjoined to cooperate in the enforcement of
the trade laws.[22] A surveyor of the woods had also been
appointed in 1685 to protect the royal forestry rights in the
colonies;[23] while various special commissioners were designat-
ed to observe the operation and enforcement of these laws. This
attempt at royal administrative centralization ended in failure

because of the difficulties of royal enforcement and the continued custom of colonial opposition[24] but not until it had led to a course of events that precipitated the American Revolution.[25]

After 1713 the Board of Trade endeavored to be more active in its efforts to supervise colonial administration and in 1718 it received its first legal adviser in the person of Richard West.[26] It explained that the defects in colonial administration were due in no small measure to the fact that while colonial administrative power was theoretically lodged in the crown, the channel of communications was confused by the fact that petitions might be presented either to the Board itself or the Secretary of State or the Privy Council. It suggested that it should be made an executive department with power to enforce royal orders and cited the example of the Admiralty and Treasury departments as precedents in its own behalf.[27] The King and Council refused with the result that this functional administrative reorganization was never achieved.[28] The Board and the Privy Council also urged the need for greater centralized administration in order to oppose the French advance and regulate the Indian trade along the American colonial frontier.[29] The comparative failure of these attempts at British imperial control seem, however, to have foreshadowed such early American constitutional principles as check and balance and strictly limited powers in the field of public administration.[30]

The Board of Trade also endeavored to abolish private and proprietary grants and charters and replace them with royal colonies.[31] By 1702 it had succeeded with eight private colonies and the Bahamas, while the Carolinas and Georgia were later added to the list.[32] It was unable to follow this policy with complete consistency because Pennsylvania was returned to the proprietors in 1694 and Maryland in 1715, and thereafter these two colonies remained in private hands until the outbreak of the Revolution.[33] Connecticut and Rhode Island were also able to retain their status as self-governing colonies.[34] The proprietary governors of Pennsylvania and Maryland were, however, appointed subject to the approval of the crown and required to furnish bonds for good behavior.[35] The people of Connecticut and Rhode Island also owed a general allegiance to the crown and imperial acts of parliament;[36] yet this had little meaning when it came to the actual enforcement of trade laws within their borders. The Board of Trade, therefore, urged parliament that the charters of these two colonies be abolished, or at least modified in such a way as to make for a more uniform operation of the trade laws; that their legislative acts and judicial decisions be subject to automatic appeal; and that governors be submitted to the king for royal approval. Parliament, however, refused to interfere and insisted upon leaving enforcement in the hands of the crown and executive authorities that were weak in power and poorly organized and coordinated. Thus the Board itself had no executive power and could get little effective support from the executive or the legislature.[37] This may be cited as another example of the way in which the English custom of check and balance tended to prevent the growth of unified colonial administration. Massachusetts, in particular, remained restless and dissatisfied under its charter that was half "free" and half royal. The chief cause of the difficulty seemed to lie in its continuing Puritan tradition and the fact that the trade laws represented a more or less constant menace to its complete freedom of action.[38]

In 1731 and again in 1732 the Board informed the House of Commons that the American colonies on the mainland ought to be discouraged from the manufacturing of woolen and linen cloth since the amount that they produced would reduce the amount of exports from Great Britain; that these colonies ought to be encouraged to produce naval stores and exchange them for British goods; that these naval stores could be sold to the Scandinavian countries for specie and thus keep gold in the kingdom.[39] This method of reasoning was in accordance with the custom and tradition of the mercantilists, even though it may have failed to appreciate the force of the colonial opposition that it was destined to encounter, because, in the meantime, the American colonies on the mainland were creating traditions of their own that culminated in the Revolution.[40]

It is clear, therefore, that the period from 1689 to 1753 witnessed a series of protracted quarrels among the various functional branches of the British government in regard to the nature of the imperial policy that should be applied to the American colonies. The English constitutional system, at least in its relation to the government of its colonies on the mainland of North America, was passing through a period of check and balance and separation of powers. These years also coincided with the birth and early formative period of the American colonial-state system. It would appear, therefore, that the American principles of check and balance are not distinctively American characteristics in their inception but were inherited by the colonies from their mother country during their early and most impressionable years and were transmitted by the federal convention and the document of 1787 to our national constitutional system.

The habits and customs of British colonial administration were, therefore, to a large extent repeated by the United States in its general constitutional policy as it operated in our early national era. The United States as a young nation played the same balance of power game that England had played.[41] Its rivals were England and England's former rivals, France and Spain;[42] and it was not until the purchase of Louisiana and the termination of the War of 1812 that we were able to enter upon a period of comparative "isolation."[43] The attempt of the British administrative system to exercise control over the colonies had its American constitutional continuation and counterpart in those constitutional provisions that gave the national government control over federal territory;[44] the action of Jefferson in inducing Congress to adopt a form of government for the people of Louisiana and pass legislation without consulting them;[45] and the decision of

John Marshall that the republican government of the United States had as much right to acquire territory as any monarchical country.[46]

This period of comparative neglect of the English colonies in America had its American colonial and early national continuation and counterpart in the comparative neglect displayed by the seaboard and tidewater leaders for the people along the frontier and the region beyond the Alleghenies.[47] This was true of the so-called "governor's party" in the colonial period and the Federalists of the early national era. The first national congress had, to be sure, re-enacted the Northwest Ordinance;[48] yet the administrations of Washington and Adams consistently failed to satisfy the demands of the frontier and western peoples for roads, internal improvements, defenses against the Spanish and Indians, more equitable representation in their state legislatures, and deferred the demands for statehood on the part of the people of Vermont, Kentucky and Tennessee.[49]

The opposition to the British excise that culminated in the stamp tax riots of 1765, had their later counterpart in the whiskey insurrection in Pennsylvania.[50] In both cases a people with a relatively simple economic development felt they were unfairly represented and unjustly taxed by a dominant commercial oligarchy. Viewed in this light, the fact that in the first case the oligarchy had its seat east of the Atlantic Ocean, and in the second case directly east of the Alleghenies, sinks into comparative insignificance.

We have indicated that England's loss of its American colonies was due in no small measure to its failure in the field of imperial administration. This, too, may be in part responsible for the fact that weakness in public administration has been one of the most conspicuous failures in the evolution of American functional powers under our constitutional system.[51] The low level of ability displayed by the British colonial administration in the American colonies tended to cast contempt, odium and suspicion upon all public administration in America from which it has been slow to recover.[52]

Washington, to be sure, was not unmindful of the better phases of the British administrative tradition and endeavored to apply exacting standards in appointing men to administrative positions.[53] The election of Jefferson saw no great advance in the growth of the tradition,[54] while it suffered a severe blow when the election of Jackson ushered in a spoils system in our national politics that prevailed until long after the Civil War.[55] Yet this does not alter the fact that in our early national era we had inherited an English administrative tradition which, while it may have been replete with faults, was one that strongly influenced the Federalists under the new American constitutional system.[56] The American departure from this tradition tended also to coincide with the current English custom because the English administrative system also suffered sadly from spoils and corruption during the first half of the nineteenth century.[57] The growth of "romanticism" and the "rise of the common man" may have been responsible for the enactment of much needed social legislation and the reform of election procedure; yet it also seems to have had an unfortunate effect upon public personnel administration on both sides of the Atlantic.[58]

This "democratization" of public administration in the United States was reinforced by the fact that we had inherited from Britain the theory of the right of appeal to the courts from the decisions of administrative agencies,[59] a political and economic philosophy of laissez-faire[60] and a vast frontier in which to give it scope. England's failure to enforce the trade laws in the colonies found its continuation and counterpart in the difficulties encountered by the United States in the early national period in its efforts to regulate trade with the Spanish and Indians, the whiskey insurrection, and the obstacles encountered by Jefferson in his efforts to enforce the Embargo Act.[61] In both periods we see continuing phases of the customary and well-nigh perennial conflict between seaboard and frontier, agriculture and commerce, land and capital. The disagreements among English administrators in regard to colonial policies had their counterpart in our early

national era in the bitter disputes between Hamilton and
Jefferson in such matters as banking, the tariff, taxation and
foreign policy; and the constant bickerings and disputes between Adams and those members of his cabinet who took
their orders from Hamilton.[62] We do not mean to imply
that American leaders were generally conscious that they
were following English traditions, although Hamilton in establishing the bank seems more or less consciously to have
been following in the path of the English mercantilists who
established the Bank of England. The fact that we followed
English administrative traditions so closely in the early national era was doubtless largely because our institutions and
habits of political and economic thought were chiefly of English origin. It was not until we moved beyond the seaboard
and began to expand our frontier that our political and administrative customs became somewhat more "American."
Yet even at this point there was still a tendency to revert to
some of the older customs that had prevailed in the period of
British imperial expansion before 1760; to place emphasis
upon check and balance and separation, and consider administrative posts as part of the spoils of partisan victory. Thus
an expanding America tended for a time to follow some of
the administrative customs of an earlier expanding Britain.

CHAPTER IV

TRADITIONAL FORCES IN THE

AMERICAN REVOLUTION (1760-1789)

"Our Revolutionary Fathers were the heirs of the English 'Whig tradition.' In fact, the American Revolution was itself a phase of the struggle of the English people for freedom—at least in so far as ideology was concerned. And those who look upon the American Revolution merely as a struggle between the English nation and the American nation in process of foundation miss one of the most interesting aspects of that great historic event." Louis B. Boudin: The Anarchic Element in the Notion of a Higher Law, in New York University Law Quarterly Review, Vol. VIII, Number I, September, 1930, p. 30.

"This study of a great revolution [the French Revolution] bids us reflect again on the essentially, and sometimes dangerously conservative nature of man. He may be, as Aristotle said, a political animal. He clings to the past and to his ingrained habits with the emotional fixity of a psychiatric child, afraid to trust itself out of sight of the scene it knows. And even when man moves forward—as in the case of Magna Carta and the Declaration of the Rights of Man—he does so insisting that he is returning to the past or in any case by resisting change even while he is submitting to it." Donald G. McKay, New York Times Book Review, February 1, 1948.

We have seen that the American colonial leaders had early seized upon the ideas of fundamental law, natural law and the social contract and applied them to the development of the church, the corporation and the town—the germ cells of religion, economics and politics—in such a way as to make them forms of free association and the bases of an American liberal tradition. The new country proved to be a fruitful soil for the landless and dispossessed of Europe:[1]—free land, the need for self-reliance, the struggle with the wilderness and the Indians, the gradual decline of the older English class distinctions and the opportunities for trade combined with the spirit of English individualism to create an American tradition that was more or less indigenous to the soil.

Thus matters stood in 1760, at the beginning of the great political struggle between England and the American colonies. The event has generally been considered a great political revolution as indeed in a sense it was; yet it is still possible to trace a considerable measure of continuity beneath the surface of constitutional change. Many of the forces that created the Revolution had developed through a long period of time and had largely effected their results before the outbreak of the war.[2] A student of the period cannot fail to be impressed by the extent to which the American leaders drew upon the precedents of seventeenth century revolutionary England in waging their contest and in laying the foundations for the American national state in the eighteenth century.[3] They endeavored to arouse the people to defend their "rights" in much the same way in which the parliamentary leaders had aroused the people of England to defend their "rights" against the Stuarts.[4] There were, of course, Tories like Thomas Hutchinson, who so loved the habits and customs of the mother country that they were unable to break away from them. John Adams thought they represented one-third of the population; in wealth and education they may have represented an even greater proportion. Yet such leaders as John Adams and Jefferson took pains to rely to a great extent upon English thought and experience in advancing the revolutionary cause. As the war drew nearer they relied upon the arguments of fundamental law and natural rights that had been employed by the Puritan and Whig revolutionists of seventeenth century England.[5] In so doing they were doubtless aware that they were appealing to the traditional individualism of their fellow American colonists.[6] Many of the individualistic doctrines of the seventeenth century—the ideas of natural law, individual liberty, the social contract, balanced government, the right of revolution and a government of limited powers, as presented in the writings of Milton, Sidney, Harrington and Locke—had also been cardinal doctrines with the English Whigs and had, at least in part, been woven into the fabric of the English constitutional system.[7] This, indeed, was one of the chief reasons why the American leaders adopted such pleas: they were based upon habits, customs and traditions that could be presented before the English bar of justice. They also appealed to the traditions of American individualism that had been inherited from England and developed and grown stronger in the American environment.[8]

The political philosophy of Locke seemed especially suited to the customs of the American environment and the colonial leaders were not slow to recognize the fact.[9] Locke had endeavored to harmonize the rights of "liberty" and "property" by claiming that the right to hold property was in itself a natural right[10] and that this property was not to be taxed without the owner's consent. This argument appealed especially to the rising commercial classes in the American colonies as it had appealed to the rising commercial classes in seventeenth century England. Locke's view of the origin of property as the work of nature appropriated by man also coincided with American conditions where a large proportion of the population was engaged in agriculture and where those who had occupied land along the frontier without receiving a title from the king, reasoned that this land should by natural right belong to its users.[11] Locke's repeated references to a "state of nature" coincided with the relatively simple customs of the American frontier inhabited by pioneers who were compelled to adopt certain customs of the Indians in order to survive; while his philosophical serenity of spirit had its appeal for the more cultured leaders of the seaboard who had rejected the sterner aspects of Calvinism and were receptive towards the pantheistic deism of the eighteenth century.[12] John Adams, the lawyer,[13] Franklin, the philosopher and man of affairs,[14] and Samuel Johnson, the president of King's College, united in praising the political philosophy of Locke, or at least those phases of it which they felt coincided with American conditions and needs.[15] Thus the leaders of the American Revolution relied in no small degree upon the same arguments of natural law and natural rights that had been employed in the English revolutions of the seventeenth century and both were in no small measure indebted to the political philosophy of Locke.[16]

This attempt to justify the philosophy of the American Revolution by an appeal to certain English philosophers of the seventeenth century was strengthened by the growth of political and social customs largely derived from England even though they had been subject to certain modifications in the new American environment. Among these traditions may be cited the habits of the English yeomanry and commercial classes and their ways of agriculture and workmanship; the English common law with its individualistic bill of rights; and the English system of county and local self-government. The American colonists were able to take these customs and adapt them to their own needs partly because, as we have already indicated, the period from 1713 to 1753 saw the growth of an impasse between the executive and legislative branches in Britain which encouraged a custom of inaction and neglect in relation to the English colonies in America.[17] This, in turn, was in part responsible for the growth of self-government by the American popular assemblies.[18]

This loss of British prestige was followed by an attempt actively to implement the centralization which the British had generally maintained was implicit in imperial affairs by transferring to America the agencies of the customs and vice-admiralty.[19] It was perhaps a bit ironic that the British should have endeavored to assert their strength in their period of weakness; that they should have abandoned their older tradition of "salutory neglect" and attempted to strengthen imperial control when it was too late to make it effective. Perhaps we possess a prescience in the problem that they could not enjoy. We must, however, recognize that it was an effort to make effective the general theory of the older colonial system:—that the colonial possessions overseas should be generally subservient to the interests of the mother country. Such a system was essentially brutal and selfish and apparently destined ultimately to end in the disaster to the country that endeavored to enforce it. Nor could the British leaders plead complete ignorance of the possible results of such a policy:— the Navigation acts of the seventeenth century, implemented by British naval power, had been relatively successful in defeating Dutch competition, securing British supremacy on the high seas and its control of foreign trade.[20] They had, however, been far from successful in their efforts to regulate domestic trade within the empire.[21] They had almost invariably failed when applied to Ireland,[22] while the custom of smuggling was so prevalent in America and throughout the empire in the eighteenth century that the agencies charged with the enforcement of these trade laws had adopted the habit of disregarding their more or less open violation. They remained on the statute books yet were by no means generally enforced.[23] Nor can it be said that the British leaders were not warned that the effort to depart from the current custom of relative non-action would be fatal. Adam Smith's great book came too late to prevent the war yet timely and repeated warnings had been issued by such members of the Whig opposition in parliament as Pitt, Wilkes, Barré, Fox and Burke. The government had persisted and passed the Sugar Act of 1764, which definitely aimed to tax the colonies.[24] This constituted a more or less radical innovation. The colonies were accustomed to acts of trade established for the purpose of regulating imperial commerce. They were not accustomed to direct taxation by parliament.[25]

The colonial opposition to Britain's political and economic policy was also extended to include certain British social customs where the political implications were less important, or at least less obvious. Thus, for example, during the years 1749-1764 there were persistent rumors concerning the possible establishment of an Anglican episcopate in the colonies despite the fact that not a few Americans or their ancestors had fled from England to escape this religious tradition[26] and were definitely opposed to its establishment in America.[27] This was especially true of the colonists in New England.[28] It is doubtless significant to recall that while the period from 1763 to the outbreak of the Revolution saw the growing influence of the lawyers in place of the clergy as leaders of public opinion, nevertheless the non-Anglican clergy were far from idle in promoting the revolutionary cause. Such events as the Quebec Act and the Boston Massacre were bitterly attacked by the Puritan clergy of New England and their sermons were widely distributed in pamphlet form. Thus the Protestant clergy of the country did much to remind the Americans of the Anglican oppressions of Charles I and Archbishop Laud that had been inflicted upon the English Puritans in the seventeenth century and to warn the colonists that these same forces were again upon the march.[29]

In tracing briefly the evolution of Anglo-American custom during the period from 1761 to 1772, we should perhaps reiterate that the American colonial leaders were making an appeal for the vindication of rights which they regarded as already established within the existing British constitution.[30] In so doing they were following a course which resembled that of the English parliamentary leaders in their long struggle against the Stuarts in the preceding century. This is not surprising when we recall that both drew much of their political philosophy from the same sources: Harrington, Milton, Sidney and Locke. A considerable number of the American political leaders were lawyers who had received their legal training at the English Inns of Court[31] and their political principles were based upon "Magna Carta," the English common law and English political customs, in short, the principles of the British constitution, which, in turn, according to the British political philosophers, were based upon the law of nature and "right reason."[32] From these general theories the American colonial leaders deduced the specific political principle that there should be no taxation without "representation" and no taking of private property without their own consent. It might indeed be said that in the seventeenth century the English parliamentary leaders were appealing to a monarchy that had overstepped these bounds, while the American colonial leaders were appealing to a monarchy to protect them against a parliament that had been the transgressor. That indeed is true yet it would seem to be overshadowed by the fact that both groups were appealing against a functional political agency that had overstepped its bounds within its current constitutional framework with the result that British subjects had suffered a loss of property rights without their own consent. In England the specific complaint had been against the monopolies, the forced loans levied by Charles I after the dissolution of parliament in 1626, and tonnage and poundage. The last two forms of taxation were especially obnoxious since the Commons argued that arbitrary taxes had been abolished by the Petition of Right of 1628. These autocratic methods had culminated in the period of personal government by the king (1629-40), the levies of ship money during the years 1634-37, and Hampden's case in 1637. These events have their American counterpart in the general efforts to tax the colonies following the Seven Years War:—the plans to increase and strengthen the Navigation Acts; the desire to levy taxes to pay for the upkeep of armed forces in the colonies as a defense against the French and Indians, even as Charles I had endeavored to make new levies to strengthen his naval forces against the French; the passage of the Navigation Act of 1765 and the issuance of writs of assistance to aid the imperial revenue officers in their search for smuggled goods. Here, too, the situation was not without a precedent because such legislation had been authorized by parliament for the mother country by the acts of 12 and 14 Charles I and 7 and 8 William III; while the provisions dealing with the writs of assistance had been extended to the colonies by the act of 14 Charles I and had already been employed in Massachusetts by Governor Shirley.[33]

This act was followed by what has been called the "great debate" in the colonies in which James Otis, in making his famous plea against the writs of assistance, based his argument in large part upon the political philosophy employed by the English parliamentary party of the seventeenth century in its struggle against the Stuart tyranny. He argued that the writs of assistance were void because they were contrary to natural equity and the constitution and that even parliament could not pass an act that was contrary to the constitution.[34] This analysis contains a considerable number of the individualistic doctrines of the seventeenth century parliamentary puritans: natural law, individual liberty, the social contract, a balanced government and a government of limited powers. Even his statement to the effect that if parliament were to pass an act contrary to the constitution it would be the duty of the court to relegate such an act into disuse, is a repetition of the argument employed by Coke in Bonham's case and Calvin's case;[35] and while the principle was never accepted in England, it was destined to become one of the precedents for the establishment of the American doctrine of judicial review.[36] It is also important to recall that Coke's "Bill of Liberties" was written into the English Petition of Rights of 1628, which, in turn, became one of the leading sources of the American bill of rights. Otis, in following the path of natural law and natural right that had been blazed by Coke, was stating clearly and forcibly the viewpoint that seems to have been more or less widespread among the colonial leaders.[37] Sam Adams, writing to Dennys De Berdt under date of December 20, 1765, declared: "The primary, absolute, Natural Rights of Englishmen as frequently declared in Acts of Parliament from Magna Carta to this Day, are *Personal Security, Personal Liberty* and *Private Property,* and to these *Rights* the *Colonists* are intitled [sic] by Charters, by Common Law and by Acts of Parliament. Can it then be wondered at that the Act of levying Stamp Duties upon the Colonies should be astonishing to them since in divers Respects it totally annihilates these Rights."[38] John Adams took a similar position in arguing the case before the governor and council;[39] while a Virginia law court supported the position taken by Otis when it declared that the act was "unconstitutional."[40]

The colonies were saying, in effect, that they objected to the passage and enforcement of the Stamp Act because it violated the long established custom that direct local taxes were to be levied only by their own representatives in their own local legislatures. We have seen that this was a repetition of the position taken by the English parliamentary leaders in the seventeenth century against the arbitrary taxes levied by Charles I. They were, therefore, following the precedent laid down by the Rump Parliament when it announced the doctrine of popular sovereignty. A distinction exists in the fact that the Puritan parliament had declared that it was the agent through which the will of the people was to be expressed, while the colonial leaders declared that they owed allegiance to the king and not to parliament. Yet even here the colonists were not without a precedent in the case of the personal union between England and Scotland:—the two kingdoms were united under the same king yet the Scottish people were not to be taxed without the consent of their own legislative representatives. This seems to have been the viewpoint of Madison, who later declared that:—"The legislative power was maintained to be as complete in each American Parliament as in the British Parliament."[41] It was also the view of John Adams, who, in the debates that followed the passage of the Stamp Act, seems to have taken the position that Massachusetts was united with Britain in a personal union under the king, while the colonial assembly alone had the right to tax the people of that area.[42] In maintaining this viewpoint he was doing little more than continuing the course of independency that had characterized the conduct of Massachusetts from the beginning. It has been pointed out that parliament and the king, or the king in parliament, to employ the more exact constitutional terminology, had actually legislated for the Channel Islands, as well as Ireland and the dominions overseas.[43] This is undoubtedly true and would indeed constitute a legal precedent for such parliamentary action. It would seem, however, that it should also be balanced against such habits and traditions as the long periods of relative neglect in which parliament had actually failed to legislate for the American colonies; their comparative isolation and the fact that the American environment had created a comparatively new set of habits, customs and traditions that were more indigenous to the American soil than to that of the British Isles.[44] The political climate of the American frontier had tended to modify the political and social stratifications inherited from England. American colonial leaders were therefore exercising considerable astuteness when they ransacked the English constitution for precedents to justify their local constitutional customs against what they claimed were the unconstitutional innovations of current English leadership. We are confronted with the strange paradox of a new, dynamic "frontier" society appealing for the old ways against the new. In the principles announced by the English parliamentary leaders of the seventeenth century, the American colonial leaders felt they had found a constitutional justification for their actual faith and practice.[45] Actually they were "rugged individualists" who wished to be left alone. It would, however, have been impolitic to say so; hence this straight-faced appeal to older constitutional customs.

There was less opposition to the trade laws due in part to the fact that custom had confirmed them. Thus Burke, in speaking of the commercial restraint, declared that: "But America bore it from the fundamental Act of Navigation until 1764—Why? Because men do bear the inevitable constitution of their original nature with all its infirmities. . . . They scarcely remembered a time when they were not subject to such restraint."[46] Perhaps, too, the habit of evasion had been better established, while the Stamp Act was theoretically self-enforcing.

The repeal of the Stamp Act in 1766 was followed by the passage of the Townshend Acts in 1767; and once again the colonists based their objections upon long established laws and customs.[47] Their viewpoint was well represented by John Dickinson, who declared that parliament had never imposed a duty for the purpose of raising revenue under the guise of a power to regulate trade.[48] It should also be observed that Dickinson agreed that the general right of parliament to regulate the trade of Great Britain and its colonies was based upon long established law.[49] It is true that the preamble of the Townshend Acts of 1767 announced that the purpose of raising revenue under the acts was to make "provision for defraying the charge of the administration of justice, and the support of civil government in such provinces where it shall be found necessary; and towards further defraying the expenses of defending, protecting, and securing the said dominions. . ."[50] Yet colonial custom contradicted the wording of this preamble because it had long been the habit of the colonies to care for themselves. They had pushed westward and built an empire on their own initiative and in so doing they had paid the costs of their own government and had raised men and money for the empire.[51] The argument of Dickinson was also supplemented by Samuel Adams. Both insisted that law and custom demanded that governments should be subject to constitutional limitations. Dickinson, however, based his arguments more upon legal precedents, while Adams emphasized the idea of a custom above the formal law and based upon natural rights.[52] The argument of constitutional custom was also advanced by Massachusetts in 1769, when the legislature refused to meet in Boston because of the presence of British troops and Governor Bernard adjourned them to meet at Cambridge. In taking this step he complained of the "waste of time and treasure to no purpose." The house replied that:—"No time can better be employed than in the preservation of the rights derived from the British constitution, and insisting upon points, which, though your Excellency may consider them as non-essential, we esteem its best bulwarks. No treasure can be better expended, than in securing that true old English liberty, which gives a relish to every other enjoyment."[53] A few years later, in 1774, it advanced another step in defending its ancient and constitutional liberties when, under the tutelage of John Adams, it claimed that the union with Great Britain was a personal union under the leadership of the crown and that Massachusetts had long possessed the right to legislate for itself under its own parliament.[54]

The period that begins about 1772 and extends roughly to 1782 marks another stage in the course of revolutionary events. It is in this period that the American revolutionary leaders tend to defend their position by placing more emphasis upon natural rights, the social contract and the consent of the people as a whole.[55] The first notable step is seen in their opposition to the "intolerable acts" of 1774. They claimed that the re-modeling of the Massachusetts charter violated the English law of corporations and destroyed the customs of local and colonial self-governments that had evolved during a period of one hundred and fifty years; that the new law governing trials for English officials and the Quartering Act violated their ancient English rights of personal liberty that had been guaranteed by Magna Carta and the Petition of Rights. Here they were taking the same position that had been held by the leaders of the Puritan revolution in the struggle against the king in the preceding century. They also claimed that the Quebec Act violated their property rights guaranteed by English law since it ignored their claims within that area.[56] The recognition for Roman Catholics also ran counter to the traditional distrust for the communicants of that religion that was shared by the great majority of the colonists of English descent.[57]

Colonial opposition to the "intolerable acts" was more pronounced than had been the case with any protests up to that

time; and while the American leaders continued to rely largely upon custom in voicing their opposition, they were basing
their appeals quite as much upon the elements of natural
law and natural right in the English constitution[58] as upon
the actual practice of constitutional and functional agencies.
Jefferson was doubtless the leader of a considerable group of
more advanced political thinkers, when, in his eloquent *Summary View,* written in 1774, he took the position that "the
common feelings of human nature must be surrendered up,
before his majesty's subjects here can be persuaded to beleive
[sic] that they hold their political existence at the will of a
British parliament."[59] He added that: "The feelings of human nature revolt against the supposition of a state so situ-
ated as that it may not in any emergency provide against
dangers which perhaps threaten immediate ruin. . . The god
who gave us life, gave us liberty at the same time: the hand
of force may destroy, but cannot disjoin them."[60] Jefferson
was thus following the custom of Locke in basing his government upon the social contract and the consent of the governed, which also implied the right of the people to alter
and amend. This seemed to show a line of thought that might
lead to revolution in the eighteenth century even as a similar
train of reasoning had helped to precipitate the English parliamentary revolution of the seventeenth. These views were
soon translated into action in terms of the first and second
Continental Congresses,[61] the Virginia Bill of Rights[62] and
the Declaration of Independence.[63] Yet even the latter document based its principles not so much upon a denial of the
king's legal authority over the colonies as upon the idea that
he had forfeited that power through his failure to observe the
customary conditions of the social contract which had given
him his original right to rule.[64]

A special word should perhaps be said in regard to the
written pronouncements of the first and second Congresses
of 1774-1775. Despite the rising tide of revolutionary feeling
which culminated in the temporary triumph of the revolutionary philosophy of natural right that had also character-

ized the onset of the English parliamentary revolution of the
seventeenth century, we are compelled to conclude that in
drafting the decisions of the first Continental Congress, the
leaders were, at least outwardly, relying in no small degree
upon the established rights and customs which they maintained were theirs as citizens of the empire. The Congress
did, to be sure, base its rights upon "the immutable laws of
nature" as well as "the principles of the English Constitution
and the several charters or compacts." It did, however, in
the fourth resolution of the "Declaration and Resolves" specifically declare that the colonies were "entitled to a free and
exclusive power of legislation in their several provincial legislatures, where their right of representation can alone be preserved, in all cases of taxation and internal polity, subject
only to the negative of their sovereign, in such manner as
has been heretofore used and accustomed."[65] A few days
later in its address to the king it explicitly declared that:—
"Your royal authority over us and our connexion with Great
Britain, we shall always carefully endeavour to support and
maintain."[66] Royal disallowance by the king in council seems
to have been expressly affirmed in its reference to the "negative of their sovereign." A reliance upon established custom
was further emphasized in the "Address to the people of
Great Britain" when the Congress declared:—"Be not sur-
prized therefore, that we, who are descended from the same
common ancestors; that we, whose forefathers participated
in all the rights, the liberties, and the constitution, you so
justly boast [of], and who have carefully conveyed the same
fair inheritance to us . . . should refuse to surrender them
. . ."[67]

The reference to property rights guaranteed by the English constitution and their alleged violation by the Quebec
Act may well remind us of the part played in this period by
Sir William Blackstone and his famous *Commentaries*. It has
been said that more than one thousand copies were imported
to America[68] before the first American edition was published
by Robert Bell of Philadelphia in 1771-1772. The sale of this

edition was so extensive that "some 1400 sets had been ordered prior to publication."[69] The list of subscribers to this
edition included colonial governors and many others who became active in the revolution and the founding of the United
States.[70] The work greatly stimulated the study of law in
America[71] and became the chief reliance of both the law
student and the lawyer.[72] It may at first glance seem somewhat paradoxical that the conservative Blackstone should
have had an influence in promoting, even by indirection, the
cause of the American Revolution. The anomaly becomes
somewhat clearer if we recall that Blackstone supported his
constitution by an appeal to the ancient laws, customs and
traditions of his realm. This gave "aid and comfort" to the
American leaders who simultaneously maintained that the
current parliamentary adherents were violating these same
traditions in their treatment of America. The colonists had
defended their position by appeals to natural law and natural
right, Magna Carta and the ancient customs of the kingdom; they discovered that Blackstone had based no small
portion of his law of England upon these self-same sources
and had developed his argument with copious illustrations
and examples which gave additional weight to the American
position. The timely support which this work gave to the
American cause seemed to the colonial leaders to be almost
providential. Here was a vast arsenal of political weapons
based upon the habits, customs and traditions of the mother
country from which they hastened to borrow and adapt to
suit their current needs.

This second period of the American Revolution also bears
certain resemblances to the second stage of the English Revolution in the seventeenth century. We are not in this chapter mainly concerned with the course of military events yet
feel that they merit a brief examination to the extent that
they influenced the course of political habits, customs and
traditions in the two revolutions. We have suggested that in
the opening period both the parliamentary and the American
revolutionary leaders were inclined to be somewhat moder-

ate in their demands and insist that they were defending the
rights guaranteed them by the customs and traditions of the
existing constitution:—that they were not seeking to alter
the constitution but to maintain and protect it. This attitude
persisted for a time in both countries after the outbreak of hostilities; they insisted that they were fighting to maintain their
rights as guaranteed to them by established constitutional
customs. This conception was to a certain extent reflected in
the conduct of hostilities by which they endeavored to maintain the political position they had taken. Parliamentary leaders of the type of Manchester,[73] Essex,[74] Sir William Waller,[75] the Scottish general, Alexander Lesley, later Earl of
Leven,[76] and the elder Fairfax, had no desire to destroy the
monarchy or kill the king but merely to see the restoration
of those constitutional limitations upon the royal power which
they insisted had been established by long custom and usage
and which they maintained had been disregarded by Charles
I. They would not abolish the monarchy but restore it to
its accustomed place in the English constitutional system. It
therefore followed that these leaders did not always engage
in a vigorous prosecution of the war but spent a considerable
amount of their time and energy in diplomatic negotiations
with the royalists in the hope of effecting a compromise by
peaceful means. Thus, for example, after the great victory
of Cromwell and his Ironsides at Marston Moor, on July 2,
1644, Manchester, Leven and Lord Fairfax, fearful that the
parliamentary extremists might get control and abolish the
monarchy, sent a joint letter to the Committee of England
and Scotland, in which they urged peace with the king and
the establishment of Presbyterianism as a compromise between Anglicanism and Independency.[77] These efforts culminated in the conference between the representatives of the
king and the parliamentary forces at Uxbridge in 1644.[78] The
conference failed to effect a settlement[79] and was followed
by the ascendency of Cromwell and the younger Fairfax, the
reorganization of the army as a result of the self-denying
ordinance, and a more vigorous prosecution of the war by

the parliamentary radicals, who wished to defeat the king in battle and capture him.[80]

A situation that was somewhat similar also existed at the outbreak of the American Revolution. The American leaders felt that they were fighting for their long established constitutional rights as British subjects and continued to hope that a peaceful settlement might be effected. This attitude also had its effect upon military operations in the sense that the military leaders on both sides failed to prosecute the war with the force and vigor that might have animated them had they realized that it was destined to be a struggle to a finish. This would seem to be a partial explanation of the slowness and ineptitude of such American military leaders as Charles Lee,[81] and to a lesser degree, Horatio Gates[82] and Israel Putnam.[83] The plot of Edmund Waller, the poet,[84] had its American counterpart in the defection of Charles Lee; while the opposition of the moderate parliamentary commanders to Cromwell after his victory at Marston Moor, had its American counterpart in the alleged plottings of Conway, Mifflin, Gates and Wilkinson against Washington after his victories at Trenton and Princeton.[85] On the British side the conduct of the war by the Howe brothers was half-hearted and far from effective.[86] Yet as time advanced both sides settled down to a war to a finish. We have seen that in the English Civil War Cromwell's great victory at Marston Moor was followed by the Uxbridge Conference, the reorganization of the parliamentary army and a vigorous prosecution of the war to its conclusion. A similar parallel may be seen in the conduct of the American Revolution. The failure of the Uxbridge Conference had its American counterpart in the failure of the Staten Island Conference on September 11, 1776,[87] and this, in turn, was followed by a more vigorous prosecution of the war. Cromwell's reorganization of the parliamentary army by means of the New Model Ordinance and the appointment of the younger Fairfax and Cromwell himself as commanders, had its American counterpart in the spring of 1778 with the appointment of General Greene as

Quartermaster-General,[88] as well as the improvements in drill, discipline and tactics under the leadership of "Baron" von Steuben.[89]

This problem of developing sound military leadership on the part of the revolutionists was accompanied by a similar problem involving military personnel in the form of officers and enlisted men. At the outbreak of the English Civil War the English nobility and country gentry, who tended to support the king, seem to have had a somewhat greater aptitude for war. They were better horsemen, more accustomed to life in the open air and feats of arms, while they had also developed the habits of command in their relations with their tenants and serving men. The parliamentary party was able to recruit a certain number of men with a similar background from the gentry of the Eastern Counties but as the war progressed it found itself confronted with the difficult task of recruiting and training men who had been engaged in commercial pursuits in the towns. Cromwell's remark to John Hampden has often been quoted:—"Your troops are most of them old decayed serving men, and tapsters and such kind of quality. Do you think that the spirits of such mean and base scullions will ever be able to encounter gentlemen that have honour, courage and resolution in them?"[90] The London trained bands developed into good soldiers in time although the process was somewhat painful and prolonged. It was difficult to instill in the minds of men drawn from the ranks of shopkeepers and apprentices those ideas and habits of rank, subordination, discipline and obedience, which commanders deem so essential for military morale; difficult to find good material for officers among such men; difficult to persuade parliament that such soldiers should be properly paid and supported; difficult to induce it to increase the pay for officers with the hope of getting better candidates for such positions. Yet in the long run and despite these obstacles, the commercial classes of the towns when properly trained and led by competent officers demonstrated greater qualities of stamina and endurance than the royalist country gentry.[91]

The spirit of trade was a highly individualistic spirit yet when subdued to the purposes of warfare it also became highly acquisitive and persistent.

A similar situation existed in connection with the efforts of Washington to train and equip the American revolutionary army. His problem resembled Cromwell's in the sense that he was compelled to adapt the spirit of an individualistic acquisitive people to the exigencies of warfare. Officer material was not readily available, while the democratic spirit that induced companies to elect their own officers did not necessarily produce those best fitted to command.[92] Washington also encountered the same difficulties with Congress that Cromwell had faced with parliament:—the problems of raising men, money and supplies in adequate amounts. Congress was reluctant to provide for a well-officered regular establishment while Washington was particularly insistent that officers should be well-paid.[93] Yet Congress was so reluctant to take effective action that Washington was compelled to struggle with the problem throughout the war.[94] It did provide for a small body of regular troops, the Continental Line, that may be considered as the general counterpart of Cromwell's Ironsides. Yet the problem of arms and supplies was part of a larger political problem that vexed both Cromwell and Washington:—the need for an efficient central government to conduct a war that was constantly negated and nullified by the forces of geographic particularism. Parliament was unable to compel associations, counties, towns and boroughs to furnish their quotas even as the Continental Congress had similar difficulties with the states. Even when mustered into the service Washington found that the state militia was undisciplined and unruly and determined to come and go at its own will.[95] Congress, however, was influenced by the traditional American fear of European militarism which had been a factor in inducing certain settlers to come to America with the result that it endeavored to prosecute the war largely with short-term militia rather than employ an army of permanent soldiers.[96] Yet this failure to develop professional soldiers and the tendency of the Americans to follow the customs of Indian fighting which many of them had learned in the French wars, enabled them at times to defeat the Britishers who had been trained in accordance with the older European military traditions.[97] The story of Braddock's defeat tended to repeat itself along the American frontier throughout the war.[98]

There was a marked tendency for political leadership in the two revolutions to pass from the control of moderate men into the hands of those who were more radical and more determined and who possessed the physical strength of youth.[99] In both revolutions the more conservative groups were divided in their counsels. The supporters of Charles I were divided on such questions as conciliation with the parliamentary party, seeking foreign aid, the support of the Irish and Scots, and the problem of Anglican and Presbyterian support, while the radical parliamentary leaders grew more and more united in their single purpose to defeat and capture the king and destroy the monarchy. A similar situation existed in the American Revolution in the sense that the Tories were divided in their demands for constitutional reform; while after the outbreak of the war they were torn between their allegiance to England and the land of their birth and divided in regard to the part they should play in the contest. Should they flee to England or to the British dominions in North America? Or remain and fight against the revolutionists? Or adopt a policy of passive resistance? The revolutionary party may have been no more numerous than the Tories, while in the Carolinas and Georgia it may have been outnumbered, yet it was better organized and inspired by a greater unity of purpose:—after the Declaration of Independence it was determined to win the war and establish national independence. Those economic groups that would be benefited by British rule and the continuance of the economic status quo were inclined to be royalists; while those who had an opportunity to gain by a more rigorous expansion and revision of the economic status quo were on the American side.

Thus the more ambitious and aggressive men were behind the American cause while the more conservative and less vigorous tended to favor the traditional economic status.[100]

In both revolutions the more vigorous prosecution of the war was accompanied by the growth of a more radical political philosophy and more radical political action. In the English civil war the conduct of revolutionary affairs fell more and more into the hands of political individualists, independents and republicans, who aimed at the abolition of the monarchy and the House of Lords,[101] the disestablishment of the church and, on May 19, 1649, the establishment of the commonwealth. By this act it was "declared and enacted:—

> "That the people of England, and of all the Dominions and territories thereunto belonging, are and shall be, and are hereby constituted, made, established and confirmed to be a commonwealth and Free State; by the Supreme Authority of the Nation, the Representatives of the People in Parliament, and by such as they shall appoint and constitute as Officers and Ministers under them for the good of the People, and that without any King or House of Lords."[102]

This constituted a bold and clear announcement of the doctrine of popular sovereignty and, by implication, an announcement and vindication of such individualistic political doctrines of the late middle ages and the seventeenth century as natural law, individual liberty, the social contract and the right of revolution.

The political aspects of the American Revolution followed a similar course. After fighting for more than a year to maintain their rights within the empire, the American leaders somewhat reluctantly issued their Declaration of Independence. Cromwell's alleged remark that only "cruel necessity" dictated the destruction of the king, has its counterpart in Jefferson's words in his first draft of the Declaration of Inde-

pendence:—"We must endeavor to forget our former love
for them [the British people]. . . We might have been a free
and a great people together."[103] The Declaration marked a
culmination of the forces of political radicalism that had been
gathering strength since the close of the Seven Years War
and the definite effort to tax the colonies. In the earlier stage
the American leaders had relied upon the doctrine of natural
rights to defend themselves under the English constitution.
In this second period the doctrine is expanded and extended
to include the right of revolution. The doctrine of consent no
longer means the consent of the legislative representatives of
the people but rather the direct consent of the people themselves. The idea of the social contract is similarly expanded:—
it is a contract between the rulers selected directly by the
people and the people themselves. By placing the blame for
American conditions squarely upon King George III of England, Jefferson was able also to appeal directly to the plain
people of America. It was a war against a despotic king and
this fear of European despotism was deeply entrenched in
the public mind because so many Americans had fled from
Europe to escape the tyranny of despotism. Jefferson was
thus sounding a warning note against an ancient tyrannical
tradition.[104] Here, too, is a close parallel in the evolution of
the political ideologies of the English and American revolutions. In both cases the political radicals tended to gain control and interpret the doctrines of natural right, natural law,
social contract and the doctrine of consent in terms of direct
popular participation in the government. The result was similar in both cases:—the announcement of the doctrine of popular sovereignty as the basis of government in the establishment of the English Commonwealth and the settlement of
1689 as well as in the Declaration of Independence.[105] Yet
at the expense of being repetitious we must repeat that even
the Declaration contained almost nothing that was new. It
was in no small degree based upon the philosophy of Locke,
which in turn was based in no small measure upon the theology of the early Puritan divines who in their turn had

evolved their ideas from the theological treatises of the more liberal divines of the pre-reformation period.[106] It has even been suggested that the doctrines of the Declaration have their counterpart in the philosophy of Nicolas of Cusa of the early fifteenth century and that certain portions of the document have sources that are derived from the classical traditions of the medieval and ancient world.[107] This phase of the problem will be discussed when we consider the adoption of the American bill of rights.

The announcement of the establishment of the English Commonwealth was followed by similar declarations by county and borough governments throughout England; while the Declaration of Independence was accompanied by similar statements in the Virginia Bill of Rights and the constitutions of the new state governments. Great pamphleteers spread the gospel of the English revolutions of the seventeenth century and the American revolution of the eighteenth. England had its John Milton who acted as secretary of state for Cromwell and in a series of eloquent state papers preached the dignity and sacredness of the individual and the religion of human liberty; it had its John Locke who continued the work of Milton by acting as advocate and defender of the revolution of 1688.[108] America had its counterpart of Milton in the person of Thomas Paine, who acted as secretary without portfolio for Washington. His *Common Sense* had been published shortly before the Declaration of Independence and prepared the American mind for its reception;[109] while his *American Crisis* inspired Washington and his troops on the eve of Trenton and later in the dark days at Valley Forge.[110] America also had its counterpart of Locke in Jefferson and his Declaration of Independence, which resembled so closely many of the words and phrases of Locke in his *Second Essay on Government*.[111]

The political ideas of the English and American revolutions were accompanied by certain social movements that were by no means dissimilar. Both were followed by confiscations of landed property by the victors. In England certain estates of the old landed nobility in Ireland and the north and west of England were confiscated by Cromwell's government and distributed to his followers. In the American Revolution the landed estates of the Tories were confiscated and the property fell into the hands of the revolutionists.[112] The established Anglican church suffered a similar fate in the two revolutions. In the English Revolution church property was confiscated and sold or desecrated and destroyed. St. Paul's Cathedral was desecrated by Cromwell's soldiers, who turned it into a cavalry barracks and a stable for their horses.[113] The situation was similar in America where the revolution was followed by a trend towards the disestablishment of state churches in general and the Episcopal church in particular.[114] The opposition to the Episcopal church in the Cromwellian and American Revolutions was based largely upon the fact that the communicants of that church were more likely to be royalists and Tories and less likely to be members of the revolutionary party. The statement attributed to Charles II to the effect that Presbyterianism was no religion for a gentlemen had its American counterpart in the remark attributed to a Virginian:—"Sure I am that no *gentleman* will choose to go to Heaven otherwise than by the way of the established church."[115] The desecration of St. Paul's and its use as a cavalry barracks in the Cromwellian revolution had its American counterpart when the British made a similar use of the Old South Church in Boston,[116] which might roughly be considered as the "mother church" of the Massachusetts establishment. The damage to church property in various parts of America was not inconsiderable.[117]

This second period of the American Revolution from 1772 to 1782 saw the initial steps in the formation of the first state governments as well as the first general government in the form of the Articles of Confederation. Here, too, the American Revolution followed the tradition of the Cromwellian revolution in the sense that even before the cessation of hostilities, the civil authorities began their efforts at constitution making. In these first constitutions of the American states we see the influence of habit, custom and tradition at almost every turn.[118] The constitutions of Rhode Island and Connecticut substituted popular sovereignty for royal sovereignty yet suffered almost no structural change, while relatively few changes occurred in the other state constitutions in their transition from colonies to statehood. This was another illustration of the fact that the leaders in the formation of these new state governments still consistently maintained that they had no desire to resort to innovations on a grand scale and that the chief object of the war with England had been to preserve their well-established laws and institutions against the radical innovations attempted by the English government since the close of the Seven Years War.[119] Thus these American leaders had rebelled not so much against the abstract implications of the British political and social system as the position to which the British leaders would relegate them within that system.

The new state constitutions definitely embodied those principles of popular sovereignty, separation of powers[120] and check and balance which the revolutionary leaders had insisted were an integral part of the English constitution.[121] Thus the Massachusetts constitution of 1780 openly stated that its constitution was based upon the principle of separation of powers which it had long defended in practice.[122] It expressly stated in its preamble that:—"the body politic is formed by a voluntary association of individuals, it is a social compact, by which the whole people covenant with each citizen, and each with the whole people, that all shall be governed by certain laws for the common good";[123] while Part I, Article IV, declared that:—"The people of this common- wealth have the sole and exclusive right of governing themselves, as a free, sovereign and independent State. . ."[124]

The framers of these new state constitutions continued their custom of opposition to centralized executive power which they had displayed against the growth of the royal prerogative under George III and in their long struggle against the royal governors. It has been suggested that this attitude was illogical since the governor's power was no longer derived from the crown.[125] Yet was not their tradition of check and balance and separation of powers based in no small measure upon what we would now call their knowledge of the iron law of oligarchy and the ego drive for power? Experience and custom had taught them that power tends to corrupt and that it should therefore be strictly limited so that for every grant of power there should be a corresponding check. It is perhaps significant to note that these first state governments were also formed by bodies known as state conventions or congresses and that in English constitutional parlance the term "convention" was employed to describe an informal meeting of parliament or the House of Commons prior to its formal organization. The extended use of the term in this sense seems to have coincided with the Cromwellian revolution. Later in the century the same term was employed to describe the assembly that wrote the bill of rights and recognized the accession of William and Mary. In view of the fact that these new American state constitutions embodied not a few of the principles of the glorious revolution in their basic structure, this similarity of name would seem to be of some significance.[126] It professed to be a technique for formalizing the fruits of a popular revolution against centralized tyranny.

These conventions were somewhat more generous in their grant of power to the new state legislatures than were the colonial charters to the colonial legislatures. Yet here, also, they were tending to follow long established custom in the sense that the colonial legislatures had largely dominated the colonial political scene and had been the leading exponent of popular rights. It was only natural that the framers of the new state constitutions, since they expressly affirmed the doctrine of popular sovereignty, should continue their custom of placing more sovereign power in the branch that more directly represented the "people."

This theory of popular sovereignty was implemented by

written bills of rights that did little more than affirm the bill of rights that had already evolved in England and colonial America. They were based upon the rights guaranteed to the individual by the common law of England as it had been expounded by Coke and Blackstone.[127] Most bills of rights, for example, contained a clause to the effect that procedure involving life, liberty or property must conform to the law of the land. This clause, derived directly from Magna Carta, furnished the traditional basis for the due process clause of the fifth and fourteenth amendments.[128] The clause against self-incrimination has been said to be of more recent origin; yet even here it is perhaps significant to note that these new state constitutions were doing little more than follow an unwritten custom that had slowly developed in England since the sixteenth and seventeenth centuries.[129]

Yet despite these bills of rights, the states tended to retain the same property qualifications for voting that had existed in England and the colonies.[130] Property qualifications in the form of land or substantial personal holdings were required in all the states,[131] while various religious qualifications prevailed in all except Rhode Island and New York.[132] The representation by districts was also so arranged in practically all the states that the substantial seaboard class and the large landowners were in control of the state legislature, while the small farmers and the men of the frontier suffered a proportionate restriction in their representation. This was especially true in Virginia, where Jefferson pointed out that under the apportionment of 1780:—"Nineteen thousand men, living before the falls of the rivers, possess half of the senate, and want four members only of possessing a majority of the house of delegates. . ."[133] A similar situation existed in New York, where John Jay had been in large part responsible for the fact that the suffrage and the legislature were mainly in the hands of the large landowners.[134] Practically the same situation existed in all the other states.[135] The highly restricted suffrage and the unrepresentative character of the election districts and the state legislature closely followed the custom that had long prevailed in England and the colonies. Richard Henry Lee was inclined to think that the situation that prevailed in Virginia following the adoption of the constitution of 1776 was theoretically worse even though it was redeemed by a milder practice.[136] Even such a pronounced radical as Thomas Paine seemed at one time to see no great inconsistency in this affirmation of popular sovereignty combined with its actual lodgement in the hands of the propertied classes. He had declared that "the mercantile and manufacturing part of the nation was its great bulwark."[137] This second stage of the American Revolution was, in other words, essentially a revolution under the dominance of middle class mercantilists and property owners, aided by such professional groups as the lawyers and the military leaders.[138] Here again, the American Revolution had followed the course of that other middle class uprising, the Cromwellian revolution of the seventeenth century, to the extent that both revolutions were in defense of property and religious rights.

In the field of national constitutional development, this second period from 1772 to 1782 also saw the creation of the Articles of Confederation, which were ratified on March 1, 1781. Here, too, the student of the period is confronted with the continuing forces of habit, custom and tradition beneath the semblance of superficial change.[139] The Continental Congress had continued the loose and indefinite union that had existed between the mother country and the colonies. Yet the Articles of Confederation by themselves did comparatively little to promote national unity, since it was expressly stated in Article II, that "Each State retains its sovereignty, freedom and independence, and every power, jurisdiction and right, which is not by this confederation expressly delegated to the United States in Congress assembled." The Articles, in other words, continued the custom of independent sovereignty which the states had possessed during the life of the Continental Congress and which in practice they had also tended to exercise as colonies.[140]

The debates that developed over the Articles, as well as

those that followed in the Congress of the Confederation, represented in no small degree a discussion of the same problems that had disturbed the relations between the mother country and the colonies: the problems of sovereignty, distribution of powers, taxation, representation, regulation of commerce, the settlement of interstate disputes and the government of land beyond the Alleghenies.

The states asserted their inherent sovereign rights against the Congress of the Confederation in a way that was by no means dissimilar to the manner in which as colonies they had asserted them against parliament. Both the colonies and their successors, the states, maintained that they exercised certain reserved and inherent rights against parliament and the American Confederation. Parliament had, however, claimed that its rights were inherent and that the colonies exercised only those rights that had been expressly delegated; the government of the Confederation, on the other hand, recognized that its rights were delegated and that all other rights had been reserved by the states. This indeed represents a departure from the British imperial system yet even this innovation is perhaps modified to a certain extent by the fact that in the distribution of power between the states and the general government, there was a tendency to follow the earlier lines of demarcation in the sense that the states granted to the general government powers similar to those that had been exercised by the crown and parliament, while retaining for themselves those powers which they had normally exercised as colonies.[141] In the light of this principle, the allocation of delegated and reserved powers to central or subordinate units would seem to lapse into relative insignificance when compared with the actual continuing custom.

Even though the colonies had become independent states, they continued to fear any taxing power superior to themselves. This traditional fear of the taxing power of parliament was, in other words, merely transferred to the Congress established under the Articles. This would seem largely to explain the fact that Congress was denied the right to tax the states; that it was merely permitted to make "requisitions;" that the actual power to levy taxes and collect revenues was retained by the states themselves; that they not infrequently reserved the right to exercise their discretion in regard to the payment of the quotas assigned; that in some cases the quota was greatly reduced and in others no amount whatever was forthcoming. Virginia was requisitioned for $400,-000 to meet its share of the Confederation for 1783. The Virginia House of Delegates informed Congress that it would pay only $50,000. In the congressional debate that followed Hamilton declared that without the taxing power the Confederation was a "rope of sand."[142] Arthur Lee, speaking for Virginia, replied that "he would rather see Congress a rope of sand than a rod of iron."[143]

In the matter of representation the colonists had brought with them from England the idea of geographic representation, which seems to have been not uncommon in seventeenth century England. In the next century England departed from this practice with the result that a member of parliament did not necessarily reside in the place he represented. The Americans, however, continued to follow the earlier custom in the election of members to their colonial legislatures, the Continental Congress and the Congress of the Confederation. The delegates from the various states not only lived in their states but represented them as equal sovereign powers in a diet of delegates in which each state had an equal vote with every other state regardless of its size, wealth or population. A similar view prevailed in regard to the regulation of commerce. The colonies had so bitterly resented the enforcement of the imperial trade laws that they had evaded them at every opportunity. Under the Confederation Congress might make commercial treaties with foreign countries yet effective enforcement was strictly limited because the right to retaliate in case of foreign discrimination was reserved by the states. The continuation of the spirit of the older tradition is still clearer in the case of interstate commerce. The states denied power to Congress in this field even as the colonies had evaded the attempt of parliament to regulate intercolonial commerce.

The forces of habit, custom and tradition are no less clear in the exercise of the judicial power under the government of the Confederation.[144] There had been a number of cases in which disputes between colonies had been sent to the Privy Council for settlement with the result that the principle had become more or less definitely established.[145] The framers of the Articles of Confederation would seem, therefore, to have had this custom in mind when they established their system of judicial appeal.[146] By Section Nine of the Articles it was provided that Congress on request might hear disputes between states;

> "but if they cannot agree, Congress shall name three persons out of each of the United States, and from the list of such persons each party shall alternately strike out one, the petitioners beginning, until the number shall be reduced to thirteen; and from that number not less than seven, nor more than nine names as Congress shall direct, shall in the presence of Congress be drawn out by lot, and the persons whose names shall be so drawn, or any five of them, shall be commissioners or judges, to hear and finally determine the controversy, so always as a major part of the judges who shall hear the cause shall agree in the determination..."[147]

The complexity of this method is doubtless in part responsible for the fact that a decision was reached in only one case.[148] Viewed traditionally, however, the importance of the technique rests in the fact that it represented a continuation of the system of judicial review which began with the disallowance of colonial laws by the judicial committee of the Privy Council, was continued under the government of the Confederation and later vested in the Supreme Court by the Judiciary Act of 1789 and Marshall's famous decision.[149]

Prior to the outbreak of the Revolution cases involving the alleged violation of the Navigation Acts had been heard by the English vice-admiralty courts[150] for the hearing of customs cases, which had been established with the coming of William of Orange.[151] With the outbreak of the Revolution and the overthrow of British administration Congress suggested to the states that they create the equivalent of these courts for the purpose of commissioning privateers and hearing prize cases and also making provision for appeals from these courts to Congress or to a tribunal to be created by Congress. All of the states except New York followed this suggestion and created admiralty courts and made provision for appeals. [152] On January 30, 1777, Congress appointed five members to act as Commissioners of Appeals.[153] Following the Olmstead case, [154] in which Pennsylvania disregarded a decision of the congressional commissioners,[155] the system was reorganized in 1780 with the creation of the Court of Appeals in Cases of Capture.[156] In this case the tradition followed was that of the English Board of Commissioners of Appeals, which was a committee of the Privy Council with the power to hear appeals from the vice-admiralty courts. This American court consisted of three judges and under the Articles of Confederation an ordinance was passed to regulate its administrative procedure[157] with the result that it continued to function until it was superseded by the document of 1787 and the Judiciary Act of 1789 that created the lower federal courts. This Congressional committee of appeals and its successor, the Court of Appeals, handled about one hundred and eighteen cases and definitely established a precedent for federal jurisdiction in admiralty and maritime cases.[158] One of the more salient features of this evolution would seem to be, therefore, the fact that our system of federal jurisdiction in these cases has evolved in an almost unbroken line from the English vice-admiralty courts in colonial America and those members of the Privy Council who acted as the English Board of Commissioners of Appeals. Few cases illustrate more clearly the influence of habit, custom and tradition in our American constitutional system.[159]

The question of the government of the western lands was so long debated that ratification of the Articles of Confederation was delayed for a considerable period. It will be recalled, however, that the other states finally yielded to the demands of Maryland[160] when that state insisted that these lands should be ceded to Congress and "parcelled out at any time into convenient, free and independent governments;"[161] and that this proposal was later implemented by the Ordinance of 1787.[162] Yet parliament had also claimed the sovereign power over its general domain in North America by the Proclamation Act of 1763. Congress was thus assuming the control that parliament had been compelled to abandon.[163] Thus the Ordinance of 1787 evolved from the custom of parliamentary supremacy as it had developed in the eighteenth century rather than from the earlier seventeenth century idea of the social compact which had been embodied in the constitutions of the states. It has also been said that the American colonial system as outlined in the Ordinance of 1787, differed from the earlier English colonial system in the sense that it was merely temporary and made definite provision for ultimate statehood.[164] Yet perhaps it may not be amiss to suggest that with the concentration of capital in the east, there was a corresponding tendency for that area to engage in the economic exploitation of the west with the result that while it yielded the political shell of power, it tended also to retain its economic substance, which, in itself, would seem to be a continuation of the concept of the old colonial system under the guise of modern finance capitalism. The economic capital was no longer London but New York, while the economic exploitation of the hinterland still continued. A more comprehensive explanation and one that may better illustrate the law of political continuity would seem to lie in the fact that the passage of the Northwest Ordinance also had its roots in the English revolutions of the seventeenth century quite as much as in the American revolution of the eighteenth. The people who had gone beyond the Alleghenies were fleeing from the newer aristocracy of the Atlantic seaboard in much the same way as their Puritan forbears had fled from the newer commercial and landed aristocracies of Tudor and Stuart England.[165]

Cromwell had found lands for his turbulent soldiery in the western parts of the British Isles and this action on the part of the leaders of the Congress of the Confederation would seem to be its American counterpart. In both revolutions a large proportion of those who fought in the ranks had been underprivileged persons who had been promised land and liberty for their pains. Land in the western areas of their respective countries represented the fulfillment of these promises and lessened the danger to the property groups who feared the presence of a discharged and impoverished soldiery. These reasons were no less compelling in revolutionary America than in revolutionary England. The small farmer and frontiersman were influenced by the same individualistic and egalitarian philosophy that had permeated the ranks of Cromwell's Levellers. It had been stimulated by American frontier conditions and by American leaders who had employed the natural law philosophy of Locke, Blackstone and Paine to strengthen American military morale. The embattled farmers had been promised their liberties. It was safer to nationalize the frontier than to fail them altogether. Let the discontented elements move towards the frontier leaving the eastern seaboard safe for the commercial and planter classes. This development, however, was little more than another stage in the traditional struggle between seaboard and frontier that began when the American seaboard had developed a commercial entity of its own. The exploited had become the exploiters. It was only the presence of a vast frontier that tended to defer the operation of a long established custom to the effect that the strong are generally prone to oppress the weak.

This struggle between the strong and the weak is well exemplified in the third period of our revolutionary development which lasted from 1782 to 1789. It had its earlier counterpart in the last stage of the Cromwellian revolution that had been followed by the restoration. After the defeat of the royalists in the field the victors had quarreled so bitterly among themselves that only the iron hand of Cromwell had prevented the renewal of a general war. Following his demise the situation became still more acute. At one extreme were the old landowning nobility who would restore the kingship with its prerogatives largely unimpaired; at the other the Levellers and Fifth Monarchy men who would establish a simple communal society based upon what their leaders conceived to be the conditions and governance that had prevailed in the early Christian churches of Greece and Asia Minor. Occupying a middle ground were the merchant and commercial classes of the towns as well as the substantial farmers and yeomen of the eastern counties who wished to establish the republican commonwealth that Cromwell himself had envisaged before the force of circumstances had compelled him to resort to a virtual dictatorship. The Levellers and Fifth Monarchy men grew so rapidly in power and numbers that both the royalists and the moderate republicans became alarmed for the safety of their lives and property and decided that it would be necessary to unite against them. Employing General Monk as a leading intermediary, the two groups agreed upon a compromise to the effect that the Stuart monarch was to be restored in the person of Charles II with the understanding that he was to be a strictly constitutional monarch and that the real power behind the throne was to be a group of constitutional advisers drawn from the ranks of both the royalists and the moderate Cromwellian republicans. Translated into economic terms, the restoration represented a compromise between land and commerce for the purpose of keeping the landless agricultural laborers and the penniless servants of commerce in subjection.

These events had their counterpart in the American revolutionary developments during the years 1782-1789. America also had its nostalgic adherents of royalty consisting of a few militarists,[166] wealthy merchants[167] and certain leaders of the old landed families in New York and Virginia. The hereditary nature of their organization would also seem to indicate that some of the members of the newly organized Society of the Cincinnati were not unsympathetic with monarchy,[168] nor was this attitude wholly confined to certain officers of the army. The awards and honors of a monarchical form of government appealed to some of the young men of the upper middle class, especially the young lawyers and law students and those with substantial fortunes.[169]

At the other extreme were the small farmers and the men of the frontier,[170] the agrarians who were fast getting control of the state legislatures and passing moratorium acts and issuing large quantities of paper money.[171] These men felt they were being exploited by the large landowners and the seaboard bankers. Ready to make common cause with them were the classes whose lot was even more hopeless: the artisans of the towns, farm laborers and such underprivileged and despised persons as the apprentices, indentured servants, Indians and slaves. In the severe winter of 1785-86 discontent blazed all along the frontier culminating in Shays' rebellion in central and western Massachusetts.[172] These events also stirred the so-called moderate men to action. They, too, had been divided in their interests. Some of the large landowners were not opposed to the establishment of royalty, while the bulk of the commercial classes were more inclined to favor a republican form of government as had their predecessors in Cromwell's day. The fear of an agrarian revolt hastened to unite them as it had in the earlier period. The leaders of the northern commercial classes and the northern and southern aristocracy decided to meet and reconcile their differences in the face of the impending danger. In this movement Colonel Alexander Hamilton seems to have been the American counterpart of the English General Monk. At an earlier date General Arnold may have aspired to be the Monk of the American revolution.[173] He had perhaps aimed at a reconciliation with the mother country when it was too late; while Hamilton aimed to reconcile civil differences and avert a civil war before it was too late. The result was the Philadelphia convention and the document of 1787, which resembled the English restoration of 1660 in the sense that it guaranteed the protection of land and private property against the dangers of Levellers and Shayesites by putting the government in the actual control of the "gentlemen of property and principle" as had the English restoration. Both revolutions culminated in a guarantee of the rights of private property; both represented a compromise between land and capital in which capital and the commercial classes tended to get somewhat the better of the bargain. In both cases the cause of the men who had achieved the victory by fighting in the ranks was to a large extent disregarded.[174] They were not present at the convention and except for the belated grant of a bill of rights, the new federal system left them to the protection of the states.

CHAPTER V

TRADITIONAL FORCES IN THE FEDERAL CONVENTION AND THE DOCUMENT OF 1787

"Now every tradition grows continually more venerable the farther off its origin, the more this is lost sight of; the veneration paid it accumulates from generation to generation, the tradition at last becomes holy and excites awe..." Friedrich Wlihelm Nietzsche: Human, All Too Human, In Two Parts, Part I, Translated by Helen Zimmern, T. N. Foulis, Edinburgh and London, 1910, p. 95.

Certain national powers that Britain had exercised over its national domain were continued by the Articles of Confederation and the Document of 1787. In the struggle over the ratification of the latter document, Madison endeavored to maintain that the federal convention had revised the Articles rather than created a new constitutional document; an exaggeration which may have been based in part upon his realization that people in the mass are prone to be traditionalists and prefer present pains to the dangers that may lie in innovation. The fact remains, however, that under the Articles the new American government assumed certain central powers formerly exercised by the British crown. Among these we may cite foreign relations, war, the creation of admiralty courts, the regulation of coinage, weights and measures, jurisdiction over the Indian tribes, the regulation of post offices and post roads, the creation of a navy, issuance of letters of marque and reprisal, control of the army, the borrowing of money and the emission of bills of credit. These powers were also destined to be continuing customs under the document of 1787.

The favorable terms of the treaty of peace of September 3, 1783, with Britain, France and Spain, were negotiated under the government of the Confederation. The fact that these terms were advantageous to the United States seems to have been due in part to the continuing forces of international power politics that operated in favor of the new American nation. Britain, at war with France, Spain and Holland, hoped that terms not ungenerous to the new America would tend to counteract future French influence in the United States. Thus the Americans were permitted to inherit their former English boundaries despite the fact that actual title to the western area was based largely upon the work of George Rogers Clark and we are still uncertain in regard to the extent to which it may have influenced the determination of the western and southern boundaries.[1]

The settlement of the northeast fisheries represented another American diplomatic victory because it permitted the United States to continue to exercise practically the same fishing rights off the coast of Newfoundland that it had enjoyed as a part of the British empire. This victory was achieved in no small measure by the courage and persistence of John Adams, who definitely based his argument upon habit, custom and tradition as he declared:

"When God Almighty made the banks of Newfoundland at three hundred leagues distance from the people of America, and at six hundred leagues distance from those of France and England, did He not give as good a right to the former as to the latter? If Heaven in the creation gave a right, it is ours at least as much as yours. If occupation, use, and possession give a right, we have it as clearly as you. If war, and blood, and treasure give a right, ours is as good as yours."[2]

The Americans achieved another diplomatic triumph in regard to the royalists. They flatly refused to permit those royalists who had fled the country to return and also refused to grant them restitution.[3] The most they would concede was a statement to the effect that there should be no more persecutions and that Congress would "earnestly recommend" to the states that they restore their property, a concession that amounted to little more than a face-saving device for Britain. This represented not only a continuation of the spirit of civil strife that had characterized the relations between Whigs and Tories during hostilities but also the traditional ill-feeling that had marked the relations between the "popular" party and the "king's party" since the founding of the first American colonies.

Another triumph was the "settlement" of the western lands question. This included its cession to the national government, the preliminary act of control of 1784, and the definitive ordinance of 1787. Here again, precedents were not lacking for the position taken by the government of the Confederation. It represented, in a sense, a continuation of the imperial policy of parliament that by the proclamation act of 1763, had insisted upon undisputed control of the area. It may, indeed, be said that the American policy marked a departure from the British in the sense that the Ordinance of 1787 envisaged final equality and statehood while the British system did not. This may be granted yet we have already indicated that the northeastern seaboard has tended to maintain its economic supremacy and this in turn has enabled it to exercise a decisive influence in the public policies of the country especially in the conduct of foreign relations and the declaration of war. Almost equally important is the fact that the nationalization of the western lands represented a continuation of the struggle between seaboard and frontier in which the commercial and landed leaders along the seaboard desired to continue their political and economic dominance of the coastal area and one of the methods for pursuing this policy was to induce the malcontents and underprivileged groups to migrate beyond the mountains.

The auspicious beginnings of the Confederation in the field of foreign relations soon turned to frustration and disaster. Britain continued to view the new nation with distrust and suspicion. John Adams was coldly received as American minister,[4] while the British refused to send an accredited diplomatic representative to the United States. The Americans discovered that commercial difficulties with England continued despite the war and "independence." They soon realized that they were still subject to the navigation system in the sense that while parliament in April, 1782, voted to establish intercourse with the new nation, it was still excluded from trade with the British West Indies and must pay high duties to trade with the British home ports. The "new" regime resembled the old colonial system in the sense that it hampered trade but did not wholly prevent it. Americans resumed their former system of smuggling and evasion in the British West Indies and since they had long been accustomed to consume British goods, they renewed their trade with the British home ports and paid the high import duties. Efforts to induce the states to permit Congress to pass an American retaliatory tariff for a period of fifteen years failed to materialize[5] and showed a continuation of the old divisive factors that had long existed: the division between town and country and seaboard and frontier; the commercial north that favored the proposal and the agricultural south that opposed it. Britain, on its side, continued its pre-war policy of making flexible adjustments as expediency seemed to dictate. Within a few years it permitted certain American products to be shipped to the British West Indies provided they were carried in English ships. This, too, resembled the old colonial system except that American ships were no longer British.

Practically every problem that had presumably been "settled" by the treaty of "peace" still existed as a matter of acrimonious debate between the two countries. In almost every case the roots of the difficulty were to be found in habits, customs and traditions that had long antedated the treaty of peace and even the revolution itself. The treaty had stipulated that British creditors should encounter "no lawful impediment" in their attempts to collect their debts, and while Congress pleaded with the states to execute this clause in good faith, the state legislatures and the state courts openly violated the provision. This was largely due to the old established colonial custom by which the debts due the leading British mercantile houses remained on their books as continuing obligations, while the debt together with its accrued interest was regularly transmitted from father to son. This was especially true of the Virginia planters,[6] which doubtless helps to explain why Virginia had been one of the worst offenders in passing a series of acts preventing the recovery of these debts both during and after the revolution.[7] The treaty provision had violated a long established custom in the relations between England and this American planter class, while the war had been followed by depression and bankruptcy in America, so that it required time for the agricultural and commercial classes in the two countries to adjust themselves to the new conditions created by the peace.

A similar situation existed in regard to the loyalists. The bitter hatred which had its roots in early colonial divisions between the privileged and the under-privileged, the governor's party and the people's party, and which had been intensified by the war, continued in the form of loyalist proscriptions after the treaty of peace. Congress recommended the restoration of loyalist property but the states disregarded it. The British, in retaliation, continued to hold the military and trading posts of the northwest despite the fact that the treaty had provided for their evacuation "with all convenient speed." Britain was also acting in the interests of the Canadian fur traders and their Indian allies because these groups were strongly opposed to relinquishing their lucrative and long-established fur trade.[8]

The new American nation also inherited England's disputes with Spain that had long existed in the trans-Allegheny regions: controversies involving the navigation of the Mississippi, the southwest boundary between the United States and Spanish Florida,[9] and the Indian forays from Spanish territory.

The traditional friendship that had developed with the American-French alliance continued under the Confederation, although France repeatedly importuned Jefferson in regard to the debt that was due her. She also granted the new nation limited trading rights in the French West Indies. Yet her general policy seems to have been to see that the United States should not disturb the balance of power by developing an undue measure of strength.

Briefly to summarize the traditional elements in the problem of foreign relations under the Confederation, we may say that the new American government had inherited an area that had been a factor in European power politics since its discovery and settlement[10] and the same countries were still engaged in a struggle to control its policies and dominate it. These countries were England, France and Spain aided by their Indian allies. Since the colonies had won a precarious "independence" under the Articles, the foreign policy of England differed from its former attitude in the sense that it must endeavor to control by indirection where it had formerly exercised more direct control. Even here, however, the difference would seem to be one of degree rather than kind: Britain had not infrequently been so divided in its counsels that there had been long periods when the colonies had been permitted to conduct their relations with foreign countries and the Indians pretty much as they wished. Even when the general policy had been formulated by the British, as in the French wars, the colonies had been granted, or at least had assumed, a large measure of freedom in its implementation and execution. They, too, had been divided in their counsels in regard to the conduct of foreign relations and these divisions had continued under the Articles. These forces of particularism had yielded to the fear of British dominance and they had united temporarily to win the war. After the war the forces of particularism returned in the form of a loose confederation. The desire of Britain, France and Spain to dominate this confederation and even dissolve it, created an American fear leading to another union stronger than the one that had opposed Britain. In its efforts to control the new American nation, European power politics thus overreached itself and defeated its own aims. The long established American tradition of union in the face of a common danger which had begun with the New England confederation of 1643 proved to be stronger than the power politics of Europe.

In analyzing the element of habit, custom and tradition in the domestic politics of the Confederation, the authorities agree that Congress lacked coercive power in such matters as national defense and taxation. The states refused to give Congress the power to establish a uniform tariff law, refused to provide adequately for the national defense and refused to pay their assigned quotas to support the general government. Thus, for example, New Jersey when it found that its imports were taxed by New York and Pennsylvania, demanded that Congress be given the exclusive right to tax imports. When Congress was unable to get the consent of the states to assume this power, New Jersey refused to pay its assessed quota.[11] Yet this policy of state independence and particularism had been a pronounced characteristic of the American settlements, colonies and states from the days of their establishment. The American founders and settlers had been minority men who had refused to conform to the authority at home; they had been dissatisfied with the European society in which they had found themselves, or at least with the position which they had occupied within it, and decided to find a greater freedom in the American wilderness. They and their actual or spiritual heirs had tended to be sympathetic with the popular party that had opposed the encroachments of the royal governor and his party and had achieved a definite victory when they had gained control of the colonial legislative and taxing power.[12] They later opposed the English king and parliament on the same issue and while they had temporarily united under the Congress and the Confederation to defend their rights and win their independence, the forces of habit, custom and tradition led them to revert to their particularistic tradition as soon as they had gained the immediate end for which they had fought.[13] It would seem, therefore, that the Americans of the Confederation were the heirs of two traditions: one that stood for political unity and one that made for political fragmentation. This indeed was a phase of one of the oldest problems in politics: that of endeavoring to strike a sound balance between the extremes of freedom and authority. Prior to the establishment of the document of 1787, the tradition of freedom tended to be the stronger. This was due in no small measure to the nature of the men who had migrated to America and the nurture of the American continent with its frontier conditions and a vast wilderness that offered an opportunity to escape from political authority. It had also been the custom of the colonists to unite in time of danger as they had united to win their independence. Yet the will to unite was usually imposed by a determined few upon those who were half hearted or indifferent. Such had been the case in the union that had won their liberty and such was to be the case in the union that was to succeed the Confederation. America in its search for a uniform political equilibrium vacillated between freedom and authority and in so doing was exemplifying the operation of another general political custom known as the swing of the political pendulum.

The transition from confederation to federalism was conditioned in no small measure by the physical differences among the states themselves. Nature and geography had created three broad sectional groupings: the New England states, the middle states and the southern states. These areas had developed marked differences in their political philosophies, systems of representation, forms of local government and social politics. Jefferson once drew up a list in which he attempted to compare the northern and southern character. In the middle states and especially in Pennsylvania, he felt there was a certain commingling of these northern and southern characteristics.[14] It was, therefore, perhaps no accident that Pennsylvania became the "keystone" state playing such a vital factor in the steps toward union: William Penn had sponsored such a plan in 1696; Franklin was a leader in the work of the Albany conference and the federal convention. This, however, is to anticipate. It is sufficient for our present purposes to emphasize that during the period of the Confederation the sectional differences not only remained as powerful as ever but tended in some ways to become more acute as the time for the federal convention approached.[15] The people west of the Alleghenies were bitterly disappointed by the failure of Jay to win the navigation of the Mississippi in his negotiations with the Spanish ambassador Gardoqui.[16] Monroe felt that Jay aimed to force the west out of the Confederation and form a separate northern confederacy and declared that Jay and his friends had "held in this city [New York] committees for dismembering the Confederacy and throwing the states eastward the Hudson into one government."[17] Charles Pettit, writing to Jeremiah Wadsworth, May 27, 1786, declared that: "Our political Situation, merely from want of [ar]rangement and Combination of our Strength, is indeed wretched. Our Funds exhausted, our Credit lost, our Confidence in each other and in the federal Government destroyed. Resolutions unexecuted; Requisitions but partially complied with in the best of the States, in others not at all; Recommenda[tions] as little regarded as the cries of an Oysterman."[18] Friends of the Confederation feared its dissolution. Madison writing to Edmund Pendleton in February, 1787, declared that: "It is not possible that a Government can last long under these Circumstances. If the approaching convention should not agree on some remedy, I am persuaded that some very different arrangement will ensue. . . . The bulk of the people will probably prefer the lesser evil of a partition of the Union into three more practicable and energetic governments. The latter idea I find after long confinement to individual speculations and private circles is beginning to show itself in the Newspapers."[19]

The colonial period had seen the rise and growth of a considerable number of disputes among the colonies involving such diversified problems as boundaries, trade, taxation, the issue of coinage and paper currency, Indian affairs, the extradition of fugitives and titles to western lands. The military problems of the revolution had put some of these matters in temporary abeyance; few, if any, had actually been settled, so that after the war these quarrels were resumed with a force that evinced their long standing bitterness.[20] New York, through its great city port, was able to tax the commerce of Connecticut and New Jersey. This enabled it to lessen its tax burden upon its great landowners and may have been a factor in their opposition to yielding the power to tax customs to Congress. New Jersey was also taxed by Pennsylvania at Philadelphia, which led to Madison's oft-quoted statement that New Jersey resembled a cask tapped at both ends.[21] Virginia and Maryland demanded export duties on the products of other states while some states raised their tonnage taxes against their neighbors and established retaliatory rates.[22] These long standing disputes were by no means unimportant in shaping the course of political events. It was, for example, the attempt of Maryland and Virginia to settle their perennial differences in regard to fishing and navigation rights on the Potomac and in Chesapeake Bay that led directly to the Mount Vernon, Annapolis and federal conventions.

Scarcely less important in revealing the continuing force of habit, custom and tradition were the quarrels within the states which they had also inherited from the days of their founding as colonies. Almost from the outset there had been a conflict between those who had remained along the seaboard and those who had first penetrated the hinterland. The seaboard people were prone to have more material possessions, to be more conservative in politics, religion and economics, and less venturesome in the pursuit of new lands and new ideas. The people who penetrated the forests tended to be the under-privileged persons who were more bold and courageous, or became so by the necessity and circumstances of their frontier environment. Here were the seeds of a more or less enduring struggle: the contest between the governor's party and the people's party, seaboard and frontier, land and capital, debtors and creditors, the ruled and their rulers. It was, in a sense, a continuation of the Leveller movement that had developed in the closing years of the English Civil war. It had flamed into violence in Bacon's rebellion in Virginia in 1676. One hundred years later it had been a factor in precipitating another revolution. Delayed for a time while hinterland and seaboard were fighting a common enemy, it merely smouldered to flame again in the struggle between agrarianism and commerce under the Confederation. Developing in the form of the paper money movement, which had been a more or less traditional problem throughout the colonial period, it culminated in Shays' rebellion in central Massachusetts in the winter of 1786-87, and so alarmed Hamilton's "gentlemen of property and principle" that it became a definite factor in the calling of the federal convention.[23]

The delegates viewed the developments of the day with an eye tinged with a certain amount of reaction. Representing the commercial interests and the country gentry of an eighteenth century America, they had scant sympathy with revolutionary movements once their political independence from Britain had been achieved, while not a few of these leaders had been related to the Tories by family and social ties. They had been called to check the growth of a revolutionary agrarian movement and the document they wrote was counter-revolutionary in its effect; they drew their ideas not so much from revolutionary England of the seventeenth century as the restoration of 1660, the settlement under William of Orange in 1689 and the Whig oligarchy of their own eighteenth century England. The writers of the Federalist papers seem to have been much impressed by the arguments of Locke, Harrington, Hume and Montesquieu in favor of a government in which land and commerce would be so balanced that neither would be able to achieve an undue advantage.[24] This idea was more or less explicitly stated by Madison in his famous tenth number of the Federalist.[25]

In the economic field the founders were doubtless influenced to a considerable extent by the philosophy of the middle class mercantilists of England and France.[26] Hamilton's later plea for government aid to manufacturers[27] reveals that this did not necessarily preclude public support for commercial enterprises in which they themselves were interested. This, too, was essentially the attitude of the English commercial class. Some of the American colonial leaders had also defended the navigation acts to the extent that they had developed colonial shipbuilding and excluded foreign manufactures.[28] The founding fathers were, in effect, urging the adoption of the economic policies of the British commercial class which they had sometimes praised but more frequently denounced.

It may seem somewhat paradoxical that in this particular area, the founding fathers ended by opposing the revolution they had precipitated. The situation becomes a bit clearer if we remind ourselves that while leaders may proclaim certain principles in order to secure popular support, revolutions are in no small degree struggles for political and economic power and not infrequently result in the continuation of the old abuses and inequities under the direction of new exploiters. The Anglo-American revolutions of the seventeenth and eighteenth centuries that were largely precipitated by the growing power of the middle class, tended to be rich men's wars and poor men's fights. The "gentlemen of property and principle" in the American colonies had desired to be free from British taxation, and while they had talked eloquently about liberty and freedom and the rights of man, it soon became clear that they had no desire to share their wealth with the under-privileged people of the frontier, the small farmers of the uplands and coastal plain, and the artisans and apprentices of the towns. The fact that these persons had done the actual fighting in the ranks and played a vital part in winning the revolution itself seems not to have counted greatly in their favor. If they had misunderstood the nature of the cause for which they had made their sacrifices, it was merely unfortunate for them. Let them go into the wilderness, occupy land beyond the mountains and cease to bother their betters along the seaboard. In the meantime drastic action had to be taken lest they get out of hand. So definite was the resolve taken at Philadelphia that even the conservative jurist and historian John W. Burgess was moved

to characterize it as a "coup d'etat." [29] This comment over-
looks the conservative customs of our English and colonial
constitutional development, as well as the inherent strength of
our liberal constitutional tradition. Seen in this perspective, the
work at Philadelphia represented little more than a vital step
in the evolution of our conservative and liberal traditions.

Side by side with Shays' rebellion was the failure of the states
to comply with the requisitions of Congress with the result
that the government was unable to support itself. Washington
had urged coercive powers in the hands of a general government as early as 1783.[30] By 1787 he seems to have converted
Madison to the same viewpoint.[31] Yet while the leaders of the
movement were definitely concerned with curbing the agrarian
and levelling tendencies of the times, they preferred to "rationalize" their aims by talking about balanced government and in
so doing they were drawing heavily upon the habits, customs
and traditions of the seventeenth century. The idea of a "balanced" government had long been advanced by certain English
writers and the leaders of the American counter-revolution
were by no means unacquainted with their writings.[32] The
concept had evolved through Aristotle, the Stoics, Polybius,
Cicero and the medieval schoolmen. Declining temporarily in
the late middle ages with the current trend towards royal absolutism, it revived with Grotius, Hooker and Hobbes and
their renewed emphasis upon the compact theory of the state.
Edward Hyde, Lord Falkland and Sir John Colepepper, in
replying to the demands of parliament on the eve of the English civil war, had pleaded for a system of check and balance
and separation in which the king should have executive and
administrative powers and share in legislation; the Lords judicial power and participation in legislation; while the Commons
should have impeachment powers, the initiative in financial
legislation and a share in general legislation.[33]

Cromwell also endeavored to establish a balanced government based upon the idea of fundamental law and urged his
parliament to impose limitations upon his powers by drafting

a written constitution. When it failed to do so, his military aides drafted the Instrument of Government in which he had insisted: "That Parliament should not make themselves perpetual; Liberty of Conscience in Religion; the army should be placed so equally that no one party neither in Parliament nor out of Parliament have the power of ordering it." Parliament failed to establish these constitutional principles with the result that Cromwell continued to exercise his dictatorial powers until his death.[34]

It is surely no accident that the American Revolution in its various stages was so reminiscent of the earlier Cromwellian revolution; that both contests were succeeded by periods of constitutional reconstruction in which checks and balances and limitations were imposed upon the arbitrary exercise of power that had precipitated the two struggles; and that both periods culminated in the establishment of constitutional government. The idea of a balanced government for which Cromwell had labored, bore fruit in the constitutional limitations imposed upon the king at the time of the restoration in 1660, when parliament declared that "according to the ancient and fundamental laws of the kingdom, the government is and ought to be by kings, lords and commons." It was also the basis for the English settlement of 1689; was defended by Bolingbroke in the eighteenth century in his long struggle against the ascendency of Walpole; and was a cardinal doctrine with Burke and the English Whigs in their efforts against the resurgence of the royal prerogative after 1760. We have seen that it was employed by Blackstone and was borrowed from him by the American colonial leaders in their efforts to defend their rights as British subjects under the constitution.[35] John Dickinson in his "Farmer's Letters" had emphasized this idea of balanced federal government when he insisted that while the general government could regulate commerce for the empire, the power to tax rested exclusively with the colonies themselves.[36] In speaking thus he seems to have represented both the past and the future: Locke's seventeenth century theory of balance was later woven into the American constitutional system as it evolved after 1789.[37] John Adams drew heavily upon these precedents in defending the doctrine of balance in a work published in 1787 entitled "A Defense of the Constitutions of the Government of the United States of America."[38] In emphasizing check and balance it is therefore clear that the leaders of the federal convention were reverting to the position taken by their Whig ancestors in seventeenth and eighteenth century England and that they themselves had maintained in the early period of the revolution. They had, to be sure, claimed that the king had disturbed the balance, while now it was Daniel Shays. The principle, however, remained the same as well as the object for which it was invoked; both the king and Daniel Shays had threatened to seize the sovereign power and confiscate the material possessions of the middle class commercial group. They did not, however, in all cases deem it wise openly to admit this fact. They preferred to "rationalize" the situation by emphasizing the traditional ideas that democracy would work successfully only when it was confined to small compact areas;[39] and that the majority of men were so swayed by their emotions as to be incapable of self-government.[40] They preferred to trust the rule of "reason" which had its customary roots in ancient classicism and the renaissance and which had been strengthened by the growth of neo-classicism and the "enlightenment" of the eighteenth century. They were, therefore, under the influence of two conflicting traditions: the rule of "reason" that induced them to frame a constitutional document by means of philosophical discussion and consent; and the non-rational and emotional traditions of the seventeenth century which were to return with full force with the revolutionary "romanticism" that marked the close of their own century. They were so fearful of these impending forces that they felt they must be curbed by balance and separation.[41] They would thus employ their "reason" to check their emotions. Subconsciously they may have realized that they were largely conditioned by their own bipolarity and the swing of the political and cultural pendulum.

Closely associated with the idea of a balanced government was the concept of federalism. The first aimed at check and balance among the functional powers of government; the second at check and balance in the geographic distribution of power among the component parts of a territorial federal union. It would seem to be reasonably accurate to say that the British empire in the eighteenth century, while politically centralized in theory, represented an inchoate federalism in fact in the sense that certain political functions were exercised by the central government in London and others by its component parts in America. The thirteen American colonies in America had been an integrated part of this system; they had been born into it and had a substantial share in shaping its growth and evolution. It had also shaped and conditioned their political thinking[42] to such an extent that it is difficult to see how they could have wholly escaped its influence at the Philadelphia convention and during the struggle over ratification.[43] Those powers retained by the states tended to resemble those that they had in practice exercised as component parts of the old empire, the government of the Continental Congress and the Confederation.[44] The old British empire in North America had for certain purposes been succeeded by the new American empire. The change in name and outward form was greater than the change in internal federal function.

The American concept of union had an English precedent in the acts of union between England and Scotland, as well as American precedents in the long series of acts beginning with the New England confederation of 1643, continuing with the Albany Congress of 1754, and culminating with the Articles of Confederation, the Alexandria, Annapolis and federal conventions.[45] The Albany plan itself foreshadowed some of the features of the federal union adopted at Philadelphia.[46] The forces of colonial particularism had slowly yielded to the most powerful single group among the settlers along the Atlantic seaboard; those of English descent who had inherited the English common law with its respect for private property combined with the English habit of political combination and compromise. These centralizing forces had triumphed over the forces of particularism in the American revolution. Delayed for a time by the disorders of the Confederation, they had triumphed again in the federal convention.

There were ample precedents for the creation of a written constitutional document. Periods of political strife and disorder in England had been followed by such written documents as Magna Carta, the Petition of Right, the Declaration of Right and the Act of Settlement. The American political leaders had been accustomed to written constitutional instruments in the form of colonial charters and the various colonial acts of union.[47] In both England and America the desire for written constitutional documents had been strengthened by the customary respect for the Bible as the recorded word of God. The fear of unwarranted official acts had impelled legislative and judicial bodies to create and preserve records of their proceedings which constituted a written body of constitutional precedents. The eighteenth century had also seen the rise of a powerful commercial class accustomed to the binding force of contractual agreements and eager to see their political rights similarly embodied in written documents.[48]

The affirmation of popular sovereignty in the document of 1787 was based upon those ideas of natural law and natural rights which the American colonies and states had inherited from the individualistic philosophy of Locke and the English revolutions of the seventeenth century.[49] It is perhaps significant that the idea of the electoral college, which was derived from a provision in the Maryland constitution of 1776, prescribing the method for the election of its state senators,[50] and more remotely, perhaps, from the idea of the electors of the Holy Roman Empire, and which was one of the few features of the document for which there was no clearly established precedent within the English constitutional system, was also one of the first to lose its force and validity and lapse into virtual desuetude.

The work of the federal convention was only a step—a long step, it is true—but still only a step in American constitutional development. It did little more than attempt to formalize certain areas within a vast constitutional system that was already established: state constitutions based largely upon colonial charters, which in turn were derived largely from English guilds and English trading corporations; town and county government that had largely evolved from English town and county government as it had existed in the seventeenth century; a legal system derived in large measure from the English common law;[51] and a body of political practice that in the colonial and early national period bore definite marks of its English origin; limited government, English precedents in the administration of justice, and a simple administrative structure with office holding as the prerogative of a country gentry and commercial oligarchy. These features characterized our government at the time of the ratification of the document of 1787 and until the next century was well advanced.[52]

The leaders of the federal convention were able to influence men of liberal leanings by an appeal to the English republican traditions of the seventeenth century as embodied in the theories of Sidney, Harrington and Locke,[53] as well as the habits and customs of the eighteenth century Anglo-American Whigs who believed in the rationalized ethics of work and free enterprise as preached in the economic gospel of Adam Smith.

In the English constitution sovereignty was vested in the crown; in the American constitution it was said to reside in the people. In both cases the power to exercise it was largely delegated to certain elected and appointed persons.[54] The concept of delegated and reserved powers was based upon the ideas of natural right and social contract[55] which had played such a vital part in the English revolutions of the seventeenth century and had been given a classic presentation by Locke.[56] While the idea of check and balance had developed in England as the result of a long struggle involving the crown, the aristocracy and the commons, the principle had suffered a definite check with the accession of William of Orange in 1689 and his recognition of parliamentary government. It is true that Bolingbroke in his long struggle with Walpole had insisted that the older custom of a balanced government was still an integral part of the English constitutional system.[57] The same concept was also maintained by such enlightened leaders as Blackstone and Burke. Blackstone had written that: ". . . herein indeed consists the true excellence of the English government, that all the parts of it form a mutual check upon each other."[58] Burke voiced a similar view when he declared that: "The great end undoubtedly of a mixed Government like ours, composed of monarchy, and of controuls, [sic] on the part of the higher people and the lower, is that the Prince shall not be able to violate the laws."[59] Bolingbroke, however, may have been influenced by his spirit of partisanship, Blackstone by his worship of ancient precedent, Burke by his inherent conservatism combined with his desire to curb the current growth of the royal prerogative, and all three by a nostalgic regret for the waning customs of an earlier age. A formal affirmation of the newer constitutional tradition may have had to wait for the passage of the Great Reform Act of 1832. Yet parliamentary supremacy tended to be the actual constitutional custom of eighteenth century England. The temporary resurgence of royal power under George III would seem to be an exception more apparent than real. This particular ruler, at the instigation of his German mother, endeavored to give actuality to a carefully nurtured myth with results disastrous to the British empire. The completeness of the collapse may indicate that England had been pursuing the shadows of a departed constitutionalism. Had it based its policies upon the political actualities of its own age, it might have achieved a greater measure of national unity and a happier issue of its imperial afflictions.

The so-called great compromise of the federal convention, establishing representation in the lower house on the basis of population and providing for equal representation in the senate, was a continuation of the struggle between the commercial and landed classes in England and America.[60] The commercial leaders of eighteenth century England and America also made similar concessions to the landed classes: in the west of England and in England's late western empire, the agricultural interests possessed representation in the national legislature far in excess of their numerical strength. As a part of the compromise between the American commercial and agricultural states, it was agreed that revenue bills should originate in the House of Representatives and require a mere majority vote. This was a continuation of the custom which had enabled the House of Commons in England and the lower houses of the colonial and state legislatures to exercise a major voice in appropriations and supplies.

Gouverneur Morris and the more conservative eastern leaders would have imposed limitations upon the evolution of self-government and statehood for the western area in much the same way that Britain had endeavored to impose limitations upon its western territory which Morris now represented.[61] Morris was unable to induce the federal convention to impose any specific limitations upon states to be admitted from the western area although he was able to defeat a proposal for the admission of new states "on the same terms with the original states." The clause as adopted declared that "new states may be admitted by the Congress into this union." [62] This would seem to imply that Congress had the right to impose limitations upon them and was a potential denial of state equality.[63] Thus the attitude of the federal convention was by no means dissimilar to the attitude that Britain had earlier taken in regard to the evolution of self-government within the American colonies along the Atlantic seaboard.

The American executive was given large powers while powerful checks were imposed upon their exercise. These powers bear the impress of the English constitution as it had existed before 1689 and as it had delegated strong executive powers to the American colonial governors. The presence of powerful checks shows the influence of the Anglo-American Whig oligarchy in the eighteenth century and its desire to increase the power of the legislature.[64] The power to remove "the President, Vice-President, and all civil officers of the United States" by impeachment exemplified a still older tradition: the right of the national community to depose its rulers which had existed in England and continental Europe from medieval times.[65]

Custom was not absent in connection with a considerable number of powers delegated to the new national Congress. Its power to legislate in such fields as piracy, paper money, coinage, postal affairs, naturalization, bankruptcy, Indian affairs and public lands, had an earlier English counterpart in the sense that parliament had enacted legislation in these areas for the government of the colonies.

In the establishment of the judicial power the framers of the document were also endeavoring to maintain the principles of check and balance and separation which they had inherited from Locke and the English revolutions. The conservative leaders were gravely disturbed by the growth of legislative power. In the Federalist Madison had declared that: "The legislative department is everywhere extending the sphere of its activity and drawing all power into its impetuous vortex . . . The conclusion which I am warranted in drawing is, that a mere demarcation on parchment of the constitutional limits of the several departments, is not a sufficient guard against those encroachments which lead to a tyrannical concentration of all the powers of government in the same hands." [66] The conservative leaders in Pennsylvania were alarmed by the growth of legislative power in that state;[67] while Madison felt the same alarm at a similar trend in his own state and was disturbed because the legislature possessed the sole right of interpreting the constitution.[68]

The first section of Article Three of the document of 1787 declared that: "The judicial power of the United States shall be vested in one Supreme Court, and in such inferior courts as the Congress may from time to time advise and establish. The judges both of the Supreme and inferior courts shall hold their office during good behavior." The first statement was in accordance with Locke's principle of check and balance and separation; while it has been suggested that the second was in accord with the precedent established by the English Act of Settlement of 1701 "which provided that the Judges' commissions should for the future be made *Quam diu seo bene gesserint* (during good behavior), and not *durante bene placito* (at the king's pleasure)." [69]

We have seen that in Bonham's case Sir Edward Coke had declared that "in many cases the common law will control acts of parliament and sometimes adjudge them to be utterly void . . ."; [70] while the American colonists had long been acquainted with the disallowance of laws by the Judicial Committee of the English Privy Council. The problem of judicial review was raised by James Otis, on February 24, 1761, in his speech against the Writs of Assistance, when he declared that "an act against the Constitution is void . . . The executive Courts must pass such acts into disuse." [71] It was also raised by the Massachusetts House of Representatives in a message to Governor Bernard, on October 24, 1765 when it referred to the "unconstitutional burdens" of the Stamp Act; [72] while on February 11, 1766, a court in Northampton County, Virginia, "unanimously declared it to be their opinion that the said act did not bind, effect, or concern the inhabitants of this colony, inasmuch as they conceive the same to be unconstitutional . . ." [73] The custom of judicial review had also developed in some of the states during the Confederation. It was formerly said that the Supreme Court of New Jersey in Holmes v Walton in 1780, had refused to recognize the validity of a state legislative act permitting the trial of certain cases before a jury of six on the ground that the state constitution required twelve. Research has revealed that six-man juries were employed until the adoption of the new constitution in 1844 so that the existence of such a decision has been seriously questioned.[74] The members of the federal convention were, however, acquainted with the case of Trevett v. Weeden in which the Supreme Court of Rhode Island had, in the autumn of 1786, declared the state paper money statute unconstitutional on the ground that it had failed to provide a trial by jury;[75] and while the convention was in session some of the delegates saw in the newspapers an account of the case of Bayard v. Singleton, in which the Supreme Court of North Carolina had declared unconstitutional a legislative act establishing trial by jury in certain cases.[76]

The document was relatively silent in regard to the general principles that were to govern public administration. Yet in the provision that no money was to be drawn from the public treasury except as authorized by law, it may be reasonable to assume that the founding fathers were recalling their unfortunate experiences with Stuart and Hanoverian rulers and their royal governors, who, to put it mildly, had sometimes strained at the colonial legislative leash in this area of public administration. Beyond this stipulation the founding fathers seem to have preferred to follow the English constitutional precedent of permitting public administration to evolve by habit, custom and tradition.

The sole direct reference to the federal electorate was the one declaring that "The House of Representatives shall be composed of members chosen every second year by the people of the several states, and electors [i.e. voters for members of this house] in each state shall have the qualifications requisite for electors of the most numerous branch of the state legislature." The qualifications for voting in the national elections were thus determined by the states, which were prone to retain certain property and religious qualifications they had inherited from England until the nineteenth century was well advanced.

The struggle over ratification represented a repetition of the struggle between land and commerce which had existed in

England prior to 1689 and its American continuation in terms of frontier and seaboard. The English restoration of 1660 represented a compromise between the leaders of land and commerce who feared the agrarian and artisan unrest of the Leveller movement; the document of 1787 represented a similar compromise and a similar victory for the leaders of the two groups. The tactics employed by the constitutionalists in Virginia in appointing Edmund Randolph as Attorney-General under the new government after he had at first opposed ratification and later favored it;[77] in making Hancock their candidate for the presidency of the constitutional convention in Massachusetts and later supporting him for the governorship,[78] had their earlier counterpart in the English restoration when the leaders won the support of Monk and other parliamentary generals by assuring them of positions of power and responsibility under the new government.[79] The American struggle over ratification thus represented a continuation of the traditional stake in society principle in the sense that economic and social elites may exert an influence upon the course of public events that is considerably in excess of their numerical strength. This was affirmed by Madison when he declared: "Had the constitution been framed and recommended by an obscure individual instead of a body possessing public respect and confidence, there cannot be a doubt that, although it would have stood in the identical words, it would have commanded little attention from those who now admire its wisdom." [80] Richard Henry Lee declared it promised benefits to military officers, lawyers, creditors, the clergy, salaried men and those dependent on money payments.[81] His statement in regard to the military men was attested in Pennsylvania, where it was said that commissions in the state militia were freely given to men of no previous military experience with the understanding that they vote for delegates pledged for ratification.[82] His remark in regard to the lawyers was verified when the country lawyers who had opposed ratification were induced to change their minds by promises of "prothonotaryships, attorney-generalships, chief

justiceships and what not . . ." [83] Thus ratification was aided
by a union of the leading merchants and the large landowners
who feared the artisans and agrarian unrest that had developed
in Shays' rebellion. This was especially true in Massachusetts,
the home of the rebellion;[84] while in Delaware, New Jersey,
Connecticut and Georgia, which were the first states to ratify,
there was the additional factor that smaller states would continue to exercise their traditional equality in law making
through their equal representation in the Senate. The abolition
of interstate taxation would also restore their traditional freedom of interstate commerce which had been threatened under
the Confederation. Even Georgia had found a considerable portion of its northeastern trade diverted to the port of Charleston, while it continued to suffer from Indian forays along its
southern and western borders, and hoped that a stronger central government would alleviate that condition.[85]

Extra-constitutional means prevailed in the action of the federal convention in drafting the new document despite its
express mandate merely to amend; in the extra-constitutional
decision that nine states be considered requisite for ratification;
as well as in the methods employed by certain leaders in the
struggle over ratification. In Pennsylvania the proponents for
ratification in the state legislature insisted upon passing a resolution calling for the election of delegates to a state constitutional ratifying convention before the members of the legislature had even received a copy of the document. The opponents
of the resolution refused to attend the sesssion on the last day,
hoping that the absence of a quorum would defer legislative
action until the next session; the constitutionalists raided their
lodgings, seized them, dragged them through the streets to the
legislative chamber and forcibly held them in their seats until
the affirmative vote was taken.[86] These tactics would seem to
represent a continuation of the revolutionary force and violence
that had existed between Whigs and Tories during the war and
the struggle between seaboard and frontier that had culminated
in Shays' rebellion. It might even be said that the founding

fathers were the spiritual heirs of the force and violence that had accompanied the extra-constitutional acts of the Cromwellian revolution. The turbulent scene in the Pennsylvania legislature represented a repetition of the extra-constitutional tactics employed by Cromwell in usurping the powers of his duly elected parliaments and those employed by Monk in demanding the dissolution of the Tory parliament in 1660 and taking the "responsibility" for negotiating with the exiled Charles. These extra-constitutional acts of the English revolution were almost invariably those of a relatively small number of persons and the same may be said of the extra-constitutional means employed by the federalists in forcing ratification through the state constitutional conventions. The election for delegates in Pennsylvania was held in such haste that many of the rural sections did not even hear of it until after it had taken place. Of the seventy thousand voters in the state only thirteen thousand actually voted, while the forty-six members of the convention who voted for ratification had been elected by sixty-eight hundred voters, or less than one-tenth the voting population of the state.[87]

The officers of Washington's army, many of whom had joined the newly organized Society of the Cincinnati, generally favored ratification. They represented the traditional conservatism of a military caste, while their experience with the weakness of the Continental Congress had impressed them with the need for stronger national powers. John Marshall, who had served as a captain under Washington at Valley Forge and Monmouth, had told the Virginia convention that the new document was necessary to provide for the common defense.[88] Basing his argument largely upon the weakness of Congress during the war,[89] he also declared that the habits, customs and traditions of mankind proved that weak nations had always been at the mercy of the strong.[90] This was the attitude of the majority of the military men in the Virginia state convention.[91] Washington was known to favor the proposed government and although he was not a delegate, his influence was thought to be considerable.[92] Some of the members of the Virginia convention had been Tories, yet they, too, were federalists.[93] This would seem to indicate that they felt the proposed document more truly represented the British traditions in government than did the Confederation.

The under privileged classes clung more or less closely to the older political tradition. Experience under the royal governors and the attempt at British centralized control prior to the outbreak of the Revolution had taught them to distrust concentrated political authority with the result that they feared the unifying tendencies of the federalists and the work of the Philadelphia convention.[94] There was a fear that this centralized political power would be supported by a large standing army. Patrick Henry expressed this traditional fear which Americans had inherited from their English forbears when he told the Virginia convention that: "If Congress shall say that the general welfare requires it, they may keep armies continually on foot . . . They may billet them on the people at pleasure."[95] Richard Henry Lee declared that: "By means of taxes, the government may command the whole or any part of the subject's property."[96] This would seem to be an appeal to the traditional fear that still lingered in the popular mind at the memory of the arbitrary taxes Britain had endeavored to impose on the eve of the Revolution.

Those opposed to ratification also feared that the new central government would assume payment of the continental currency. The decision of the Rhode Island Supreme Court in the case of Trevett v. Weeden was based upon the English common law principle of the inviolability of a contract. The proposed documentary constitution expressly stated that there should be no abrogation of the right of contract. The federalists were thus aiming directly at the state legislatures that under the influence of the agrarian and debtor elements, were issuing debt moratoriums and passing paper money laws. Patrick Henry warned the Virginia delegates that the new government would require the state to pay its share of this paper currency[97] despite the fact that much of it was in the hands of northern speculators.[98] He also added: "Is it not their business to appreciate this money? Yes, and it will be your business to prevent it. But there will be a majority against you, and you will be obliged to pay your share of this money, in its nominal value." [99]

The western people also feared that the proposed government would continue the traditional attitude of the British in viewing their interests as subordinate to the eastern seaboard[100] and to be balanced against the national need for placating the Spanish and Indians, although it has also been said that in Virginia and Georgia, the traditional fear of the Indians may have been a factor in inducing ratification.[101] It is perhaps significant that ten out of the fourteen members of the Kentucky delegation in the Virginia convention voted against ratification.[102] They were bred in a tradition that had developed a profound distrust and fear of executive, administrative and judicial powers as exercised by royal governors, administrators and judges. They were less opposed to legislative action because the tradition of parliamentary neglect in the era prior to 1763 still lingered in their minds, while they felt that under colony and confederation the legislatures had been less hostile to their views. Cherishing their tradition of personal liberty as embodied in the English bill of rights, they feared that the "gentlemen of property and principle," the lawyers and men of education, were conspiring to deprive them of their heritage.[103]

We realize the strength of this older tradition when we read that the failure of forty-six towns to send delegates to the Massachusetts convention may have been decisive. They were so bitterly opposed to ratification that had they been represented Massachusetts might well have failed to ratify.[104] This might have led to rejection in Virginia and the failure to secure the requisite nine states. It is another illustration of the continuing force of habit, custom and tradition that Massachusetts, with its long cherished religious freedom and fear of an Anglican episcopate, was one of the states in which the religious issue was raised. John Holmes feared that the proposed government gave Congress the power to establish an inquisitional church[105] and Thomas Lusk feared "that Popery and the Inquisition may be established in America."[106]

Thus the leading argument against ratification had been that the people were in danger of losing their traditional liberties because the proposed document did not contain a bill of rights, and strong as were the constitutionalists in wealth and organization, it is doubtful if ratification would have been achieved had they not at last definitely promised such a written guarantee. Here, too, the course of American constitutional evolution resembled the English pattern. The theory and philosophy of the American bill of rights was based upon Locke's theory that personal and property rights were natural, inalienable, indefeasible and reserved,[107] and that it was the chief duty of the state to preserve and protect them.[108] The English restoration of 1660 and the settlement of 1689 were accompanied by special guarantees affirming English liberties and a considerable degree of religious toleration.[109] The American Revolution also saw the principle of religious liberty imposed upon the national government by groups purporting to represent the states and embodied in the first amendment of the bill of rights.[110] The American fear of a standing army was inherited from the military rule of Cromwell and his major generals, the efforts of James II to overawe London by his encampment on Hounslow Heath, and the Massachusetts Quartering Act on the eve of the American Revolution. The English military abuses had been followed by the British Quartering Act which permitted the people to bear arms and forbade the billeting of soldiers on householders in time of peace without their consent.[111] These two provisions of the English bill of rights were also embodied in the state documentary constitutions and became a part of the national bill of rights as limitations imposed upon the national government by the states.

The Bill of Rights, like the document of 1787, was based upon habits, customs and traditions of America's past. These traditions differed considerably, however, from the traditional bases of the written documentary constitution. The latter were based largely upon traditions that had their roots in collective and cooperative action, while the former was derived in no small degree from the traditions of European individualism and its particularistic fragmentation. It embodied the seeds of an ancient and honorable tradition that has been traced from the Babylonians and Hebrews to the ancient Greeks. Developed by the Sophists and peripatetic philosophers who dared to oppose the will of the Greek tyrants with their own individualistic theories, it was perpetuated by the Stoics, who, while they taught that man was a citizen of the world, also emphasized the idea that he must retain the mastery of his own will and spirit. This concept was transmitted to ancient Rome and incorporated into Roman jurisprudence by Cicero and the later Roman jurists, Gaius, Ulpian and Gratian, in terms of the indefeasible and inalienable rights of the Roman citizen. Adopted by St. Augustine and the early Christian fathers, it became a cardinal doctrine of Thomas Aquinas and the medieval schoolmen. With the decline of the empire, it was transmitted to the middle ages through the civil and canon law. The former recognized the innate right of the citizen in his relations with his community—his city state, his guild, his church; while the canon and ecclesiastical law proclaimed his inalienable rights as a communicant of the city of God.[112]

These doctrines of natural law and natural right survived the medieval period to become a part of the heritage of the early national states. Their influence may have waned temporarily with the rise and growth of royal absolutism in the sixteenth and early seventeenth centuries, yet they were also employed to limit the political power of these new national monarchs. They survived in the English legal writings of Bracton, Fortesque and Saint German and through them to Coke and Blackstone, and thus to colonial and early national America.[113]

This spirit of English individualism was not confined to its juristic and political leaders. It possessed that sense of personal freedom which was inherent in English religious movements from the days of Wyclif and the Lollards[114] to the rise of those staunch protagonists of human rights, the Puritans.

These doctrines reappeared in the English Civil War among the more radical Cromwellian groups known as the Independents and still more radical Levellers. They seem to have based their appeals in part upon the idea of natural rights, and perhaps even more upon the principle of natural law which was more or less synonymous with the medieval churchman's concept of the innate justice of God and His constant concern for the freedom and welfare of the individual soul. This debate between Cromwell and the Levellers was followed by the dictatorship, the restoration and the glorious revolution. It may be suggested, however, that the bill of rights of 1689 represented a compromise between conflicting forces in the sense that the tradition of collective power was recognized in the form of a constitutional monarchy under such limitations as the Whigs insisted represented a continuation of the idea of social contract; while the bill of rights represented a continuation of the spirit of the Levellers and their insistence upon the political fragmentation of power.

This tradition of independency was a portion of the American heritage which was accentuated and strengthened by American frontier conditions with the result that our bill of rights, both in its wording and the spirit that animated it, was one of the traditions that we inherited directly from England. Its formulation in 1689 owed much to Harrington and Locke and these two authorities were known and quoted by exponents of our American bill of rights. Harrington intrigued John Adams,[115] while the influence of Locke upon Jefferson is well known.[116] The European continental influences also penetrated colonial America. James Otis had quoted Vattel, Grotius, Pufendorf and Rousseau in defense of his theory of fundamental law.[117] Yet their impact upon American colonial thought was naturally less direct and powerful than that of the English philosophers.

The result was an American constitution that contained not

a few of the habits, customs and traditions of the English constitution.[118] Our political independence of Britain, our Articles of Confederation and our document of 1787 by no means destroyed the continuity of our constitutional growth. The political philosophy of the founding fathers was derived in no small measure from that of the English middle class. It may have been liberal in theory since it substituted the idea of "popular" sovereignty for the older principle of an autocratic kingship; yet it was not democratic in the current sense of that term since the actual exercise of political power and the legal right to vote remained in the hands of the educated and propertied groups.[119]

It was not until the American political revolution of 1800 and the extension of statehood beyond the Alleghenies that we see the quickened tempo of certain political habits and customs that were more definitely indigenous to the American climate and soil.

CHAPTER VI

CHAPTER VI

TRADITIONAL ELEMENTS IN THE EARLY AMERICAN CONSTITUTIONAL PERIOD

"... Republics are famous for their superstitious attachments to old customs; they are afraid that changes for the better may destroy the stability of the state, and the government of aristocratic Venice still preserves its original Greek character." The Memoirs of Casanova De Seingalt. Twelve volumes. The Venetian Society. London and New York, 1929. Vol. VII, pp. 239-240.

"... The mythology of a people is not determined by its history, but on the contrary, its history is determined by its mythology—or rather, mythology does not *determine,* but is itself the people's destiny, its lot fallen to it from the beginning..." Fritz Wittels: Freud and His Time. Liveright Publishing Corporation, New York, 1931, p. 122.

There was no king and court at the capital cities of New York and Philadelphia. Yet Jefferson and his republican followers insisted that there was a strong tendency for Washington and his circle to create a court and ape the manners of English royalty.[1] Some of the republicans had even objected to the parades and pageantry with which the news of ratification had been received.[2] Despite the fact that these were ancient and well-tested political devices for gaining popular support for public action, the republicans insisted that they savored of the trappings of royalty and were reminiscent of the pageantry and display that accompanied a royal coronation.[3] It seemed to them that the people were being taught to say: "King Confederation is dead. Long live King Constitution." Jefferson even professed to feel that such ceremonies would culminate in a government that closely resembled the British monarchy.[4]

The new documentary constitution was launched upon a wave of prosperity and the federalists were not averse to taking the credit for it, while placing the blame for the depression from which the country had just emerged upon the absence of a strong government under the Articles. To the republicans this savored of fulsome flattery. They were not unacquainted with the fact that English monarchs had been greeted with addresses of welcome in which sycophantic subjects referred to the "unhappy events that preceded your reign" and "the era of peace and prosperity which your gracious majesty has inaugurated." The republicans felt that this savored of the flattery that had greeted Charles II at the restoration. They felt that although they were the heirs of the English revolution of 1688, their tradition had been rejected in favor of the royalist tradition of the restoration of 1660. Jefferson even maintained that there was a tradition to establish a monarchy. John Adams seemed at times to believe that a constitutional monarchy would evolve because the precedents seemed to indicate that democratic and aristocratic extremes tended to capitulate to limited monarchy.[5] There seems also to have been an attempt to maintain the idea that the American president, like the English king, was above the strife of partisan faction.[6] This would help to explain why Jefferson and Hamilton could remain in office under Washington: they remained bitterly antagonistic and yet without any sense of disloyalty to the president. In Washington's case there seems also to have been the desire to maintain the traditional idea of a constitutional check and balance even within the cabinet itself.[7]

Certain habits of Washington supported by Adams[8] and Hamilton,[9] gave color to the republican statements that he aped the customs of monarchy: his public receptions or "levees"; his coach and four; his journeys about the country which were compared with royal progresses; the fact that he was greeted with cries resembling the salutations formerly reserved for royalty;[10] and the fact that his birthday was celebrated as a festival.[11]

The English tradition of respect for the king and the royal prerogative soon reappeared in the form of a worship of the document of 1787 and the laws and ordinances that evolved under it, so that the habit and custom of worshipping the symbols of sovereignty continued largely unabated. It resembled the earlier worship of the sovereign in the sense that political factions could differ widely in matters of policy and simultaneously protest that they were the true defenders of the constitution. It also tended to unite and stabilize the government and place it beyond the reach of party faction, even as the English sovereign had been so placed by the Act of Settlement of 1689. As early as January, 1776, Thomas Paine in his *Common Sense* had urged the worship of a supreme organic law in place of the king.[12] Many of the framers of the document of 1787 had been doubtful of the success of the new government; yet the custom which had expressed itself in veneration for the king and the royal prerogative soon reasserted itself in its praise. Thus Washington in his Farewell Address emphasized: "Respect for its authority, compliance with its laws, acquiescence in its measures," and urged "that you resist with care the spirit of innovation upon its principles..."[13]

This emotional worship of the document of 1787 represented the evolution of a social myth in the field of domestic power politics: a process by which a small revolutionary group after having seized the political controls, seeks to invest their *fait accompli* with an odor of sanctity by ascribing the event to the decree of heaven,[14] or at least to the voice of the people, which in the popular revolutionary parlance of the late eighteenth century was said to be the voice of God; and this, too, despite the fact that the great majority of the people had little or no share in creating the document of 1787 and had been either indifferent or actively opposed to its adoption.

This would seem to imply that the founding fathers were not unaware of the importance of habit, custom and tradition as a stabilizing force in the conduct of public affairs. Voltaire's remark to the effect that if God did not exist it would be necessary to create Him, has its parallel in the need for political traditions: the founding fathers may have felt that if political habits, customs and traditions were relatively non-existent it would be sound political wisdom to create them. They had worshipped many of the traditions of the British constitution and that worship they transferred to the newly established American constitution. During the early revolutionary period they had maintained that they were the true defenders of the English constitution as it had been stabilized by the great events of the latter half of the seventeenth century and that the king and parliament by their arbitrary conduct since 1763 were the innovators. Thus the Federalist leaders, while they did not openly praise the British constitution in the first decade of our constitutional development, were still inclined to worship not a few of its seventeenth century traditions. In the federal convention Hamilton had definitely avowed his respect for the British constitution in general and the House of Lords in particular;[15] while James Wilson of Pennsylvania confessed his respect for the English republican tradition of the seventeenth century when he observed that the English revolution of 1688 did more than "set a mere precedent in England." He declared that: "This revolution principle—that the sovereign power residing in the people, they may change their constitution and government whenever they please—is not a principle of discord, rancor, or war; it is a principle of melioration, contentment, and peace." [16] We know, too, that Jefferson strongly favored this English republican tradition. He would also have America continue its simple agricultural way of life as the best guarantee of individual liberty.[17]

It would seem, therefore, that the differences between the Federalists and Republicans represented an American continuation of the English constitutional struggle between the royal and republican traditions.[18] The Federalists were the heirs of the more aristocratic tradition, while Jefferson represented the tradition of the English Independents and Levellers as strengthened by the spirit of the newer American frontier.[19] The Republicans felt that one of their first opportunities to continue their tradition was to propose and ratify the bill of rights which had evolved from the Leveller movement of the Cromwellian revolution and which had been promised them during the struggle over ratification. Thus the Republicans, no less than the Federalists, became political myth makers and insisted that they were the true guardians of the constitution despite the fact that they had done their best to defeat its ratification. Drawing their strength in no small measure from English seventeenth century republicanism, they insisted that this republican tradition would be in safe hands once they had defeated the Federalist leaders and driven them from office. This was essentially the position taken by Jefferson, the great founder and leader of his party.[20]

We have already indicated that the document of 1787 represented a written embodiment of a considerable number of the principles of the English constitutional system. Since it is generally agreed by modern students of political science that all constitutions must of necessity be partly written and partly unwritten and that the distinction between so-called written and unwritten constitutions is one of degree rather than kind, it is also important to observe that while the American document of 1787 represented a written statement of a considerable number of the principles embodied in the English constitutional system, it also continued the customary and unwritten tradition of the English constitutional system by omitting to reduce many vital matters to writing and preferring to trust to the evolution of events and the habits, customs and traditions of the future. The importance of the American document lies almost as much in its "masterly silences" as in its written statements and in this respect it was following the great tradition of the so-called unwritten elements in the British constitutional system. In refusing definitely to define the question of ultimate sovereignty it was following the English constitutional principles of the seventeenth century which had suffered a temporary eclipse under the so-called "personal" rule of George III; but the hour of the new English revolution had not struck, for the American Revolution was soon followed by the French Revolution and the Napoleonic wars with the result that the principle of parliamentary supremacy was not formally recognized until the passage of the great reform bills in the nineteenth century. The American document of 1787, in failing to designate the final arbiter in a dispute among functional or territorial powers, was repeating the custom of seventeenth century constitutional England, which had failed to provide for a final arbiter in a dispute between king and parliament, or between southwestern agricultural England and eastern commercial England. The results of this omission were by no means dissimilar: the English civil war tended to be the English arbiter even as the American civil war was later destined to be the American arbiter.

The American constitutional system therefore resembled the English in the sense that it gave ample scope for its evolution by means of functional and customary change. Hamilton as the leader of the Federalists was determined that this customary evolution should mainly follow the program of the English commercial group as it had evolved since the revolution of 1688 and the accession of William of Orange.[21] Blackstone in his Commentaries had declared that: "A certain proportion of debt seems . . . to be highly useful to a trading people ..."[22] This would seem to explain the founding of the Bank of England, stabilizing the national debt and the creation of the sinking fund. Hamilton endeavored to enlist the support of the corresponding middle class in America—the bankers, merchants, manufacturers and speculators—in favor of the new government by similar means: a national bank, the assumption of a national debt and its payment by means of a sinking fund created by national taxation.[23] In his famous first report on the public credit, he had urged the assumption of the state debts.[24] The proposal met with the bitter opposi-

tion of the agricultural interests,[25] as it had in England a
century earlier[26] when a similar plan of creating a permanent funded debt had led to the founding of the Bank of
England.[27] It has also been suggested that Hamilton was
also influenced by such later English financial legislation as
the Sinking Fund Act of 1786 sponsored by the younger
Pitt.[28] Hamilton's proposal met with bitter opposition in
Virginia where that state by the sale of its public lands had
paid a large proportion of its debt.[29] The Virginia House of
Delegates protested to Congress in a memorial drafted by
Patrick Henry, in which it insisted that it was the duty of the
states to act as "sentinels" in protecting the rights of their
people against federal encroachment.[30] Here was a continuation of the English republican tradition that had petitioned so
vigorously in the seventeenth century against the growth of
the royal prerogative under the Stuarts. Yet Hamilton persisted and in the defense of his plan evolved his theory of implied and resultant powers,[31] which was strongly reminiscent
of the arguments advanced by the English court party in defending the abuses of the royal prerogative by the Stuart kings.
It is significant that the bank aimed to establish a monopoly in
the form of a government fiscal agent, and monopolies, benev-
olences and forced loans had been favorite devices with the
Tudor and Stuart kings; that the opposition to monopolies
under James I had become so violent that the king had been
compelled to abolish their worst abuses by proclamation; and
in 1624 parliament had aimed at their more general abolition.
The attempt of Charles I to revive them had been so bitterly
resented that it was one of the forces leading to his downfall.

Madison in opposing the bank in the House of Representatives declared that: "The doctrine of implication is always a
tender one. The danger of it has been felt by other Governments. The delicacy was felt in the adoption of our own; the
danger may also be felt if we do not keep close to our chartered authorities . . . It takes from our constituents the opportunity of deliberating on the untried measures, their hands are

also to be tied by the same terms . . . It involves a monopoly which affects the equal rights of every citizen." [32] This would seem to be a clear implication that he felt the doctrine of implied powers was a counterpart of the royal prerogative as abused by the Stuart kings in the grant of monopolies and the exercise of the dispensing power on the eve of the revolution of 1688. Madison might also have reminded the Federalists of certain events that had precipitated the American Revolution. He was confronted with the edifying spectacle of Washington, Hamilton and their Federalist followers, who had professed to rebel against the theory of inherent power when exercised by a "despotic" king, resorting to the same concept to defend their own extensions of power.

The bill was bitterly opposed by the republicans and of the twenty negative votes in the House, nineteen were from the South. This would seem to show that the opposition felt the plan was for the advantage of the commercial north [33] even as the Bank of England had been strongly supported by the commercial classes and opposed by the agricultural areas. Ames in writing to Dwight had declared that "I do not believe that the hatred of the Jacobites towards the House of Hanover was ever more deadly than that which is borne by many of the partisans of State power towards the government of the United States." [34]

Jefferson, true to his republican traditions, had opposed Hamilton's doctrine of implied and resultant powers to justify the establishment of the bank. The roots of Jefferson's thinking stemmed from the thought and practice of the earlier agricultural England of the seventeenth century and not the later England that had seen the ascendency of the commercial class. A believer in the check and balance of Locke, he also preferred a sound balance between town and country and feared that a powerful commercial group would impose its power upon agriculture as it had done in eighteenth century England when the newly ennobled commercial groups had framed the enclosure acts, appropriated the common lands and driven the impoverished agricultural workers to the towns. He seems to have viewed the American constitutional system of 1789 not as a monopolistic agency to be dominated by any one group but more akin to the English corporations and chartered companies of the Elizabethan and early seventeenth century periods, which were to be strictly construed under the terms of their express grants and changed only with the consent of the grantee, which meant the people of the states acting through their state legislatures or state constitutional conventions.

Hamilton had his way and proceeded to put his financial principles into effect and vindicate them by the use of coercive power in the case of the whiskey insurrection in western Pennsylvania in 1794.[35] His excise bore most heavily upon the western farmers, who had been the most bitterly opposed to his fiscal policy and who were less likely to be touched by his tax on imports, since the lack of roads and transportation prevented their consumption of imported commodities.[36] In resorting to the excise he was also following the same custom employed by Britain that had led directly to the war. The western farmers were not unmindful of this fact[37] and they, too, responded with a rebellion.

Jefferson had hoped that the federal courts would declare these acts unconstitutional. Since they failed to do so, he turned to the states and following the passage of the Alien and Sedition Acts of 1798, he and Madison formulated the Kentucky and Virginia resolutions[38] that expanded Virginia's early theory of sentinelship and announced the compact theory of the constitution: the states as sovereign political bodies granted certain powers to the national government while retaining sovereignty in all other matters. In viewing the Alien and Sedition laws as a serious threat to the bill of rights in general and freedom of speech and press in particular,[39] Jefferson and Madison were heirs of the seventeenth century revolutionary tradition that had emphasized the compact theory of government and formulated the English bill of rights in 1689. Jefferson had expressed the same view in the Declaration of Independence. The spirit of 1689 and 1776 animated the resolutions of 1798.

Turning from the traditional elements in the interpretation of the document of 1787 to those involved in the exercise of its functional powers, we shall see that traditional elements were not lacking in the evolution of the presidency. The influence of the English kingship still lingered in the relation between the new American executive and the national legislature. At the outset it had appeared that the Senate might become an advisory body to the president after the manner of the English Privy Council. Soon, however, it proceeded to assert its independence to such an extent that the tendency was checked as certain members from the agricultural states expressed their seventeenth century sense of independence and check and balance. Yet Washington was reluctant to depart from the ancient forms and still continued to address the two houses in a manner reminiscent of the king's speech from the throne.[40] In recent years the administrative functions of the British and American governments have tended in fact, if not in theory, to be more or less separate and independent branches of their respective governments. In the time of which we write, however, it would seem to be more correct to think of national public administration as appertaining more or less to the executive power. The English system of a ministry executing sovereign powers and responsible to parliament had become more or less definitely recognized under the ministry of Sir Robert Walpole and American political leaders were not unacquainted with this customary evolution. It may be significant that while administrative functions were implied by the document of 1787 in the clause stating that the executive might ask the advice of heads of departments on writing, practically no provisions were stipulated for their administrative exercise. Since the founding fathers knew that British administration had largely evolved by custom and tradition, they may have felt it would be best to trust to the growth of custom in this functional area. The customs that actually developed did not wholly differ from the British customs as they were known to the American leaders in the period prior to American independence. We have already seen that the attitude towards Washington was reminiscent of the English attitude towards the kingship. He was the head of the state and its various functional activities, including its functional administration.[41] Hamilton was so enamored of the English governmental model that he endeavored to emulate its example. He issued directives to the other departments while he was administering his own much as though he were the English prime minister and chancellor of the exchequer.[42] He informed the Attorney-General that "there appears to be too much tartness in various parts"[43] of a certain draft. Despite the opposition of Secretary of War Knox, he continued to make purchases for the War department and even induced Congress to pass an act confirming his action in this area.[44] Jefferson submitted a report on negotiations with Spain for the free navigation of the Mississippi for his approval;[45] while he also asked him for suggestions in regard to the wording of a proposed commercial treaty with the same country.[46] Finally, however, Jefferson felt that Hamilton was exercising undue influence in the negotiations with Britain and France that preceded the neutrality proclamation of 1793.[47] To Jefferson's plea of departmental autonomy, Hamilton countered with concepts of concerted cabinet action.[48] It is perhaps no accident that this administrative conception had its earlier counterpart in the principles of cabinet unity, responsibility and solidarity that had already evolved in Britain and with which Hamilton could not have been unacquainted. Another precedent would seem also to exist in the administrative unity that had tended to prevail in the English privy council and the council of the American colonial governors.

Hamilton also wished to have the House of Representatives appeal to him directly for reports dealing with public policy. This, however, was opposed by Jefferson and perhaps by Washington with the result that he appears to have abandoned the practice. Yet it also tends to indicate that at the outset he was definitely influenced by the English parliamentary model of a chief minister endeavoring to direct legislative action.[49]

The office of the Secretary of the Treasury seems to have been organized with the idea that it owed a special responsibility to Congress. The Secretary was specifically enjoined to perform such financial duties as should be required of him by Congress, and also to make reports and give information to either branch of the legislature, in person or in writing.[50] This would seem to indicate a continuing Anglo-American tradition to the effect that legislative bodies were jealous of their right to control the purse and determined to hold officers of fiscal administration to a strict accountability.[51] Hamilton, on the other hand, seems to have had in mind the more recent tradition of an eighteenth century English chancellor of the exchequer, endeavoring to control the conduct of financial legislation.[52] After he was denied the privilege of addressing the House in person,[53] he proceeded with considerable success to dictate financial policy by indirection and political manipulation until 1794. By that time the House was able to hold its own through the rise and growth of its own finance committee.[54]

This, however, was not until Hamilton had formulated his excise tax that precipitated the Whiskey insurrection and drafted the proclamation of September 15, 1792, in which the leaders were ordered to desist.[55] It has been suggested that he deliberately provoked a crisis by issuing writs commanding persons to appear at Philadelphia despite the fact that a law had been passed permitting their appearance in the state courts of the area affected.[56] Following a conference between the leaders of the national government and the state government of Pennsylvania, in which the two groups were unable to agree upon a plan of action,[57] it was Hamilton again, who pleaded with Washington to exercise such a display of force "as will deter the opposition, save the effusion of the blood of citizens, and serve the object to be accomplished."[58] He had urged the use of 12,000 militia, yet Washington called for 12,950 "which indicates, in striking fashion, the great influence of his Secretary."[59] This number was later increased to

15,000.[60] In justice to Washington it should be added that he made every effort to impress the expedition with the idea that it was to support the civil authorities and not supplant them. The regular courts remained open and at no time was martial law declared.[61] The new country was continuing the tradition of the old to the effect that military power should always be strictly subordinate to the civil authorities.[62]

The next important case of civil disorder occurred during the administration of John Adams in 1798 when a considerable number of persons in three counties of eastern Pennsylvania opposed the federal assessments levied to meet the expenses of the expected war with France. Adams acted more largely on his own initiative than had Washington in sending troops and in pardoning John Fries and the other leaders who had been convicted of treason.[63] He may have employed greater force than was necessary yet once the disorder was quelled, he followed the English traditions by giving precedence to the civil authorities over the military.

In the field of foreign relations Jefferson favored the recognition of the new French government largely on the basis of the social contract which he had presented in the Declaration of Independence,[64] and which in turn had been based upon the ideas of Locke and the revolutionary philosophy of the seventeenth century. The policy of "neutrality"[65] tended to represent a continuation of his ideas of political independence in the diplomatic field. This concept also had to be balanced against the fact that the new country was continuing its colonial inheritance as a factor in European power politics. It was certainly far from "isolation" in the decade that followed the ratification of the document of 1787. In playing the balance of power game in its relations with Britain, France and Spain to the extent that its limited resources permitted,[66] it was following the traditions of power politics as it had been played by Britain since the accession of Henry VII.

The proclamation of 1793 also gave Hamilton an opportunity to present his concept of executive power in the conduct of foreign relations. Here, as in the field of finance, he demonstrated that he was a strong eighteenth century traditionalist with a decided preference for continuing the customs of the British constitution within the framework of the newly established government.[67] He took the position that the general conduct of foreign relations, including the right to issue a proclamation of neutrality, was constitutionally conferred upon the president as a part of his executive power, subject only to the qualifications and exceptions specifically indicated in the written instrument.[68] This interpretation was bitterly opposed by Jefferson and Madison, who countered with the seventeenth century traditions of Locke,[69] and the principles of check and balance and separation, that would vest a larger measure of such power in the legislature.[70] In writing to Jefferson, Madison referred to: "An assumption of prerogative not clearly found in the Constitution and having the appearance of being copied from a monarchical model . . ."[71] Spurred by Jefferson, Madison also attacked Hamilton's arguments in his famous Letters of Helvidius.[72] Asking Hamilton specifically for the sources of his ideas, he answered his own question by declaring: "There is but one answer to this question. The power of making treaties and the power of declaring war, are *royal prerogatives* in the *British government,* and are accordingly treated as *executive prerogatives* by *British commentators.*"[73] He also objected to the fact that Hamilton had referred to the proclamation as emanating from the "government" and added: "The 'government' unquestionably means, in the United States, the whole government, not the executive part, either exclusively, or *pre-eminently:* as it may do in a monarchy, where the splendour of prerogative eclipses, and the machinery of influence directs every other part of the government."[74]

We concluded the Jay treaty[75] with Britain in 1794, in which we yielded much and gained little since we were so weak that we could not well do otherwise.[76] This, too, was representative of European power politics: a weak state must yield to a stronger and bide its time with the hope that it may grow stronger. The Federalists also inherited from Britain a traditional distrust for France which was rendered acute by the XYZ Affair[77] and the various acts of hostility between the two countries from 1798 to 1800. Adams, in endeavoring to work for peace, disappointed the conservative wing of his own party, that was not wholly averse to war,[78] because of its hatred of French republicanism and its feeling that a war would strengthen national unity and enable it to win the election of 1800.[79] Here again, these leaders were following a device long practiced in Europe: a party in control of the government and finding its leadership threatened, may seek to strengthen its position by precipitating a foreign war.

The organization and procedure of Congress was based to a considerable extent upon the habits, customs and traditions of the English parliament which had been transmitted through the customs of the colonial and state legislatures. Thus in the selection of members for the House of Representatives, we employed methods that did not differ widely from the English system of electing members for the House of Commons: the single, undifferentiated geographic district and the property and religious qualifications for voting that existed in most of the states. The American system lacked many of the minor, medieval inequities of the English development, although the major injustice of the English rotten borough system continued in the United States in the form of vast inequities of representation between seaboard and frontier. Thus the American seaboard deprived its own frontier of representation in much the same way that it had been denied representation when it had been the frontier of an expanding Britain. In both countries the older propertied groups were endeavoring to check the representative wishes of a newer society. Religious and property qualifications restricted the suffrage in both countries and the movement for universal manhood suffrage did not develop in either Britain or the United States until the next century was well advanced.

The organization and procedure of the House of Representatives had much in common with that of the House of Commons. The first rules of procedure were based largely upon a manual prepared by Jefferson, which was in turn based upon the parliamentary procedure of the House of Commons. The fact that each house was to make its own rules and be the judge of the qualifications of its own members represented a principle that had been won by the House of Commons in its long struggle for parliamentary privilege and had been transmitted to our House of Representatives by way of the American colonial and state assemblies. It was also understood that the elected speaker was to resemble the English speaker in the sense that he was to be merely an impartial presiding officer and our system saw no departure from this principle until the election of Henry Clay as speaker in 1811. The early House of Representatives also resembled the Commons in its system of standing committees, its committee of the whole, its rules for debate and the conduct of its members.

For a time it appeared as if the Senate might become an advisory body of the executive after the manner of the English Privy Council and the council of the colonial governor. Soon, however, it proceeded to assert its independence to such an extent that the tendency was checked,[80] although vestigial remains continued in the form of secret executive sessions. Yet elements of habit, custom and tradition were not absent in its organization and work. Its share in the treaty making function had its earlier counterpart in the English Privy Council and its vital part in the conduct of foreign relations under the Stuarts and Hanoverians. It also had its American origins in the conflict between seaboard and frontier and the agricultural and commercial states. Hamilton and Gouverneur Morris of New York, as representatives of the centralizing traditions of the English kingship and a commercial oligarchy, preferred to vest the conduct of foreign relations largely in the executive;[81] while James Wilson of Pennsylvania and George Mason of Virginia, as representatives of the more independent landed traditions, hoped that a larger measure of its direction would be lodged in the Senate and House.[82] The resulting compromise, in which it was shared by the executive and the Senate, again exemplifies the influence of Locke and the English republican tradition of the seventeenth century with its emphasis upon check and balance as a means of limiting executive power. It also bears a marked resemblance to Locke's theory that the conduct of foreign relations was a "federative" power which involved the defense of the whole community and should therefore be the common concern of both the executive and the legislature.[83] The Senate also represented the continuing tradition of federalism which had evolved by inchoate custom within the British empire and which had also developed in America in periods of colonial crisis. The two-thirds rule in Senate action upon treaties seems to have had its roots deep in American sectional traditions in the sense that the New England area felt it must protect its traditional rights to the Newfoundland fisheries; while the southern states felt they must defend their long continuing interest in the Mississippi region.[84]

We have already suggested that the framers of the document of 1787 seem to have intended that the Senate should resemble the English Privy Council in giving advice to the executive in the conduct of foreign relations. The fact that treaties were to be negotiated with the "advice and consent" of the Senate, gives additional color to that view. Yet Washington's first appearance before that body with a proposed treaty with the Creek Indians led the Senate to request a postponement for additional study. Senator Maclay recorded that the president withdrew with an air which he was tempted to call "sullen dignity." He returned another day and the business was concluded but the senator sensed an air of restraint that kept his colleagues silent.[85] This ended the attempt to continue direct personal contact between the executive and the entire senate in the negotiations of treaties.[86]

With the outbreak of the war between England and France, Hamilton took the view that the president's general executive power resembled the British in the sense that subject to express constitutional limitations, he might declare and interpret the law governing the conduct of foreign relations by means of executive action, with the understanding that Congress might later modify it by legislative enactment. Madison, in his Letters of Helvidius, pointed out that this concept of executive power was based upon the English royal prerogative and added that: "The power of the legislature to declare war, and judge of the causes for declaring it, is one of the most express and explicit parts of the Constitution." [87] Yet we have tended to follow the English royal tradition by vesting the general conduct of foreign relations in the hands of the executive with the result that the power of Congress to "declare war" has tended to become merely the power to approve a fait accompli which has largely evolved under executive direction.

Although the House was denied access to the papers pertaining to the negotiation of the Jay treaty, it definitely asserted its power on the question of appropriations to put the terms of the treaty into effect.[88] It declared that:

> "When a Treaty stipulates regulations on any of the subjects submitted by the Constitution to the power of Congress, it must depend, for its execution, as to such stipulations, on a law or laws to be passed by Congress. And it is the constitutional right and duty of the House of Representatives, in all such cases, to deliberate on the expediency of carrying such Treaty into effect, and to determine and act thereon, as, in their judgment, may be most conducive to the public good." [89]

The appropriation was thereafter affirmed by a vote of 51 to 48. More, however, had been affirmed than the appropriation: the long shadow of Locke's federative power had been affirmed in England's former dominion. The House had spoken in no uncertain terms and it was recognized that in the future a treaty dealing with matters that required an appropriation, must have the approval of both houses and that as a matter of practical politics, the leaders of the House of Representatives should be consulted in advance.[90] Yet even with this concession the actual conduct of foreign relations gravitated into the hands of a comparatively small number of persons. Here, too, the English and European pattern tended to repeat itself. The alleged need for secrecy was pleaded to re-inforce the iron law of oligarchy in the conduct of foreign affairs.

Turning from the legislative to the judicial power under the document of 1787, we have already traced the traditional elements in the evolution of the national judiciary during the Revolution and the Confederation, where we saw the influence of the Privy Council, and particularly its members who acted as Commissioners of Appeal from the decisions of the vice admiralty courts in America. We have also explained the traditional factors in the federal judicial power as outlined in the document of 1787, and the fact that the founding fathers were aware of the precedents for judicial review and doubtless intended that it should be exercised. Not a few of these habits and customs were embodied in the Judiciary Act of 1789,[91] which resembled the British system of a centralized judiciary in giving the Supreme Court virtually the same control over the legislative acts and judicial decisions of the states that the high judicial and administrative courts of Britain had exercised over the colonial courts and legislatures;[92] and while the part played by the federal judiciary in the first decade of our national constitutional period was by no means unimportant, its power was greatly enhanced by the appointment of John Marshall and his decision in the case of Marbury vs. Madison in 1803,[93] which lies slightly beyond the province of our study. We have already discussed the English precedents for judicial review and the fact that they were in accordance with some of the English constitutional principles of the seventeenth century, which was a period that had so profoundly influenced the founding fathers. The decade that followed the Judiciary Act of 1789 saw the first steps in national judicial review in the sense that there were several cases in which the lower federal courts held state statutes invalid.[94] In the First Hayburn case the federal circuit court for the district of Pennsylvania also declared that the Invalid Pension Act of 1792 was unconstitutional because judicial decisions involving the act were subject to review by the Secretary of War.[95] It is perhaps worthy of note that the decision of the court aroused no particular partisan controversy.[96] This, also, may perhaps indicate that the English seventeenth century constitutional principle of check and balance, which had been implemented by the doctrine of judicial review, was more or less definitely a part of the American constitutional consciousness.

In dealing with the elements of habit, custom and tradition in their relation to the electorate we have already seen that the property and religious qualifications for voting which we had inherited from England and the American colonial period remained virtually unchanged in federal elections. We have also indicated that the English system of discrimination by area was transmitted to the United States in the form of discrimination between seaboard and frontier, by which the seaboard areas were much more heavily represented in the state legislatures than those beyond tidewater.[97] Yet the Anglo-American tradition also contained within itself certain levelling customs which were destined to bear fruit in Jacksonian democracy and the movement for universal white manhood suffrage. The Ordinance of 1787 was a definite force working for the extension of the suffrage in the western area and indirectly along the Atlantic seaboard. Early in Washington's administration the republican tradition was strengthened by the outbreak of the French Revolution with the result that the artisans in the towns along the seaboard were demanding white manhood suffrage. As early as 1776 the mechanics of Pennsylvania had compelled that state to give a broader popular basis to its franchise by means of a low tax paying qualification.[98] In 1791 Vermont was admitted into the union minus its property qualification for voting[99] and New Hampshire followed suit the next year.[100] In 1792 Delaware also gave the vote to all white men who paid taxes.[101] This tradition of the English seventeenth century Levellers was even more marked beyond the Alleghenies, where Kentucky, by its constitution of 1792, vested the right to vote and hold office in all free male citizens who had resided in the state for two years.[102] Tennessee, in its constitution of 1796, also abolished its property qualifications for voting although it required land ownership for those who were candidates for the assembly or the governorship.[103] Doubtless, however, it was not especially difficult to become a landowner and thus eligible for state office in the Tennessee of that day.[104]

The French Revolution found its greatest pamphleteer in Thomas Paine and his *Rights of Man,* in which he declared that: "Every age and generation must be . . . free to act for itself *in all cases* as the ages and generation which preceded it. The vanity and presumption of governing beyond the grave is the most ridiculous and insolent of all tyrannies . . . Every generation is, and must be, competent to all the purposes which its occasions require."[105] These words seemed to imply the departure from all traditions yet they but repeated the ideas of the English Levellers of the Cromwellian revolution. The plain people of seaboard and frontier were deeply moved by these words of Paine.[106] Hundreds of American democratic societies in imitation of the French Jacobin clubs, arose throughout the country.[107] John Quincy Adams felt that at least in France they had stemmed from ". . . the rabble that followed on the heels of Jack Cade . . ."[108] Thus the "mob" spirit that had characterized the conduct of large masses of people in London and Paris in the latter half of the eighteenth century had its counterpart in scenes enacted in New York and Philadelphia. The London mobs that had shouted for "Wilkes and Liberty," precipitated the Gordon riots and campaigned for Charles James Fox, and the Paris mobs that marched to Versailles and stormed the Bastille, had their smaller but no less actual counterpart in the American mobs that favored the new French republic and opposed the neutrality proclamation of 1793 and the Jay treaty of 1794. This contest between the American Jacobins and their opponents represented a continuation of the traditional conflict between republicanism and aristocracy that we have already traced. American Jacobins tended to represent the traditions of those less privileged persons who had fought in the ranks against England, favored the continuance of the Confederation and opposed the ratification of the document of 1787: the debtor classes, the artisans of the towns, the small farmers and the people of the frontier. The anti-Jacobins represented the people of "property and principle" who had favored the adoption of the document of 1787 and who for the most part lived along the Atlantic seaboard and its navigable rivers: the commercial and professional classes, the large landowners, creditors and holders of government securities. The first group represented the party of Jefferson, the second of Hamilton.

The passage of the Bank Act helped to unite Jefferson and Madison and greatly strengthened the republican cause.[109] Jefferson was quick to take advantage of the charge of speculation in connection with the banking and assumption acts and the attitude taken by the government in crushing the Whiskey rebellion; while the federalists placed the blame for the unrest in western Pennsylvania at the doors of the Jacobin societies.[110] The struggle continued in the field of foreign relations, where the federalists were prone to prefer England and the republicans revolutionary France. It culminated in the Alien and Sedition Acts and the Kentucky and Virginia Resolutions. The Alien and Sedition Acts proved to be the most serious tactical blunder committed by the federalists because it enabled the republicans to put themselves squarely on record as defenders of the Anglo-American bill of rights and its basic traditional principles of compact, delegated and reserved powers and natural rights. It also enabled them to achieve the "political revolution" of 1800 and establish a government which they claimed more truly represented the American republican tradition.

CHAPTER VII

SUMMARY AND CONCLUSION

"Politics cannot stop to study psychology. Its methods are rough; its judgments rougher still." Henry Adams: The Education of Henry Adams, Boston, 1918, p. 166.

"The burden of our civilization is not merely, as many suppose, that the product of industry is ill-distributed, or its conduct tyrannical, or its operation interrupted by embittered disagreements. It is that industry itself has come to hold a position of exclusive predominance among human interests, which no single interest, and least of all the provision of the material means of existence, is fit to occupy. Like a hypochondriac who is so absorbed in the processes of his own digestion that he goes to the grave before he has begun to live, industrialized communities neglect the very objects for which it is worth while to acquire riches in their feverish preoccupation with the means by which riches can be acquired." R. H. Tawney: The Sickness of an Acquisitive Society. London, 1920, p. 86.

Our brief survey of habit, custom and tradition in the growth of American constitutionalism prior to 1800, would seem to raise certain questions of a general nature. What, for example, were the underlying forces that conditioned these habits, customs and traditions? How did they evolve and what were some of the results of their evolution? What are some of the tests for a sound development in the growth of these forces and how may society promote it?

The field of political motivation in general and of political habit, custom and tradition in particular is so largely unexplored and uncharted that we can do little more than make a few tentative suggestions as signposts for future students. Why, for example, were the forces of habit, custom and tradition

124

important in shaping our early political life and what impulses lie behind the continuity of our political institutions? The answer would seem to lie partly in the fact that men consciously or unconsciously endeavor to shape their conduct in the light of their experience, accepting, modifying or rejecting it as it seems beneficial and expedient. If we ask ourselves to what extent such a course of conduct is conscious and rational or unconscious and irrational, we must reply that our present state of knowledge does not entitle us to speak with any great degree of assurance. What, for example, is the relation between the "unconscious" mind and the forces of habit, custom and tradition? Following the fruitful pioneering of Freud, the social psychiatrists may have opened new vistas. They have suggested that each social group has inherited an unconscious "social memory" that compels it to repeat its past in much the same way that the human embryo recapitulates its biological heritage. It has also been said that the individual may be similarly impelled to re-live his former experiences. The strongly extroverted person would recapture the satisfactions implicit in his former leadership; while weaker, introverted souls might revert to the past as a flight from reality, a form of infantile regression and a disguised death wish. Interesting and even intriguing as these theories may be, we feel that they lack sufficient substantiation and demand an attitude of suspended judgment. We shall be on safer ground if we suggest certain other forces that seem definitely to have influenced the evolution of our political habits and customs.

Certain elements of the rational and the non-rational would seem to be blended in most areas of conduct with the result that many acts generally considered rational contain an element of the non-rational; while many so called non-rational acts may not be wholly devoid of certain elements of rationality. Recent studies in the psychology of the emotions seem to suggest that the so-called element of "rationality" is somewhat smaller, and the degree of non-rationality considerably greater than the proportion professed by the leaders of the enlightenment in the so-called "age of reason." It is perhaps not unimportant to recall that the "age of reason" was succeeded by the emotional extremes of the "romantic" period. This would seem to indicate that the effort to restrain the emotions created a certain amount of psychic tension; that the age of "reason" in its denial of the emotions was in itself not wholly rational. Its insistence upon "reason" may have contained certain elements of distrust and fear resembling what the psychologists of today sometimes call a "self-defense mechanism."

It would appear, therefore, that the general problem of habit, custom and tradition cannot easily be separated from the general problem of emotional drives; that to the extent that it contains elements of the non-rational—and we have already suggested that the non-rational is seldom altogether absent—to that extent it is doubtless in itself an emotional drive that can with difficulty be wholly dissociated from other emotional drives. Perhaps we may even suggest that as the elements of emotion in habit, custom and tradition tend to increase, to that extent, also, do the number and extent of the emotions associated with it tend to increase. It would therefore follow that those factors of habit, custom and tradition that are the most potent, powerful and prolonged, would also tend to be inextricably interwoven with other emotional drives, including such non-rational forces as acquisitiveness and the economic factor, gregariousness and consciousness of kind, physical force and militarism, fear, the ego, religion, the procreative impulse, art and the creative forces and the emotional desire for the good life. This by no means completes the list, since social psychologists have suggested the existence of scores of emotional drives.

As a possible example of association, let us briefly analyze such a well-known political-economic force as the rise and decline of the old colonial "system" since its effects upon the founding and early political evolution of the American colonies and states is more or less definitely established. We have in this instance a well established custom which, however, was subject to more or less constant modification and change, and which in turn was succeeded by a considerable measure of laissez faire, although laissez faire at its strongest also contained more than a trace of the old colonial system which it in large measure superseded. Mercantilism was a national policy in which the forces of continuity and change were engaged in a more or less constant struggle for the mastery and the result was a series of compromises in which neither achieved a clean-cut victory. Yet mercantilism and laissez faire were by no means wholly separate and distinct from the acquisitive drive since there was a marked tendency for individuals and groups to view these forces in the light of what they conceived to be their own acquisitive interests and endeavor to shape their conduct with that aim in view. Nor were the psychological forces of gregariousness and consciousness of kind altogether absent; persons who held similar views in regard to the operation of these laws, their enforcement or non-enforcement, naturally tended to form their own associations and organizations. This in itself was a factor in the American colonial revolt, which in turn involves a study of the custom and psychology of force and militarism, although, as a matter of fact, the old colonial system from its inception, was itself closely associated with force in general and navalism in particular, so that the entire problem involves a study of the habits and customs of national force. Yet force also involves a study of the psychology of fear, which in turn is a factor in the psychology of the ego and its struggle for survival and growth. This old colonial system, as well as the idea of laissez faire which partially superseded it, also partook at times of some of the characteristics of a religion. Thus Adam Smith and his more devoted followers insisted that if each were permitted freely to seek his own in a society absolved from state restrictions, each in some mystic way would find his own best interests, and in so doing promote the will of God and the welfare of the state. Mercantilism and its modifications may not be wholly dissociated from the procreative drive since as individuals prospered or declined under its influence, it might tend to affect their attitudes and activities in the field of family responsibilities. It was not altogether devoid of influence upon the artistic and cultural standards of the age as the rising commercial class became a patron of the arts and to a certain extent the arbiter of taste; while we have already intimated that the proponents of laissez faire professed to see in its beneficence a harbinger of the good life.

It would appear, therefore, that various emotional drives were associated with the political forces of habit, custom and tradition during the period under discussion. It is also fairly clear that these habits, customs and traditions were subject to modification by such general political forces as the stake in society principle, the iron law of oligarchy, the abuse of political power and the swing of the political pendulum. There was a general tendency for those groups in the community that possessed the most economic power to be in a position to exercise the largest amount of influence in the evolution of habit, custom and tradition. If the commercial classes of England and seaboard America tended to have the most influence in the evolution of the political customs of the period, it was doubtless because society tended to be dominated by these expanding commercial groups. There were times, to be sure, when the more powerful landed groups were not devoid of considerable influence in the evolution of public affairs; yet in the wars, compromises and working agreements that were struck, the former tended to get the better of the bargain and to the extent that it did so, its ability to write the political habits, customs and traditions of the period was of corresponding importance.

Closely associated with this evolution is the iron law of oligarchy in the sense that since the actual control of political power tends to gravitate into the hands of a comparatively small number of persons, it naturally follows that the molding and shaping of political habits, customs and traditions tends also to be in their hands. These persons, in placing emphasis upon those phases of the past which they feel will be most likely to promote the ends they have in view, strive to employ the past for the purpose of shaping the present and future in accordance with their own aims and desires. They may not at all times be fully conscious of their "rationalizations" in regard to the "usable past" and its adaptation to their present urgencies; they may not, in other words, be fully aware of the fact that they are attempting to create social myths; yet this lack of complete consciousness on their part need not wholly nullify the effectiveness or the importance of what they do. In the period under review we have seen that the actual power tended to rest largely in the hands of the leaders of commerce and agriculture. In England these two groups tended to merge their identity as leaders of the Whig oligarchy, intermarry with the older landed oligarchy, purchase their impoverished estates and set themselves up as country gentlemen. The vast frontier of the American continent made it considerably more difficult to develop an equal degree of hegemony between commerce and agriculture, nor has it even yet been completely achieved; yet it is perhaps significant to recall that even as the leaders of these groups in England united to restore the monarchy in 1660, and achieve the compromises of the glorious revolution of 1688, so also were the leaders of these two American groups able to unite for the purpose of fighting Britain in the American Revolution, achieve a common front against agrarian and frontier unrest, and write the compromises of the document of 1787.

Closely associated with the iron law of oligarchy, and indeed one of its results that seems to be more or less inevitable, is the abuse of political power. One is reminded of Lord Acton's famous dictum that all power tends to corrupt and absolute power tends to corrupt absolutely. To the extent that this is true it would seem to follow that those who have the most influence in the shaping of habit, custom and tradition endeavor to employ it in ways that they feel will best provide their own advancement and the welfare of their group and this in turn not infrequently results in the exploitation of the lesser and weaker groups subject to their control. Thus in the period under consideration there was a strong tendency both in England and

America for the more powerful agricultural and commercial groups to exploit the smaller landowners, agricultural laborers, and the artisans of the towns, while the lot of those bound to serve as apprentices, indentured servants and slaves was even more unfortunate and pitiable.

Closely associated with the stake in society principle, the iron law of oligarchy, and the abuse of political power, is the swing of the political pendulum. Its application to our present study may be briefly stated as follows: one set of habits, customs and traditions will advance to a certain point when the tide will turn, a reaction will develop and a group of habits, customs and traditions that are more or less the reverse of the former will succeed them. The situation would seem to be representative of the "law" of bi-polarity in human affairs by which the long range course of events is established by striking a balance between opposite extremes.[1] The situation may be seen rather clearly in the case of wars and revolutions when periods of dynamic change and arbitrary reaction tend to alternate. Thus, for example, in the English Civil War and the American Revolution the struggles began with the efforts of the commercial groups, their allies and associates, to achieve their "rights" within the framework of the existing government; this was followed by the rising power of a more radical group that foreswore allegiance to the king, proclaimed the doctrine of popular sovereignty and pushed its fortunes vigorously in the field until it had achieved a military victory. Its military triumph was followed by dissensions within its own ranks that brought the two countries to the verge of renewed hostilities and was prevented only by a strong swing to the right in which the oligarchic leaders of the commercial and agrarian groups established a working compromise that was strongly in their favor and imposed powerful limitations upon English levellers and American artisans and "Shayesites." Thus the English settlement of 1689 and the American settlement of 1787 more closely resembled the situation that had existed prior to the outbreak of hostilities than the demands of levellers and agrarians. Under the dominance of the Whig oligarchy this settlement remained the standing order in England where it was subject to few substantial modifications until the next swing of the political pendulum saw the establishment of the great revisions of the nineteenth century that began with the Reform Act of 1832. In the United States the swing of the pendulum began somewhat earlier, when the political blindness and ineptitude of the Federalists, the political astuteness of Jefferson and the political and social unrest of a vast frontier, culminated in the "revolution" of 1800, which represented a swing to the left and resembled the spirit of the agrarian demands as they had existed in the second and more radical stage of the American Revolution. John Adams may have had these political swings of the pendulum in mind when near the close of his long life, he remarked that it had always seemed to him that the "constitution was a game of leap frog."

In the United States there was no marked extension of the national suffrage until the period of Jacksonian democracy, which corresponded almost precisely with the establishment of a similar custom in England. Thus the two revolutions in England and America evolved through certain stages that were by no means dissimilar. The political customs of the American Revolution and its results resembled the customs of the English revolution and its aftermath that had occurred one hundred years earlier in the mother country.

At this point it may be well to ask a few questions in regard to the speed and tempo of change in matters involving political habits, customs and traditions. The rate of change would seem to coincide directly with the changes in the main currents of public events. In static groups it will be slow and comparatively slight; in dynamic periods more rapid and far-reaching. Peace, "isolation", agrarianism, stratified social classes, fixed modes of thought, and the absence of "great" leaders, accompany established customs and traditions; while war, dynamic foreign contacts, the growth of a commercial and industrial society and the development of science and invention, represent forces making for the modification of older customs and the creation of newer traditions. The rate and tempo of change would seem to vary directly with the force of the newer factors and their impact upon the older social order.

It is, therefore, fairly clear that in the evolution of habit, custom and tradition in the field of politics there is a more or less constant interplay between the forces of continuity and change. Some of the older forces linger and seem virtually to repeat themselves, while forces that are relatively new develop, coexist with the older forces and may in time largely supersede them. Actually, however, there may be considerable periods of time in which the older and newer customs become more or less inextricably intermingled with the result that there are generally elements of the old in the new and new in the old so that the present as the meeting ground of the older and newer customs, represents a working compromise between these two forces. It follows, therefore, that much that seems to be new is little more than the old that has assumed a somewhat newer guise; while many established customs that seem to be relatively free from change are subject to corroding forces that are not yet apparent to the eye, yet are in reality producing a hidden transformation within the inner substance of the custom or institution itself. It is the duty of the student of political habits and customs to trace the elements of continuity in those customs that appear to be new, and the elements of change beneath the appearance of their continuity. Few political customs are wholly new, while few remain precisely the same for any considerable length of time.

Since we are dealing with forces engaged in more or less constant conflict, it would seem that the balance that should be struck should be one that will promote the general welfare and this we conceive to be the ideal that ought to actuate the democratically governed service state. We must also hasten to add that the question of what constitutes the general welfare is not infrequently difficult to determine in advance, although the perspective derived from the study of our political past should aid us in evaluating the customs that may influence our future. The record of our earlier political customs is not devoid of certain unfortunate developments. America was the child of the renaissance and the commercial revolution.[2] It was thus compounded of dream and hard reality. There had once been a blessed estate from which man had forever fallen. St. Augustine had therefore bade him put aside all thought of earthly felicity and consider the city of God eternal in the heavens. It was not until the thirteenth century that the cathedrals of the middle ages became symbols of a richer spiritual life, intensified city rivalry, increasing material wealth and the growth of a new bureaucracy born of commerce and trade. The jurists from this group served the rising power of kings against the older bureaucracy of the churchmen who had drawn their precedents more directly from the Roman law. In much the same way the English jurists served their royal masters in England by developing a body of national precedents later known as the English common law. These spiritual, artistic, material, juristic, political and administrative forces developed with increasing strength until they culminated in the high renaissance of the sixteenth century with its works of art and science and the discovery of distant lands. This expansion of the human horizon naturally led the men of that age to think they had outsoared the darkness of their night. The golden age was yet to be. Man had risen again upon this earth.

The sixteenth and seventeenth centuries saw a great deal of political writing in which men dealt with the state and endeavored to reform it in accordance with their conceptions of what it ought to be. The English writers in this group—Sir Thomas More and his *Utopia,* Richard Hooker and his *Ecclesiastical Polity,*[3] Milton, Sidney, Hobbes, Harrington and Locke[4]—were the men whose political ideas exerted the most influence upon the political thought of emerging America. Unable to build Jerusalem in England's stratified land, the discovery and settlement of America seemed to them a little less than providential. It meant a chance to establish those habits, customs and traditions that they thought should ultimately prevail. Colonial America thus became a political battleground upon which these contending forces endeavored to establish their conflicting customs. To the theocratic Puritan it was a place where men should conform to the Bible as expounded by Calvin and thus establish the habits and customs of true liberty and freedom.[5] John Winthrop declared that "it is a liberty to that only which is good, just and honest." [6]

Other men had other views and other methods of bringing them to pass. Moderate men of the type of Thomas Hooker saw in the new land a chance for men to unite freely for common purposes provided they imposed no limits upon the traditional freedom of their fellow men. Franklin in the next century expressed the view of moderate men of good will when he declared that: "The happiness of individuals is evidently the ultimate end of political society." [7] He embodied much of the optimism and hope of colonial America in the eighteenth century and exemplified the traditions of the European enlightenment at its best. It was indeed unfortunate that human nature did not find itself represented by more Americans with the same amount of good sense and good will.

There were others who saw the new land as a place where they could be free from all traditional restraints. At their best they could produce a Roger Williams who, although he became a restless seeker, had many points in common with moderate men who desired to establish the custom of free societies united by the bonds of social contract. Others desired complete freedom from the irksome rules and customs of "civilized" society. They drifted towards the frontier where they were ever impatient of "law and order." It was their passion to slay the wild beasts and the Indians, destroy the forests, exploit the natural resources, and resist as much as possible the encroachment of the older customs of the seaboard as represented in terms of courts and legislatures. Here were sown the seeds of lawless customs that we have never quite outgrown and that may help to explain our traditionally high ratio of homicides and crimes of violence. Yet these people of the frontier felt they had fled from ancient eastern evils intent upon their exploitation. They would have agreed with Rousseau that man was born free but was everywhere in chains. Their way of life meant danger and privation yet they preferred it to the corruptions and cruelties of "civilization."

Yet theocratic conservatives, moderate men and even the radicals saw the new land in terms of their acquisitive drives. The theocratic Puritan became the New England Yankee hungry for land and success in trade and commerce.[8] As symptomatic of this transformation we see the decline of the clergyman and the rise of the lawyer who became so useful as an arbiter in helping men divide their spoils. This custom continued through the eras of the Revolution, Confederation, federal convention and early national period. Hamilton and Adams believed that men were justified in their "rational" attempts[9] to satisfy their acquisitive desires. Since, however, they were prone to be predatory in this pursuit, they felt that society should establish such rules and customs based upon still older traditions of right and justice[10] as might be necessary to restrain them. The Federalists would also continue the custom of giving the most weight to property and since they had the largest proportion of it, they were therefore assigning themselves the largest share of political power. Thus those who had been the most successful in gratifying their acquisitive desires were proving themselves insatiate for additional acquisitions. Such an attitude also had the traditional sanction of the English Puritan theocracy which had blessed the seizure of Catholic church property, Spanish galleons and African Negroes and laid the foundations for the English commercial oligarchy and its overseas colonial expansion. America was founded and developed by an acquisitive people. Surely God had blessed its acquisitions. The Good Book itself had declared that to him that hath shall be given.

The Federalist leaders realized that it might be said that this was a system in which the strong continued the ancient custom of exploiting the weak and endeavored to answer it. Madison in the famous tenth number of the Federalist had declared that: "Means must be provided to reform and enlarge the public views, by passing them through the medium of a *chosen* body of citizens whose wisdom may best discern the true interests of their country." [11] He was saying in effect that his group should rule because they were best equipped for it. Yet this was what old England's Whig oligarchy had said. It was what New England's theocratic oligarchy had said. It was what those in power always say.

Jefferson replied that he had never seen any tendency for the principles of men to improve as their property increased. He believed that the political evils of the past were due to the leviathan state controlled by the few and exploiting the many. He would, therefore, continue the customs of our simple agrarian economy, keep the natural resources open to all, improve the lot of the common man and prevent his exploitation. It seemed to him that here in America with its vast natural resources untouched and even unexplored, it was possible to come within a measurable distance of realizing these ideals. If these great natural resources were wisely conserved and administered in the public interest they would provide support and substance for countless generations. America was a land rich in possibilities for human happiness if men of good will united to make it their aim.

These views of Jefferson were colored by the humanitarian concern for the common man that had developed with the French Revolution. They found a ready response in the hearts of the plain people and the men of the frontier in emerging America. They knew little of the causes of the French Revolution, yet like the small tradespeople and peasants of France, they wished to be free from the restrictions imposed by a state church and an arbitrary central government. They would have agreed with Rousseau that the state of nature was kind compared with the harsh, impersonal and inexorable character of the excise gatherer. In the small towns and along the frontier

Americans had developed the custom of helping each other at log rollings and barn raisings; while the gentlemen of property along the seaboard had also developed the custom of exploiting them through the techniques of heavier taxes and minority representation; depriving them of their just share for roads and schools and refusing to give them adequate aid in their defense against the Indians.

Thus despite the temporary influence of Jefferson and his followers, the customs of English liberalism rather than French liberalism prevailed in the United States and our political philosophy was more influenced by English precedents than by French. The country was largely peopled by English middle class individualists and their descendants, while the land itself provided a powerful temptation for exploitation. Most of these people had inherited a political philosophy which justified a person in seizing all he could get without much thought for his fellow-man or any concern for posterity. No other theory can provide so complete and rational an explanation of the dispossession and slaughter of the Indians, the exploitation of women and children in the factories of New England and the rapid growth of a harsh system of slave labor in the lower South. This way of life had been shaped by the philosophers and economists of the English middle class, by John Locke in the seventeenth century and Adam Smith in the eighteenth: the chief duty of the state was to protect private property and if it attempted to interfere with the individual in his pursuit of private gain, its powers should be strictly limited. Most Americans wished to acquire material possessions and when the state gave them the freedom to engage in this pursuit, the custom was thereby sanctified, strengthened and stabilized.

A saving remnant of humane liberalism survived in New England; the Emersons and Thoreaus who saw the good life in terms of gentleness and peace. Yet this traditional quest of the artist for spiritual mastery was of little avail against the acquisitive customs of the age: the rising power of the Lowell mills, the mounting piles of money in the counting rooms of

State Street, the larger acreage of cotton in the deep South. These were the more dynamic customs that were shaping public events, producing the Civil War and the orgy of crime and violence that followed that great national calamity. Emerson and Thoreau were the still small voices of the spiritual world crying in a wilderness of material things. So, too, the great New England humanitarians, William Ellery Channing and Theodore Parker. Were they not unbalanced persons preaching against the gods of materialism, slavery and war, when all practical men knew that these forces represented the continuing customs of human nature. Life had always been a struggle in which the strong survived and the weak perished and no amount of humanitarian preaching could ever make it otherwise. It was a hard world in which a man must take his profits where he could get them. So sensed the hard headed "practical" man of affairs who drew his wealth from his Lowell mills, his Boston counting house and his plantations of the lower South. Slavery had its faults yet people had always lived in a faulty world. The slaves had been here for a long time and one who owned them must make the best of it and seek his recompense in the fact that the world needed cotton. Surely the southern Negro was as well protected as the people in the northern mills and factories who were turned out to starve when they were too old to work. Some of the southern men of letters thought of southern society as a revival of the age of chivalry or even the classical culture of ancient Greece. Yet the plantation owner and his overseer in the lower South seldom voiced such illusions. They knew their life was one of alarms and constant danger. Yet they accepted the customs of the age as they found them and struggled as best they could with a difficult situation.

In the meantime the west was developing a set of customs that were somewhat more indigenous to the American soil. The Atlantic seaboard had long been the cultural fringe of Europe, while the west had inherited more of the freedom of Indians, hunters and pioneers. In the mind of Lincoln, who was to become its great spokesman, a man should be free to develop as far as his powers permitted him, provided he did not encroach upon the rights of his fellow man. Here was the traditional freedom of Rousseau and the traditional spirit of English individualism fused in free land and a more flexible environment. Despite all the disappointments and hardships of the western frontier a poor man had a greater chance to rise by his own efforts than he had in New England or the South.

Thus ends our account of early American constitutional custom. Compounded of many forces, two have led all the rest: the traditions of freedom and authority. They have clashed to our hurt and blended to our health. The tradition of freedom at its best gave us Sir Edward Coke, John Milton, John Lilburne, Roger Williams, Patrick Henry, George Mason and Thomas Jefferson; carried to excess it gave us the Levellers, Fifth Monarchy men and the Diggers of the English Commonwealth, the lawlessness of our American frontier and the disorders and mob violence of our confederation and early constitutional periods. Authority, too, has had its heartening and disturbing traditions. At its best it could give us a Cromwell, a Washington and a Hamilton; at its worst the tyranny of the Stuarts and the third Hanoverian, the colonial despotism of a Berkeley and Andros.

May we not, therefore, say that American constitutional custom bore its best fruit when it united freedom and authority in sound and just proportions? Thus balanced it gave us Locke, Madison, Jefferson and Lincoln: a balanced government in the settlement of 1689, the document of 1787, the election of 1800 and the union that Lincoln saved. As our study comes to a close, Lincoln was about to be born in the wilderness of Kentucky. Yet it seems as though he best embodied these two great traditions. At Cooper Union he pleaded for freedom in our federal territories and invoked the habits and customs of the founding fathers in its behalf. In his first inaugural he upheld our freedom of elections as one of our great traditions when he declared that:

"In your hands, my dissatisfied fellow-countrymen, and not mine, is the momentous issue of civil war . . . You have no oath . . . to destroy the government, while I shall have the most solemn one to 'preserve, protect and defend it.'

"I am loath to close. We are not enemies, but friends. We must not be enemies. Though passion may have strained, it must not break our bonds of affection. The mystic chords of memory, stretching from every battle-field and patriot grave to every living heart and hearthstone all over this broad land, will yet swell the chorus of the union when again touched, as surely they will be, by the better angels of our nature." [12]

A sound balance between the traditions of freedom and authority was the major note that Lincoln sounded in his two inaugurals, his message to Congress and his Gettysburg address. Implicit in this balance is its willingness to compromise. Lincoln, the great Kentuckian, inherited a spirit of compromise that had developed more or less inevitably in a buffer state. The compromising spirit of Clay and Crittenden reached in him its culmination. He even waged a great civil war in a compromising spirit.

This is indeed a heartening heritage. May we be worthy of this great tradition.

NOTES

INTRODUCTION

1. Havelock Ellis: Studies in the Psychology of Sex. Six volumes, Philadelphia, 1926-27. Vol. VI, Sex in Relation to Society, pp. 641-642.

2. "When the stream of history has once carved its channel, we assume that it could have followed along no other path." R. M. MacIver: European Doctrines and the Constitution, in M. Conyers Read, Editor: The Constitution Reconsidered, New York, The Columbia University Press, 1938, p. 58.

CHAPTER I

1. "The declaration of the royal charters . . . acted as a powerful factor in the spread throughout the colonies of English constitutional principles—including the rights and liberties secured by Magna Carta and its confirmations." H. D. Hazeltine: The Influence of Magna Carta on American Constitutional Development, Columbia Law Review, Vol. XVII, January, 1917, Vol. I, p. 6. See also Raymond G. Gettell: History of American Political Thought, New York, The Century Company, 1928, p. 38; Max Savelle: Seeds of Liberty—The Genesis of the American Mind, New York, Alfred Knopf, 1948, pp. 284-289.

2. Sir Henry Sumner Maine: Ancient Law. Fourth American edition, New York, Henry Holt, 1906, p. 353.

3. Christopher Saint German: The Doctor and Student, or Dialogues Between a Doctor of Divinity and a Student in the Laws of England . . . Revised and Corrected by William Muchall, Gent. Cincinnati, Robert Clarke & Co., 1874, p. 2.

4. 7 Co I, 4b(1610). See also Edward S. Corwin: The "Higher Law" Background of American Constitutional Law, Harvard Law Review, Volume XLII, Number 3, 1929, pp. 369-370; W. S. Holdsworth: A History of English Law, Third edition, Twelve volumes, Methuen & Co., London, 1922-1938, Vol. IV, pp. 279-281, 289-290, Vol. V, p. 216, Vol. VI, pp. 218-220.

5. "Even in the Fleet loaded down with chains, or in the Tower with

a sentinel at the door of his cell and his friends kept at more than arm's length, he would manage to write and smuggle out the copy for a pamphlet to be printed in Holland, or in a secret press in London, and when deprived of pen and ink would write them in his own blood . . . Of the latter series of pamphlets those written when the so-called Commonwealth was coming, or had recently come to birth, 'Foundations of Freedom' and 'England's New Chaines Discovered', and 'The Legall Fundamentall Liberties of the People of England Revised, Asserted and Vindicated', are the most notable. On these three alone Lilburne might rest a valid claim to respect as a great constitutional lawyer. Indeed, every written constitution drawn up since his day does in some part derive from the first-named." H. Halliday Sparling: John Lilburne as a Pamphleteer, in The Bookworm, Vol. Six, New York, A. C. Armstrong and Son, and London, Elliot Stock, h.d. pp. 315, 317.

6. Lewis Mumford: The Golden Day, New York, Boni and Liveright, 1926, pp. 27-29; Gettell: op. cit. p. 71.

7. Savelle: op. cit. pp. 318-326.

8. John Milton: Doctrine and Discipline of Divorce, London. Printed by T. P. and M. S. 1643, pp. 1-48.

9. John Milton: The Tenure of Kings and Magistrates, London. Printed by M. Simmons, 1649, pp. 1-42.

10. Algernon Sidney: Discourses Concerning Government, London. Printed by the Booksellers of London and Westminster, 1698. Section VI, pp. 83-87, Section XXXI, pp. 242-247.

11. James Harrington: The Commonwealth of Oceana. With an Introduction by Henry Morley, London. George Routledge and Sons, 1887, pp. 20-21.

12. J. Russell Smith: Harrington and His Oceana, London, 1914, pp. 199-200, 215, 497-498, 501-514. See also F. J. C. Hearnshaw, Editor: The Social and Political Ideas of Some Great Thinkers of the Sixteenth and Seventeenth Centuries, George G. Harrap, London, 1926, Chap. VIII, pp. 174-203; T. W. Dwight: Harrington and His Influence Upon American Political Institutions and Political Thought, in Political Science Quarterly, Vol. II, 1887, pp. 1-44.

13. Carl Becker: The Declaration of Independence, New York, Alfred A. Knopf, 1942, pp. 78-79; William Seal Carpenter: The Development of American Political Thought, Princeton University Press, Princeton, 1930, pp. 22-23; Ralph Barton Perry: Puritanism and Democracy, New York, The Vanguard Press, 1944, pp. 186-187.

14. John Bowle: Western Political Thought, Jonathan Cape, London, Second impression, 1948, pp. 203-210; R. W. and A. J. Carlyle: A

History of Mediaeval Political Thought in the West. Six volumes. William Blackwood and Sons, Edinburgh and London, 1927-36, Vol. III, pp. 5-6; F. J. C. Hearnshaw, Editor: The Social and Political Ideas of Some Great Mediaeval Thinkers, George G. Harrap, London, 1921, Chap. IV, pp. 85-106.

15. Bowle: op. cit. pp. 236-241; R. W. and A. J. Carlyle: op. cit. Vol. VI, pp. 9-11, 41-43; Hearnshaw, Editor: Some Great Mediaeval Thinkers, Chap VI, pp. 167-191.

16. Jan Herben: Huss and His Followers. Geoffrey Bles, London, 1926, Chap. II, pp. 35-78, Chap. VIII, pp. 193-204; Johann Loserth: Wiclif and Hus. Translated by the Rev. M. J. Evans, London, Hodder and Stoughton, 1884. Introduction, pp. XV-XLVII, Book II, Chap. X, pp. 280-291.

17. William Archibald Dunning: A History of Political Theories— Ancient and Modern, New York. The MacMillan Company, 1935, pp. 260-265; James Gairdner: Lollardy and the Reformation in England. Four volumes. London. MacMillan and Co., 1908-13, Vol. I, pp. 3-21.

18. For a brief but excellent summary of this survival, see Perry: op. cit. pp. 66-67. See also H. L. Cannon: The Poor Priests: A Study in the Rise of English Lollardy, in Annual Report of the American Historical Association for the year 1899. Two vols. Washington, Government Printing Office, 1900, Vol. I, pp. 451-482; Gairdner: op. cit. Vol. 3, pp. 308, 392-395; Thomas Cuming Hall: The Religious Background of American Culture, Boston, Little Brown and Company, 1930, pp. 3-5, 7-8, 10, 12-13, 15-16.

19. Dunning: op. cit. pp. 266-270; J. N. Figgis: Studies in Political Thought from Gerson to Grotius, 1414-1625, Second edition, Cambridge University Press, 1916, Lecture II, pp. 41-70.

20. Bowle: op. cit. pp. 241-242; Dunning: op. cit. pp. 270-276.

21. Giorgio Del Vecchio: The Formal Bases of Law, New York, The MacMillan Company, 1921, pp. 27-31; Gettell: op. cit. Chap. VII, pp. 133-135.

22. Perry: op. cit. pp. 78-81; Hall: op. cit. pp. 87-89; R. H. Tawney: Religion and the Rise of Capitalism, London, John Murray, 1926, p. 233; John Winthrop: History of New England, 1630-1649, edited by James Kendall Hosmer. Two vols. New York, Charles Scribner's Sons, 1908, Vol. II, pp. 279-282.

23. "The common law, the ancient statutes of England, had been all carried by the English settlers, into the American colonies, as their birthright, or afterwards adopted by usage, or sometimes recognized by the positive acts of their subordinate legislatures." George

Chalmers: Opinions On Interesting Subjects of Public Law and Commercial Policy Arising From American Independence, A New Edition, Corrected, London, J. Debrett, 1785, p. 161.

24. W. S. Holdsworth: op. cit. Vol. II, pp. 354, 584-585; Sir Frederick Pollock and Frederick W. Maitland: History of English Law, 2 vols. Cambridge University Press, Second edition, Cambridge, England, Vol. II, pp. 32-34.

25. A. E. Mckinley: The Suffrage Franchise in the Nineteen English Colonies in America. Ginn and Company, Philadelphia, 1905, p. 65.

26. C. H. McIlwain: The High Court of Parliament and Its Supremacy, New Haven, Yale University Press, 1910, pp. 363-364.

27. "This financial middle class began its influential career when it acquired the lands of the church under Henry VIII, and in so doing supplanted the impoverished nobility which had been broken and ruined by the Wars of the Roses the century before." Charles M. Andrews: The Colonial Period of American History, New Haven, Yale University Press, 4 vols. 1934, Vol. 1, p. 26.

28. Sir Charles P. Lucas: The Beginnings of Overseas Enterprise, Oxford, Clarendon Press, 1917, pp. 35, 198.

29. McIlwain: op. cit. p. 363.

30. Andrew C. McLaughlin: The Foundations of American Constitutionalism, New York University Press, New York, 1932, Chap. II, pp. 31-39.

31. Harold Laski: The Foundations of Sovereignty, New York, Harcourt, Brace & Company, 1921, pp. 200-203.

32. Robert Charles Winthrop: Life and Letters of John Winthrop. Second edition, 2 vols. Boston, Little Brown & Company, 1869, Vol. II, p. 430.

33. McLaughlin: op. cit. Chap. I, pp. 3-29.

34. Winthrop: op. cit. Vol. II, p. 277.

CHAPTER II

1. Ralph Lane to Sir Philip Sydney. August 12, 1585, in Calendar of State Papers, Colonial Series, 1574-1660, Vol. I, p. 3. George Louis Beer: The Origins of the British Colonial System, 1578-1660, New York. The MacMillan Company, 1908, Chapter III, The Economic Theory of Colonization, pp. 53-57.

2. For an account of the administration of Virginia under the crown

and Privy Council see Calendar of State Papers, Colonial, Vol. IV, 1626-1628, pp. 77-80, 86, 88. See also A. Berriedale Keith: Constitutional History of the First British Empire, Oxford, The Clarendon Press, 1930, p. 18.

3. See, for example, the growth of direct control over Newfoundland and its fisheries, Calendar of State Papers, Colonial, Vol. I, 1574-1660, pp. 20, 26, 92-93, 173-174, 236, 303, 315, 355, 376, 381, 403, 441; Beer: op. cit. Chap. XII, pp. 360-370; Carl J. Friedrich: Constitutional Government and Democracy, Boston, Little Brown and Company, 1941, pp. 19-20; Henry Robinson: Certain proposalls in order to the peoples freedome and accomodation in some particulars. With the advancement of trade and navigation of this commonwealth in generall . . . London, Printed by M. Simmons, 1652, p. 11.

4. "The decade which was dominated by Cromwell's vigorous personality was marked by the devotion of especial attention to commercial and colonial expansion." Beer: op. cit. p. 372.

5. Calendar of State Papers, Colonial, Vol. I, pp. 254, 308, 393, 402; Keith: op. cit., p. 55.

6. Calendar of State Papers, Colonial, Vol. I, p. 429. See also The Narrative of General Venables. Edited by C. H. Firth. Longmans, Green, New York, 1900, pp. 1-42.

7. Calendar of State Papers, Colonial, Vol. I, p. 453, December 17, 1656. See also Beer: op. cit. pp. 423-424; Andrews: The Colonial Period of American History, Vol. III, pp. 6-7.

8. For text see J. D. Richardson, Editor: Messages and Papers of the Presidents, 1789-1897, 10 vols. Washington. Published by the authority of Congress, 1898-1899. Vol. II, p. 209. "It was inseparable from the continental expansion of the United States." Samuel Flagg Bemis: John Quincy Adams and the Foundations of American Foreign Policy, New York, Alfred A. Knopf, p. 407.

9. John Bassett Moore: Digest of International Law. 6 vols., Washington. Government Printing Office, 1906, Vol. III, pp. 130-210.

10. Thomas A. Bailey: A Diplomatic History of the American People, Third edition, New York, F. S. Crofts & Co., 1946, pp. 166, 294-295, 307-309.

11. Moore: op. cit. Vol. 6, p. 220.

12. W. H. Callcott: The Caribbean Policy of the United States, 1890-1920. Baltimore, Johns Hopkins University Press, 1942, p. 210.

13. Frank Strong: A Forgotten Danger to the New England Colonies. Report in American Historical Association Reports, 1898. Washington, Government Printing Office, 1899, p. 85.

14. Calendar of State Papers, Colonial, Vol. I, p. 158, Dec. 19, 1632. Beer: op. cit. pp. 312-313.

15. Andrews: op. cit. Vol. I, p. 411.

16. George Louis Beer: The Old Colonial System, 1660-1754. Two vols. New York. The MacMillan Company, 1912, Vol. I, p. 57.

17. J. Allen Smith: The Spirit of American Government, New York. The MacMillan Company, 1907, Chapter 2, pp. 12-26; J. Mark Jacobson: The Development of American Political Thought—A Documentary History, New York, D. Appleton-Century Company, 1932, pp. 164-179.

18. In 1641 Charles I was forced to submit to an act declaring that no duties were to be levied without the consent of parliament. 16 Ch. I. c.8. See also Beer: The Origins of the British Colonial System, pp. 340-342; Charles M. Andrews: British Committees, Commissioners & Councils of Trade & Plantations, 1622-1675. Baltimore. Johns Hopkins Press, 1908, pp. 16-23; Keith: op. cit. pp. 19-22.

19. Gaillard Thomas Lapsley: The County Palatine of Durham, A Study in Constitutional History. Harvard Historical Studies, Vol. VIII, Longmans, Green and Company, New York, 1900, pp. 196-203.

    For text of the Gorges grant of the Province of Maine in 1639, see Francis Newton Thorpe: The Federal and State Constitutions, Colonial Charters and Other Organic Laws . . . Seven volumes. Washington, Government Printing Office. 1909, Vol. III, pp. 1625-1637. See also J. E. A. Jolliffe: The Constitutional History of Medieval England. London. A. & C. Beach, 1937, pp. 397-398.

20. Thorpe: op. cit. Vol. III, p. 1628; James P. Baxter: Sir Ferdinando Gorges, Three volumes, Boston, Prince Society, 1890, Vol. I, pp. 234-237, Vol. II, pp. 65-70.

21. ". . . as ample Rights, Jurisdictions, Privileges, Prerogatives, Royalties, Liberties, Immunities and Royal Rights, and Temporal Franchises whatsoever, as well by Sea as by Land, within the Region, Islands, Islets, and Limits aforesaid, to be had, exercised, used and enjoyed, as any Bishop of Durham, within the Bishoprick or County Palatine of Durham, in our Kingdom of England, ever heretoforth hath had, held, used, or enjoyed, or of right could, or ought to have, hold, use or enjoy." Thorpe: op. cit. Vol. III, p. 1679. For complete text, see ibid. Vol. III, pp. 1677-1686.

22. The Fundamental Constitutions of Carolina, 1669. For text see Thorpe: op. cit. Vol. V, pp. 2772-2786.

    "Lord Baltimore and the Carolina proprietors followed in much the same line [as Gorges] though with abundant variation in detail." Herbert L. Osgood: The American Colonies in the Seventeenth Century. Two vols. Columbia University Press, 1930, Vol. II, p. 7.

23. For a concise summary see J. Franklin Jameson: The American Revolution Considered as a Social Movement. Princeton University Press, 1940, pp. 29-31. See also Keith: op. cit. pp. 41-42.

24. "And because in a Country so farr distant and seated amongst soe many barbarous nations the Intrusions of Invasions as well of the barbarious people as of Pirates and other enemies maye be justly feared Wee Doe therefore for us our heires and successors give and graunte unto the said Sir Fardinando Gorges his heires and assignes full power and authoritie . . ." Thorpe: op. cit. Vol. III, p. 1630.

For a similar statement in the Maryland charter, see Thorpe: op. cit. Vol. III, p. 1681. For an interesting statement to the effect that the English proprietors were obsessed with the idea of transplanting English customs of government to the American wilderness, see Andrews: The Colonial Period of American History: Vol. I, pp. 328-329.

25. Osgood: op. cit. Vol. II, p. 15.

26. Jameson: op. cit. pp. 34-36.

27. Andrews: op. cit. Vol. III, pp. 273-275; Osgood: op. cit. Vol. II, p. 8.

28. "Our sovereign lord the King having out of his royal grace and bounty granted unto us the province of Carolina, with all the royalties, properties, jurisdictions, and privileges by a county palatine, as large and ample as the county palatine of Durham, with other great privileges..." Opening statement of The Fundamental Constitutions of Carolina, 1669. Thorpe: op. cit. Vol. V, p. 2772.

29. Keith: op. cit. p. 86.

30. "...many of the conventions of a landed aristocracy took root. And if it be said that the aristocracy of later Carolina was distinctively America, its place won by enterprise and merit with the aid of favorable land policies, it must also be admitted that the aristocracy envisioned in the proprietors' plan was essentially the same." Wesley Frank Craven: The Southern Colonies in the Seventeenth Century, 1607-1689. Louisiana State University Press, 1949, p. 341.

31. Albert J. Beveridge: Life of John Marshall. 4 volumes. Boston and New York, Houghton Mifflin Company, 1916-1919, Vol. I, p. 49.

32. Leonard Woods Labaree: Royal Government in America, New

Haven, Yale University Press, 1930, p. 5; Louise P. Kellogg: The American Colonial Charter: A Study of English Administration in Relation Thereto, Chiefly After 1688, in Annual Report of the American Historical Association for the Year 1903. In Two Volumes, Washington, Government Printing Office, 1904, Vol. I, p. 252.

33. Kellogg: op. cit. p. 194.

34. "Throughout the seventeenth century and the first six decades of the eighteenth, the colonies were recognized as dependencies of the English crown and not of the English people nor even of their representatives in parliament." Labaree: op. cit. p. 3.

35. Thus in the seventy year period from 1696 to 1765 nearly 400 American colonial laws were disallowed. See Oliver Morton Dickerson: American Colonial Government, Cleveland, Ohio, The Arthur H. Clark Company, 1912, pp. 22-235.

    "Of 8563 acts submitted by the continental colonies, 469 or 5.5 per cent were disallowed by orders in council." E. B. Russell: The Review of Colonial Legislation by the King in Council, Columbia University Studies in History, Economics and Public Law, New York, 1915, Vol. LXIV, No. 2, p. 221.

    See also C. M. Andrews: The Royal Disallowance, in Proceedings American Antiquarian Society, April 1914-October, 1914, Worcester, Massachusetts, Published by the Society, 1914, New Series, Vol. XXIV, p. 343; Kellogg: op. cit. p. 209.

36. Kellogg: op. cit. p. 252; Labaree: op. cit. pp. 99, 223-229.

37. Roscoe Pound: Organization of Courts, Boston, Little, Brown and Company, 1940, pp. 22, 24.

    "In judicial matters . . . the interference of English authorities was successful . . . The right to take appeals from all colonies, whether protected by charters or not, was asserted as a prerogative of the crown, and was successfully maintained against all resistance." Kellogg: op. cit. p. 272.

38. Beer: Origins of the British Colonial System, 1578-1660, p. 342.

39. Proceedings and Debates of the British Parliaments Respecting North America. Five volumes. Edited by Leo Francis Stock. Washington, D. C. Published by the Carnegie Institution of Washington, 1924-1941. Volume I, Preface, p. XI and pp. 3-6.

40. House of Commons Debates, 1621, Vol. III, pp. 408, 441-442. For a comprehensive account of the struggle, see Harold A. Innis: The Cod Fisheries—The History of An International Economy, New Haven, Yale University Press, 1940, Chapter IV—The Struggle Against Monopoly, 1600-1650, pp. 52-94.

41. House of Commons Journal, Vol. I, p. 592. Quoted in Beer: op. cit. p. 302.

42. C. H. Firth and R. S. Rait: Acts and Ordinances of the Interregnum, 1642-1660, London, H. M. Stationery Office, 1911, Three vols., Vol. II, p. 122.

43. "...at the American Revolution and later at the French Revolution, 'the people' were thought of as succeeding to the sovereignty of the British Parliament or of the French king..." Roscoe Pound: Interpretations of Legal History, Cambridge University Press, Cambridge, England, 1930, p. 3.

44. "The Statute is not a revolutionary measure. It represents the outcome of a long process of development..." Arthur Berriedale Keith: The Dominions as Sovereign States. London, MacMillan and Co., 1938, p. 61.

45. William MacDonald: Documentary Source Book of American History, 1606-1913, New York, The MacMillan Company, 1916, pp. 55-56.

46. For text see MacDonald: op. cit. pp. 90-92.

47. D. L. Keir: The Constitutional History of Modern England, 1485-1937, London, 1938, p. 347; Osgood: op. cit. Vol. II, p. 441.

48. Andrews: The Colonial Period of American History, Vol. I, p. 293. For text see Thorpe: op. cit. Vol. III, p. 1841.

49. McLaughlin: Foundations of American Constitutionalism, pp. 21-25.

50. Homer C. Hockett: The Constitutional History of the United States, 1776-1826. Two vols., The MacMillan Company, 1939, Vol. I, p. 26, note.

51. John Wise: A Vindication of the Government of the New England Churches, Boston. Printed by J. Allen for N. Boone, 1717, pp. 44-45; Andrews: op. cit. Vol. I, pp. 291-292.

52. For text of Sir Edmund Andres' Commission for the Dominion of New England see Thorpe: op. cit. Vol. III, pp. 1863-1869.

53. Andrews: op. cit. Vol. III, p. 68.

54. W. S. McKechnie: A Commentary on the Great Charter of King John. Glasgow, Scotland, James MacLehose and Sons, 1914, pp. 123, 125-126.

55. The Reports of Sir Edward Coke, edited by J. H. Thomas and J. F. Fraser, 6 vols., London, 1826, Vol. IV, pp. 21, 375.

56. "The presence of Coke's doctrines in the colonies during the latter two-thirds of the seventeenth century is widely evidenced by the repeated efforts of colonial legislatures to secure for their constituencies the benefits of Magna Carta and particularly of the twenty-ninth chapter thereof." Edward S. Corwin: The 'Higher Law' Background of American Constitutional Law, Harvard Law Review, Vol. XLII (1929), p. 394.

See also the numerous examples given in H. D. Hazeltine: The Influence of Magna Carta on American Constitutional Development, in Columbia Law Review, Vol. XVII, January, 1917, No. 1, pp. 6-20.

57. Richard B. Morris: Government and Labor in Early America. Columbia University Press, New York, 1946, pp. 513-531.

58. Claud Mullins: The Law and Poor Persons, in The Quarterly Review, No. 563, London, January, 1945, p. 74.

59. Roscoe Pound: Interpretations of Legal History, p. 41; McLaughlin: Constitutional History of the United States, pp. 25-27.

60. Jefferson to Benjamin Rush, Jan. 16, 1811, in Jefferson's Writings, edited by Paul Leicester Ford, 10 vols. New York, G. P. Putnam's Sons, 1892-1899, Vol. IX, p. 296; Dumas Malone: Jefferson the Virginian, Boston, Little, Brown and Company, 1948, p. 175; Ralph Barton Perry: Puritanism and Democracy, New York, The Vanguard Press, 1944, pp. 126-127, 148, 185-187.

61. George Catlin: The Story of the Political Philosophers, New York, Whittlesey House, 1939, p. 282.

62. William Archibald Dunning: A History of Political Theories from Luther to Montesquieu, New York, The MacMillan Company, 1938, p. 368.

63. "... he [Locke] was in essence the official apologist for the revolution of 1688." Keith: Constitutional History of the First British Empire, p. 354.

64. McLaughlin: The Foundations of American Constitutionalism, pp. 63-71.

65. "The creation of the new Board of Trade and Plantations [in 1696] was due ... to the desire of the commercial class for an improvement of the trade of the Kingdom." Kellogg: op. cit. p. 215.

66. Carl Becker: The Declaration of Independence, New York, Alfred A. Knopf, 1942, p. 79; C. H. Van Tyne: The Influence of the Clergy and of Religious and Sectarian Forces on the American Revolution, in American Historical Review, Vol. XLX, Number 1, October, 1913, pp. 48-52.

67. Hockett: Vol. I, op. cit. pp. 5-6.

68. Keith: Constitutional History of the First British Empire, pp. 3-4.

69. Kellogg: op. cit. p. 320.

70. W. Seal Carpenter: The Development of American Political Thought, Princeton University Press, 1930, p. 102; Henry Jones Ford: The Rise and Growth of American Politics, New York, The MacMillan Company, 1911, p. 56; McLaughlin: Constitutional History of the United States, pp. 14-16.

71. Kellogg: op. cit. p. 194.

72. MacDonald: Documentary Source Book of American History, 1606-1926, Third edition, New York, The MacMillan Company, 1928, No. 2, Second charter of Virginia, pp. 9-14.

73. McLaughlin: The Foundations of American Constitutionalism, pp. 37-52.

74. See James Otis' Rights of the British Colonies Asserted and Proved, in S. E. Morrison, Editor: Sources and Documents Illustrating the American Revolution, 1764-1788, and the Formation of the Federal Constitution, Oxford, Clarendon Press, 1923, pp. 4-5.

75. "The common law of England is the common law of the plantations and all statutes in affirmation of the common law, passed in England antecedent to the settlement of a colony, are in force in that colony unless there is some private act to the contrary, though no statutes made since those settlements are there in force, unless the colonies are particularly mentioned. Let an Englishman go where he will, he carries as much of law and liberty with him as the nature of things will bear." Richard West, Counsel of the Board of Trade. Quoted in George Chalmers: Opinions of Eminent Lawyers in Various Points of English Jurisprudence, Chiefly Concerning the Colonies, Fisheries and Commerce of Great Britain. Two volumes, Reed and Hunter, London, 1814, Vol. I, pp. 194-195.

   See also to the same effect Sir Edward Coke's decision in Calvin's case (1610), 7 Co. Rep. I, 2 State Trials, 559; Pound The Spirit of the Common Law, pp. 1-31; Keith: Constitutional History of the First British Empire, pp. 9-10.

76. Morrison: op. cit. p. 8.

77. McLaughlin: Constitutional History of the United States, p. 69.

78. William Seal Carpenter: The Separation of Powers in the Eighteenth Century, in American Political Science Review, February 1928, Vol. XXII, pp. 32-44; William Bondy: The Separation of

Governmental Powers, in Columbia University Studies in History and Public Law, New York, 1896, Vol. V, No. 2, pp. 135-318.

79. J. H. Robinson: The Original and Derived Features of the Constitution, in Annals of the American Academy of Political and Social Science, October, 1890, Vol. I, pp. 202-243; McLaughlin: Constitutional History of the United States, pp. 91-105.

80. McLaughlin: op. cit. pp. 33, 58-59, 95, 98.

81. McLaughlin: op. cit. p. 15 note. See also McLaughlin: The Background of American Federalism, in American Political Science Review, May, 1918, Vol. XII, pp. 215-240; Carl Brent Swisher: American Constitutional Development, Houghton Mifflin, Boston, 1943, pp. 12-13.

82. Edward S. Corwin: The 'Higher Law' Background of American Constitutional Law, in Harvard Law Review, Vol. XLII, No. 2, December, 1928, pp. 149-185; Vol. XLII, No. 3, January, 1929, pp. 365-409. Note especially pp. 366-369, 373-374, 379-380, 395, 399, 408-409.

83. "The conception of indefeasible rights played a leading part in Locke's defense of the Revolution of 1688 . . ." Holdsworth: op. cit. Vol. II, p. 445.

84. Ibid: Vol. I, pp. 544-568.

85. Pound: Organization of Courts, pp. 51, 53, 92. The American federal courts were, however, given a much wider jurisdiction by the Judiciary Act of 1789. See Westel Woodbury Willoughby: The Constitutional Law of the United States, Three volumes, New York, Baker, Voorhis and Company, 1929, Vol. III, pp. 1339-1340.

86. "The powers of the Supreme Court of the United States to declare state laws unconstitutional is scarcely more than an American version of the constant practice of the Board of Trade." Dickerson: op. cit. p. 365.

87. Madison reported that in the federal convention the proposal to give the national congress the power to nullify state laws was so seriously considered that the "votes on it more than once equally divided." Max Farrand, Editor: The Records of the Federal Convention of 1787. Revised edition in four volumes, New Haven, Yale University Press, 1937, Vol. III, Appendix, A, CCCCI, p. 549.
See also Labaree: op. cit. p. 5; A. M. Schlesinger: Colonial Appeals to the Privy Council, in Political Science Quarterly, Vol. XXVIII, September, 1913, pp. 433-450.

88. 8 Co. 114 (1610) and 7 Co. I, 4b (1610). See also Holdsworth: op. cit. Vol. I, pp. 99, 462, II, 442, IV, 186, 323, 403, V, 345, 425, 475,

477, 478, VIII, 240 (Bonham's case); I. 226, III, 56, 290, 373, 464, IV, 173, 183, 186, 201, 203, 209, 277, V. 49, 50, 163, 232, 234, 247, 364, 369, 434, 463, VI, 23 24, VII. 95, 483, 484, VIII. 409, IX. 5, 72, 74, 76, 77, 78, 79-84, 86, 87, 93, 98 (Calvin's case).

89. Charles A. Beard, Editor: The Enduring Federalist, Doubleday & Company, Garden City, New York, 1948, Number 82—Relation of Federal and State Courts, pp. 353-356. Signed Publius (Hamilton). See also McLaughlin: op. cit. p. 11.

90. For text of the New England Confederation see William MacDonald: Select Charters, New York, The MacMillan Company, 1899, pp. 94-101. For a comprehensive account of the Confederation see Osgood: The American Colonies in the 17th Century, Vol. I, Chap. X, pp. 392-423.

91. MacDonald: Select Charters, pp. 400-401.

92. Ibid: p. 401.

93. Ibid: p. 399.

94. Hockett: op. cit. Vol. I, pp. 130-131.

95. MacDonald: Select Charters, pp. 253-257.

96. Hockett: op. cit. Vol. I, p. 134. See also Lois K. Mathews: Benjamin Franklin's Plan for a Colonial Union, 1750-1775, in American Political Science Review, Vol. VIII, pp. 393-412, August, 1914; Rayner Kelsey: The Originator of the Federal Idea, in The Nation, Vol. XCIV, pp. 562-563, June 6, 1912.

97. Pound: Organization of Courts, Chap. II, pp. 26-57.

98. See The Federalist, No. 23, entitled General Powers Necessary for an Effective Union, in The Enduring Federalist: op. cit. pp. 93-96. See also ibid., No. 42, Powers over Foreign and Interstate Affairs, pp. 181-185.

99. Especially by means of the first ten amendments popularly known as the bill of rights. Farrand: Records of the Federal Convention: Vol. IV, pp. 93-95.

100. Carl J. Friedrich: Constitutional Government and Democracy, Boston, Little Brown & Company, 1941, pp. 80-81.

CHAPTER III

1. Letter of the Massachusetts House of Representatives to Lord Camden, January 29, 1768, in Documents of American History, edited

by Henry Steele Commager, Second edition, F. S. Crofts and Company, New York, 1940, p. 65.

2. W. F. Reddaway: Rivalry For Colonial Power, 1660-1713, in The Cambridge History of the British Empire, Eight volumes, Cambridge. At the University Press, 1929-1936. Vol. I, Chapter X, pp. 300-329.

3. J. Holland Rose: Sea Power and Expansion, 1660-1763, in Cambridge History of the British Empire, Vol. I, Chapter XVIII, pp. 507-537.

4. "After the abolition of the Star Chamber, there was no tribunal which would punish a breach of a proclamation unless the conduct ordered or forbidden by it was illegal." Holdsworth: Vol. 6, p. 303. See also ibid. Vol. 6, pp. 254, 302-312.

5. See also the rebukes administered to the Board of Trade in 1721 by "certain proprietors." Documents Relative to Colonial History of the State of New York, by John Romeyn Brodhead. Edited by E. B. O'Callaghan, M. D. Vol. V, Albany, Weed, Parsons and Company, 1855, p. 627.

6. See the excellent summary of this point in Holdsworth: Vol. VI, pp. 287-290.

7. Sir William Blackstone: Commentaries on the Laws of England. Second edition, Two volumes. Callaghan and Company, Chicago, 1872. Edited by Thomas Cooley, Volume I, p. 146.

8. "The pulpit gave way to the bar, and the preaching of brimstone was soon to yield to the teaching of Blackstone." James Truslow Adams: The Adams Family. The Literary Guild, New York, 1930, p. 16.

9. Young John Marshall was given a copy of Blackstone by his father and read it "with delight." Albert J. Beveridge: The Life of John Marshall, Houghton Mifflin Company, Boston and New York, Four volumes, 1916-1919, Vol. I, p. 56.

10. Andrews: op. cit. Vol. IV, p. 367.

11. Debate in the House of Commons on colonies and home duties for February 8, 1747/8. Proceedings and Debates on the British Parliaments Respecting North America. Edited by Leo Francis Stock, Vol. V (1739-1754), pp. 256-263.

12. Andrews: op. cit. Vol. IV, p. 366.

13. For a discussion of smuggling and the proposed smuggling amnesty, see Proceedings and Debates: Vol. V (1739-1754), pp. 213-214.

14. Note Grenville's efforts to improve enforcement, in Acts of the Privy Council, Colonial Series, 1613-1783, London, 1908-12, Vol. IV, pp. 569-572. See also the violations listed in Keith: Constitutional History of the First British Empire, pp. 339-341.

15. See the comprehensive report of Mr. Blathwait from the Commissioners of Trade and Plantations presented to the House of Commons on February 5, 1701/2. Proceedings and Debates Respecting North America, Vol. 2, 1689-1702, pp. 426-442.

The report specifically states that: "And it appears by what we have before represented, that the propriety-colonies are in a state wholly defenceless; and that the proprietors and charter-governments have not complied with what has been demanded of them, in reference to trade, or with what may be necessary for the common safety . . . that they have made laws contrary and repugnant to the laws of England and directly prejudicial to trade . . ." Ibid. p. 441.

16. By the act of 11 and 12 William III, c 7(1700) a special statute was passed creating commissioners for the trial of piracy. See Proceedings and Debates, Vol. 2, 1689-1702, pp. 383-384.

17. Ibid. Vol. II, pp. 204-207.

18. For text see Commager: op. cit. No. 27, pp. 38-39.

19. For list of duties see Proceedings and Debates, Vol. 2, p. 365.

20. Ibid, Vol. 2, p. 197, notes 66 and 67; Board of Trade Journal, Vol. I, November 16, 1704, pp. 58-59.

21. For references to the vice admiralty colonial courts, see Proceedings and Debates, Vol. 2, pp. 192, 193, 400, 404-406.
For an adverse critique of the Board by Captain Charles Desborow and other navy personnel, see Ibid: Vol. 2, pp. 285-286.

22. See especially, Ibid: Vol. 2, pp. 202-206.

23. Ibid. Vol. 2, p. 388. See also Calendar of State Papers, Colonial, 1700, pp. 563-567; Robert Greenhalgh Albion: Forests and Sea Power—The Timber Problem of The Royal Navy, 1652-1862, Cambridge, Harvard University Press, 1926, p. 110.

24. Albion: op. cit. p. 280; Herbert L. Osgood: The American Colonies in the 18th Century, 4 volumes, New York, The Columbia University Press, 1924, Vol. I, pp. 39-41; New York Colonial Documents, Vol. V, p. 629.

25. Calendar State Papers Colonial, 1724-1726. Sections 193, 214; Andrews: Vol. IV, pp. 374-377.

26. "A letter from Earl Stanhope . . . signifying His Majesty's having

appointed Richard West, Esqr. one of his Majesty's counsel at law, to attend such law business relating to trade and plantations, as this Board do not conceive of that importance, to require the opinion of His Majesty's Attorney or Solicitor-General, was read." Board of Trade Journal, April 23, 1718, p. 369.

27. New York Colonial Documents, Vol. V, p. 630.

28. Andrews: Vol. IV, p. 391.

29. New York Colonial Documents, Vol. V, pp. 625-626, 627-628; Vol. VII, pp. 634-641; Calendar State Papers Colonial, 1708-1709, pp. 327-328. See also Board of Trade Journal, June 2, 1709, p. 41 and September 6, 1709, p. 70.

30. Leonard D. White: Introduction to the Study of Public Administration, New York, The MacMillan Company, 1939, pp. 18-20; Oliver Morton Dickerson: American Colonial Government, 1696-1765. Cleveland. The Arthur H. Clark Company, 1912, p. 365.

31. For a statement of the attempt against Rhode Island and Connecticut, see Board of Trade Journal, January 19, 1725/26, p. 213. See also New York Colonial Documents, Vol. V, p. 628.

32. Andrews: Vol. IV, p. 394.

33. Ibid., Vol. IV, pp. 394-395.

34. For the replies of Rhode Island and Connecticut to the requests for the surrender of their charters, see Kellogg: op. cit. pp. 322-334.

35. Dickerson: op. cit. p. 225.

36. Ibid., pp. 357-358.

37. Andrews: Vol. IV, pp. 401-402.

38. Parliamentary Debates: Vol. IV, pp. 91, 104, 117, 120, 121 note, 122, 133, 173, 174, 224-226, 230 (trade and manufacturing). In regard to naval stores see Vol. IV, pp. XVI, XVIII, 63, 67-71, 233, 237, 238, 240 note.

39. "It will be seen . . . that commercial restriction was the chief characteristic of colonial legislation for this period." 1728-1739. Leo Francis Stock: Preface Parliamentary Debates, Vol. IV, p. XVI.

40. Andrews: Vol. IV, pp. 403-404.

41. For a detailed account of these intrigues see Beveridge: Life of John Marshall, Vol. II, Chapters VII-IX, pp. 257-373.
    See also the statement of John Adams written in his Paris diary: "It is obvious that all the powers of Europe will be continually manoeuvring with us to work us into their real or imaginary bal-

ances of power." The Works of John Adams. C. F. Adams edition, Boston, 1865. Vol. III, p. 316, November 18, 1782.

42. "In a very real sense the narrow commercial policy of Great Britain, as well as that of Spain and France, transformed the United States from thirteen squabbling states into one nation." Thomas A. Bailey: A Diplomatic History of the American People, Third edition F. S. Crofts, New York, 1926, p. 52.

43. Bailey: op. cit. p. 106.

44. Dickerson: op. cit. p. 366.

45. See U. S. Statutes at Large, II, 283; Annals of Congress, 8th Cong. 2d Session, 1597.
    John Quincy Adams thought that such laws were "oppressive to the natural rights of the people of Louisiana." Samuel Flagg Bemis: John Quincy Adams and the Foundations of American Foreign Policy, New York, Alfred A. Knopf, 1950, p. 120.

46. American Insurance Company et al vs. Cantor, I Peters, 511-546.

47. Thus, for example, the western part of Virginia was definitely under-represented by the constitution of 1776. See Beveridge: Life of Marshall, Vol. I, pp. 217, note 1.

48. Commager: op. cit. Number 82, pp. 128-132.

49. For a concise summary of the grievances of the westerners, see Frederick Jackson Turner: The Significance of Sections in American History, New York, Henry Holt, 1932, Chapter IV—Western State Making in the Revolutionary Era, pp. 136-137.

50. McMaster: History of the People of the United States, Vol. II, Chapter IX, pp. 189-203.

51. See the statement in the Report of the President's Committee on Administrative Management, Washington, Government Printing Office, 1937, p. 36. See also Marshall E. Dimock: The Meaning and Scope of Public Administration, in John M. Gaus, Leonard D. White and Marshall E. Dimock: The Frontiers of Public Administration, The University of Chicago Press, Chicago, 1936, pp. 1-2.

52. Leonard D. White: Introduction to the Study of Public Administration, p. 20.

53. Leonard D. White: The Federalist—A Study in Administrative History, New York, The MacMillan Company, 1948, p. 514.

54. For Jefferson's statement of his position in the matter see his famous New Haven letter, in Works: Federal edition, Vol. IX, pp. 273-274, July 12, 1801. See also Leonard D. White: The Jefferson-

ians. A Study in Administrative History, 1801-1829, New York, The MacMillan Company, 1951, pp. 354, 553-559.

55. For Jackson's defense of the spoils system, see James D. Richardson, editor. A Compilation of the Messages of the Presidents, 1789-1897, 10 volumes, Washington, 1898-1899. Vol. II, pp. 448-449. See also Carl Russell Fish: The Civil Service and the Patronage, New York, Longmans Green, 1905, Chapter V, pp. 105-133.

56. Carl J. Friedrich: Constitutional Government and Democracy, Little Brown and Company, Boston, 1941, p. 43; White: The Federalist, p. 508.

57. Friedrich: op. cit. p. 40.

58. "At the middle of the nineteenth century members of the House of Lords were so successful in getting their impecunious relatives on the public payroll that John Burns once referred to the civil service as the outdoor relief department of the British aristocracy ... So Andrew Jackson and his friends did not invent the spoils system; they merely transplanted an old-world institution to a new soil." William Bennett Munro: The Governments of Europe. Third edition. The MacMillan Company, New York, 1939, pp. 120-121.

59. For the English principle see Holdsworth: op. cit. Vol. IV, pp. 274-275. For the continuation of the principle in American public law, see W. F. Willoughby: Principles of Judicial Administration, The Brookings Institution, Washington, 1929, p. 18; White: Introduction to the Study of Public Administration, p. 581.

60. Gaus, White and Dimock, op. cit. pp. 92-95; White: op. cit. p. 20. See also Jefferson's statement to the effect that public works were less well managed than private enterprises and that he thought it unwise "to abstract the high executive officers from those functions which nobody else is charged to carry on and to employ them in superintending works which are going on abundantly in private hands." Jefferson's Writing, Memorial edition, Vol. XII, p. 108, July 28, 1808. Quoted in White: The Jeffersonians, p. 25.

61. White: The Jeffersonians, pp. 423-452. "Resistance to the embargo was ... substantial and violations were frequent." Ibid. p. 451. See also Beveridge: Life of Marshall, Vol. IV, pp. 12-16.

62. Hamilton's Works, Lodge edition, Hamilton to McHenry, Vol. X, p. 307; White: The Federalists, pp. 241-252; Beveridge: op. cit. Vol. 11, pp. 485-488.

CHAPTER IV

1. T. V. Smith: The American Philosophy of Equality, University of Chicago Press, Chicago, 1927, pp. 5, 7.

2. "The Revolution was effected before the war commenced. The Revolution was in the minds and hearts of the people . . ." John Adams to H. Niles. Quincy, 13 February, 1818. John Adams Works, edited by Charles Francis Adams, Vol. X, p. 282.

See also Adams to Jefferson: "I think, with you, that it is difficult to say at what moment the Revolution began. In my opinion, it began as early as the first plantation of the country." John Adams to Thomas Jefferson, Quincy 29 May, 1818. Adams: Works, Vol. X, p. 313.

3. "As the Patriots were guided by the historical precedents established by England in the seventeenth century, so they followed the political theory developed at that time by the revolutionary party." Charles E. Merriam: A History of American Political Theories, New York, The MacMillan Company, 1906, p. 88. See also the tribute to Locke by James Otis, in Adams: Works, Vol. X, pp. 311-312. See, again, the statement of Luther Martin at the Federal Convention, in Farrand: Records, Vol. I, pp. 437-438, June 27, 1787.

4. Thomas Edwards, in his Gangraena, published in 1646, had declared that the Puritan leaders were saying that all persons ought to enjoy "their naturall and just Liberties agreeable to right reason . . . For by naturall birth all men are equally and alike born to like propriety, liberty and freedom . . ." Thomas Edwards: The Third Part of Gangraena, or a New and Higher Discovery of the Errors . . . of the Sectaries. London, Printed for R. Smith, 1646, pp. 16, 17.

5. See the reference to "our just, antient and constitutional rights" in An Association Signed by 89 Members of the Late House of Burgesses of Virginia, 27 May, 1774, in Papers of Thomas Jefferson. Julian P. Boyd, Editor. Four volumes to date (April 22, 1952), Princeton, New Jersey, Princeton University Press, 1950-1951. Vol. I, p. 107. See also Merriam: op. cit. p. 93.

6. Merriam: op. cit. p. 95.

7. Holdsworth: op. cit. Vol. VI, pp. 287-289.

8. Papers of Thomas Jefferson—Resolutions of the Freeholders of Albermarle County, 26 July, 1774. Vol. I, p. 117. See also his Notes on Locke, ibid., Vol. I, pp. 544-551.

9. John C. Miller: Origins of the American Revolution, Little Brown and Company, Boston, 1943, p. 178.

10. John Locke: Two Treatises of Government. London. Printed for Awansham and John Churchill, 1698. Book II, Chapter 5, p. 202; Sterling Power Lamprecht: The Moral and Political Philosophy of John Locke, New York. Columbia University Press, 1918, pp. 123-124.

11. Locke: op. cit. pp. 198-199; Paschal Larkin: Property in the Eighteenth Century with Special Reference to England and Locke. Longmans, Green. London, 1930. Chapter V—Locke and America, pp. 141-142.

12. H. D. Foster: International Calvinism through Locke and the Revolution of 1688, in American Historical Review, Vol. XXXII, April, 1927, pp. 498-499.

13. John Adams: A Defense of the Constitutions of Government of the U. S. A. Philadelphia, 1787, p. 365. See also Adams: Work, edited by Charles Francis Adams, Vol. IV, pp. 463-464.

14. Carl Van Doren: Benjamin Franklin. New York, The Viking Press, 1938, pp. 14, 190, 192; H. D. Foster: op. cit. p. 475.

15. R. M. MacIver: European Doctrines and the Constitution, in Conyers Read: The Constitution Reconsidered, pp. 51-53.

16. "... when the Virginia Convention on June 12, 1776, declared that all men, having a permanent interest in the community 'cannot be taxed or deprived of their property for publick uses, without their own consent, or that of their representatives' . . . it was converting into a text for the American Revolution a doctrine which formed the prologue of the English Revolution. It was the language of Locke." Larkin: op. cit. p. 145.

17. Andrews: op. cit. Vol. IV, p. 408.

18. Beveridge: The Life of John Marshall, Vol. I, 1916, pp. 4-6.

19. Andrews: op. cit. Vol. IV, pp. 422, 423, 424-425.

20. J. Holland Rose: Sea Power and Expansion, in The Cambridge History of the British Empire, Vol. I, Chapter XVIII, pp. 507-560.

21. J. F. Rees: Mercantilism and the Colonies, in Cambridge History of the British Empire, Vol. I, Chapter XX, pp. 593-602.

22. Stock: Parliamentary Debates, Vol. IV (1728-1739), pp. XII, 88n, 130n, 179-188, 240n, 252, 272, 824.
Under date of February 21, 1732/3, Mr. Dodington, Lord of the Treasury, declared: "that English Parliaments seldom touch upon Ireland but to their own hurt, witness the act for restraining Irish cattle from coming to England, and the restraint of their woollen manufacture, which has been the occasion of the French and other countries rivalling us in that trade. That the revenues of Ireland sink and the Kingdom is in a bad way, and must be worse if not suffered to dispose of their commodities in exchange for foreign goods . . ." Ibid. Vol. IV, p. 179.
See also Charles M. Andrews: The Acts of Trade, in Cambridge

History of the British Empire, Vol. I, Chapter IX, pp. 279-281, 284-285, 287-288.

23. The Parliamentary Debates abound with references to measures for the prevention of smuggling. See especially Parliamentary Debates: Vol. IV, p. 315 and note 105. For the serious situation in Massachusetts in the 1680's see Beer: The Old Colonial System, Vol. 2, p. 301.

24. 4. Geo. III, c. 15. For text see Macdonald: Select Charters, New York. The MacMillan Company, 1899. No. 56, pp. 272-281.

25. Edmund Burke: Works and Correspondence. A new edition. Eight volumes. London. Francis and John Rivington, 1852. Vol. II, p. 424-428.

26. Winthrop's Conclusion for the Planting of New England, in Old South Leaflets. Vol. II, Boston, Directors of the Old South Work, n.d. Number 50, pp. 4-5; Nellis M. Crouse: Causes of the Great Migration, 1630-1640, in New England Quarterly, Vol. V, January, 1932, pp. 3-36.

27. Van Tyne: The Causes of the War of Independence, pp. 346-347.

28. Arthur Lyon Cross: The Anglican Episcopate and the American Colonies, New York, Longmans, Green and Company, 1902, Chapter V, pp. 113-138.

29. Adams: Works, Vol. IV, p. 55 footnote; Van Tyne: The Influence of the Clergy, and Of Religious and Sectarian Forces, on the American Revolution, in American Historical Review, Vol. XIX, Number 1, October, 1913, pp. 44-64.

30. See the Letters of the Massachusetts House to the Ministry, January, 1768, in Commager: Documents of American History, Two volumes, New York, F. S. Crofts & Co., 1935, Vol. I, p. 65.

31. Charles Warren: A History of the American Bar, Boston, Little Brown and Company, 1911, Chapter IX, pp. 188-194. "Probably from twenty-five to fifty American-born lawyers had been educated in England prior to 1760; and it has been stated that 115 were admitted to the Inns, from 1760 to the close of the Revolution..." Ibid. p. 188.

32. Holdsworth: op. cit. Vol. IV, pp. 279, 280, 281.

33. John Adams "Autobiography" in Adams: Works, Vol. II, p. 124, note 1. Quoted in Hockett: op. cit. Vol. I, p. 74, note 1.

34. For Otis' Speech Against the Writs of Assistance, see Commager: op. cit. Vol. I, pp. 45-47.

35. Bonham's case (1609) 8 Co. Rep. 107, 118. Calvin's case (1609)

7 Co. Rep, 13a and 25a. See also Holdsworth: op. cit. Vol. 4, p. 186, note number 3.

36. Edward S. Corwin: The "Higher Law" Background of American Constitutional Law, in 42 Harvard Law Review, pp. 365-376 (1929). See also Theodore F. T. Plucknett: Bonham's case and Judicial Review, in Harvard Law Review, Vol. XL, 1926-1927, pp. 68-70.

37. Edward S. Corwin: Court Over Constitution, Princeton University Press, 1938, pp. 21-23; Plucknett: op. cit. Vol. XL, 1926-1927, pp. 61-65.

38. The Writings of Samuel Adams. Collected and edited by Harry Alonzo Cushing. Four volumes, G. P. Putnam's Sons, New York, 1904, Vol. I, p. 65.

39. John Adams: Works, Vol. 9, pp. 390-391.

40. McLaughlin: op. cit. pp. 47-48 and note 28, p. 48. McLaughlin quotes the Virginia Gazette, March 21, 1776 as his source and suggests that this may have been the first case in which an act was held void because it violated a "constitution."

41. Writings of James Madison. Edited by Gaillard Hunt, 9 vols., New York, G. P. Putnam's Sons, 1900-1910, Vol. VI, p. 373.

42. John Adams: Works, Vol. IV, pp. 37-38.

43. Robert L. Schuyler: Parliament and the British Empire, Columbia University Press, New York, 1929, Chapter I, pp. 1-39. Much of the legislation for the Channel Islands in the eighteenth century seems to have dealt with trade and imperial defense rather than with the passage of local statutory enactments. See, for example, Stock: Parliamentary Debates, Vol. V, pp. 81, 126, 162, 229.

44. Frederick J. Turner: The Frontier in American History, New York, Henry Holt and Company, 1928, p. 4.

45. John Adams: Works, Vol. IV, pp. 15, 17-18.

46. Edmund Burke: Select Works. Three volumes. Edited by E. J. Payne. Oxford, The Clarendon Press, 1872. Speech on American Taxation, April 19, 1774, Vol. I, pp. 118-119.

47. Thomas Hutchinson: History of Massachusetts Bay, 3 vols., Thomas and John Fleet, Boston, 1764-1768, Vol. III, p. 172.

48. The Writings of John Dickinson, Paul Leicester Ford, editor. Pennsylvania Historical Society Memoirs, Vol. XIV. Philadelphia, The Historical Society of Pennsylvania, 1895, Letter II, pp. 314-322.

49. Ibid. pp. 312-313.

50. Commager: Documents, Second edition, 1940, No. 43, p. 63. For text see ibid., pp. 63-64.

51. John Adams: Works, Vol. IV, p. 46.

52. Harry Alonzo Cushing, Editor: The Writings of Samuel Adams, Four volumes, New York, G. P. Putnam's Sons, 1904-1908, Vol. I, pp. 39, 46-48; Massachusetts Circular Letter, February 11, 1768, written by Samuel Adams, in ibid. Vol. I, pp. 184-188; statement of Burke in his speech on American taxation: "I venture to say, that during that whole period, a Parliamentary revenue from thence was never once in contemplation." Burke: op. cit. Vol. I, p. 117.

53. Massachusetts State Papers: Speeches of the Governors of Massachusetts from 1765 to 1775 and The Answers of the House of Representatives to the Same . . . Boston, Printed by Russell and Gardner, 1818. Message From the House of Representatives to the Governor, June 19, 1769, p. 173. See also a copy in Samuel Adams: Writings, Vol. I, p. 348. Adams was a member of the committee that reported the answer. Ibid. Vol. I, p. 346.

54. John Adams: Works, Vol. IV, pp. 175-177.

55. "We do declare that there their natural and legal rights have in frequent instances been invaded by the parliament of Great Britain." Draft of a Declaration of Rights Prepared for the Virginia Convention of August, 1774. 26 July, 1774. The Papers of Thomas Jefferson, Vol. I, p. 119.

56. For text of the Intolerable Acts see Commager: Number 49, pp. 71-76. For the fears of the colonials in regard to their western land claims, see Clarence W. Alvord: The Mississippi Valley in British Politics, Cleveland, The A. H. Clark Co., 1917, Two vols., Vol. II, pp. 112-114.

57. John Adams: Works, Vol. II, p. 252; Samuel Adams: Writings, Vol. I, pp. 201-203.

58. See, for example, Resolutions of Freeholders of Albemarle County, Virginia, drafted by Jefferson, July 26, 1774, with its references to "the common rights of mankind" and "those rightful powers which God has given us" . . . Commager: Number 52, pp. 77-78.

59. The Papers of Thomas Jefferson: A Summary View, Vol. I, p. 126.

60. Ibid. Vol. I, pp. 132, 135.

61. For text of the Declaration and Resolves of the First Continental Congress, October 14, 1774, see Commager: Number 56, pp. 82-90. For the Declaration of the Causes and Necessity of Taking Up Arms, of the Second Continental Congress, July 6, 1775, see Commager: Number 61, pp. 92-95.

62. Commager: Number 67, pp. 103-104.

63. Ibid. Number 66, pp. 100-103. See also the comprehensive account in The Papers of Thomas Jefferson: Vol. I, pp. 413-433.

64. "The history of the present king of Great Britain is a history of repeated injuries and usurpations." Ibid. p. 101.

65. Journals of the Continental Congress, 1774-1789. Edited by Worthington C. Ford and Gaillard Hunt. 34 Vols. Washington, Government Printing Office, 1904-1937, Vol. I, pp. 68-69.

66. Ibid: Vol. I, p. 119.

67. Ibid: Vol. I, p. 82.

68. Charles Warren: A History of the American Bar, p. 178. See also Burke's Speech on Conciliation: "I hear that they have sold nearly as many of Blackstone's Commentaries in America as in England." Burke: Select Works, Vol. I, p. 182.

69. David A. Lockmiller: Sir William Blackstone, Chapel Hill, North Carolina, 1938, p. 170.

70. Ibid. pp. 170-171.

71. Warren: op. cit. pp. 179-180; Lockmiller: op. cit. p. 169.

72. Hugh Evander Willis: Introduction to Anglo-American Law, Indiana University Studies, Bloomington, Indiana, No. XIII, 1926, p. 155.

73. Sir Bulstrode Whitelock's Memorials of the English Affairs, London, Printed for Nathaniel Ponder, MDCLXXXII, pp. 134-135. See also Sir Philip Warwick: Memoirs of King Charles the First. Edinburgh, James Ballantyne, 1813. Warwick describes Manchester as "very facile or changeable." Ibid. p. 272.

For Cromwell's quarrel with Manchester after the battle of Newbery, see Edward, Earl of Clarendon: The History of the Rebellion and Civil Wars in England, Edited by W. Dunn Macray. Six volumes, Oxford. At the Clarendon Press, MDCCCLXXXVIII, Vol. III, pp. 452-453. See also Samuel Rawson Gardiner: A History of the Great Civil War, Four vols. London, Longmans, Green, 1888-1901, Vol. I, pp. 183, 477, Vol. II, pp. 20-22.

74. Memoirs of the Life of Colonel Hutchinson, Governor of Nottingham, by his wife, Lucy, edited by C. H. Firth. Two vols. London, 1885, Vol. I, p. 336. See also the account of parliamentary laxity in the royalist attack on London, November 12, 1642, as described by Sir Philip Warwick: op. cit. pp. 256-257; Whitelock: op. cit. pp. 62-63.

Clarendon declares that Essex hoped "he should become the

preserver, and not the destroyer of the King and Kingdom." Clarendon: op. cit. Vol. II, p. 542; Gardiner: op. cit. Vol. I, pp. 192-193. Gardiner declares that Essex "was wanting . . . in that ferocity of discipline which in a great commander cuts sharply asunder the ties of personal attachment." Ibid. Vol. I, p. 192.

75. Yet at the outbreak of the war Sir William Waller had penned some lines that speak for themselves. Writing to his old friend, Sir Ralph Hopton, the royalist, he had declared: "The experience I have had of your worth and the happiness which I have enjoyed in your friendship, are wounding considerations to me, when I look upon this present distance between us: Certainly Sir, my affections to you are so unchangeable, that hostilitie itself cannot violate my friendship to your person; but I must be true to the cause wherein I serve . . . That Great God, who is the searcher of all hearts knows with what a sad fear I go upon this service, and with what a perfect hate I detest a war without an enemie, but I look upon it as opus Domini, which is enough to silence all passion in me. The God of Peace send us, in his good time, the blessing of peace, and in the meantime, fit us to receive it. We are both on the stage and must act those parts that are assigned to us in this Tragedy, but let us do it in the way of honour, and without personal animosities; whatsoever the issue of it be, I shall never resign that dear title of

Your most affectionate Friend and faithful Servant

William Waller." Vindication of the Character and Conduct of Sir William Waller . . . (Written by Himself), London, Printed for J. Debrett, 1793, pp. 12-14.

76. Samuel Rawson Gardiner: The First Two Stuarts and the Puritan Revolution, 1603-1660, Second edition, London, Longmans, Green, 1877, p. 158; Warwick: op. cit. p. 309; Clarendon: op. cit. Vol. II, pp. 460-463.

77. Whitelock: op. cit. pp. 86, 89, 95, 104, 126, 138, 147, 158, 159; Clarendon: op. cit. Vol. I, pp. 395-397, 415-416.

78. Warwick: op. cit. pp. 311-312; Clarendon: op. cit. Vol. III, pp. 468-500; Gardiner: History of the Great Civil War, Vol. II, pp. 69-75. See also Edward Walford: Greater London, 2 vols. London, Cassell & Company, n.d. Vol. I, pp. 231-232.

79. Clarendon: Vol. III, pp. 500-501; Gardiner: Vol. II, pp. 75-77.

80. Warwick: pp. 332-336; Clarendon: Vol. II, pp. 567-568, Vol. IV, pp. 259-260; Waller: pp. 82-97; Whitelock: pp. 253-259; Gardiner: Vol. II, p. 75.

Cromwell was credited with saying that: "If he met the king in battle, he would fire his pistol at the king as at another." Thomas

Carlyle: Oliver Cromwell's Letters and Speeches. Four volumes, New York, Charles Scribner's Sons, 1899-1900, Vol. I, p. 197.

81. Journals of Henry Dearborn, 1776-1783. Reprinted from the Proceedings of the Massachusetts Historical Society, 1886, Cambridge, John Wilson and Son. University Press, 1887, pp. 16-18. This excerpt contains an account of General Lee at the Battle of Monmouth.

See also J. W. Fortesque: A History of the British Army, London, MacMillan and Co., 1902, Vol. III, 1763-1793, pp. 161, 190, 193, 194, 208, 254; Carl Van Doren: Secret History of the American Revolution. Garden City Publishing Company, Garden City, New York, 1941, pp. 29-36.

82. Fortesque: op. cit. Vol. III, pp. 232, 251, 319; Van Doren: op. cit. pp. 134-137. For a more favorable view of Gates, see Bernhard Knollenberg: Washington and the Revolution — A Reappraisal, New York, The MacMillan Company, 1940, Chapter I, pp. 1-11; Samuel White Patterson: Horatio Gates—Defender of American Liberties, New York, Columbia University Press, 1941, pp. 392-396.

83. Fortesque: Vol. III, p. 235; Van Doren: pp. 3-6; Patterson: op. cit. pp. 48, 221.

84. Clarendon: Vol. III, pp. 38-48. Waller was first cousin to Hampden and also to Cromwell. He is not to be confused with Sir William Waller, the able defensive parliamentary general. For a detailed account of Edmund Waller's efforts to weaken the parliamentary party and restore the king, see Samuel Johnson: Lives of the Poets, edited by George Birbeck Hill, 3 vols., Oxford, Clarendon Press, 1905, Vol. I, pp. 256-267. Birbeck Hill's notes are most illuminating.

85. For an able summary of the leading documents in the case, see Francis Wharton: Revolutionary Diplomatic Correspondence of the United States. 6 vols. Washington. Government Printing Office, 1889, Vol. I, pp. 272-283.

See also Patrick Henry: Life, Correspondence and Speeches, edited by William Wirt Henry, 3 vols., New York, Charles Scribner's Sons, 1891, Vol. I, pp. 544-552; Louis Clinton Hatch: The Administration of the American Revolutionary Army, New York, Longmans, Green, 1904, pp. 22-34; Pennsylvania Magazine of History and Biography, Philadelphia. The Historical Society of Pennsylvania, 1905, Vol. XXIX, p. 20.

By a curious coincidence a certain Lord Conway was one of the members of Waller's plot. See Johnson's Lives: Vol. I, pp. 260, 263, 264, 266. We have been unable to discover if he were an ancestor of the Conway of the American Revolution.

86. Fortesque: Vol. 3, pp. 188, 252-253; Van Doren: pp. 10-11. See also

Wharton: Vol. 2, p. 33, where, under date of March 22, 1775, Lord Richard Howe assured Franklin of his good will and his desire for a reconciliation.

Under date of May 26, 1779, Franklin wrote to the Congressional Committee of Foreign Affairs that "General and Lord Howe . . . have formally given it as their opinion in Parliament that the conquest of America is impracticable." Ibid., Vol. III, p. 194. See also Arthur Lee's comment on General Howe: "He is a brave man, but has a very confused head, and is therefore very unfit for an extensive command." Ibid., Vol. II, p. 84.

87. Benson J. Lossing: The American Revolution and the War of 1812. Three volumes, New York Book Concern, New York, 1875, Vol. II, pp. 608-609.

88. Hatch: pp. 97-98; Washington: Writings, W. C. Ford edition, Washington to the President of Congress, August 3, 1778, Vol. VII, p. 141; same to same, November 24, 1779, Vol. VIII, p. 124.

89. "I should do injustice if I were to be longer silent with regards to the merits of the Baron de Steuben. His knowledge of his profession, added to the zeal which he has discovered since he began upon the functions of his office, leads me to consider him as an acquisition to the service, and to recommend him to the attention of Congress." Washington to the President of Congress, 30 April, 1778, Works: op. cit. Vol. 6, p. 507. See also Hatch: p. 63.

90. Gardiner: op. cit. Vol. I, p. 47. See also the account in Fortesque: op. cit. Vol. I, pp. 193-199. For a briefer version of the same statement, see Carlyle: Cromwell's Letters and Speeches, Vol. I, p. 128.

91. In speaking of the battle of Naseby Clarendon declared that Rupert's men "having, as they thought, acted their parts, they could never be brought to rally themselves again in order, or to charge the enemy . . . whereas Cromwell's troops, if they prevailed, or though they were beaten and routed, presently rallied again, and stood in good order till they received new orders." Clarendon: op. cit. Vol. IV, pp. 45, 46.

92. Washington Writings, Ford edition. August 29, 1775, Vol. III, p. 98. See also Hatch: op. cit. pp. 13-17.

93. Washington to Committee of Congress, January 28, 1778, Writings, Ford ed. Vol. VI, pp. 301-304; Hatch: op. cit. pp. 78-81.

94. Washington to the President of the Congress, Valley Forge, 10 April, 1778, Writings: Ford ed. Vol. VI, pp. 465-466; Hatch: op. cit. pp. 81-85, 196. "The officers were left unpaid for months at a time, and were subjected to the most galling mortifications." Ibid. p. 196.

For Washington's pleas for a permanent army for the duration of the war, see also John C. Fitzpatrick, editor, George Washington: Writings from the Original Manuscript Sources, 1775-1799. Washington, 1931-1940, Vol. VI, pp. 331-333; Vol. VII, p. 43. See also Philip Schuyler to the President of Congress, July 6th, 1780, in Letters of Members of the Continental Congress. Edited by Edmund C. Burnett. Eight volumes, Washington, Carnegie Institution of Washington, 1931, Vol. V, No. 294, p. 249.

95. Washington: Writings, Ford ed. Vol. III, p. 344, Vol. IV, p. 77, Vol. V, pp. 101, 154-155, 276.

96. John C. Miller: Triumph of Freedom, 1775-1783, Little Brown and Company, Boston, 1948, pp. 80-81.

97. See, for example, the work of the partisan leaders in the Carolinas, as described by Colonel Robert Gray, an American loyalist, in Colonel Robert Gray's Observations on the War in Carolina, in South Carolina Historical and Genealogical Magazine, Vol. XI, July, 1910, No. 3, pp. 139-159.

98. Brigadier General P. Horry and M. L. Weems: The Life of Gen'l Francis Marion, New York, John W. Lovell Company, n.d. Preface, p. 5, Chapter XIV, pp. 137-147. In referring to Washington and Marion, the writers remark: "they both learned the military art in the hard and hazardous schools of Indian warfare . . ." Ibid, p. 310.
See also the account of the Battle of King's Mountain, in Henry Lee's Memoirs of the War in the Southern Department of the United States, New York, University Publishing Company, 1869, pp. 198-201.

99. Carlyle: Cromwell's Letters and Speeches, Vol. I, p. 195; J. Franklin Jameson: The American Revolution Considered as a Social Movement, Princeton University Press, 1940, pp. 11-12, 15.

100. Curtis P. Nettels: The Roots of American Civilization—A History of American Colonial Life. F. S. Crofts and Company, New York, 1938, pp. 628-629; Jameson: op. cit. pp. 17-18.

101. See the statement of Colonel Whalley in 1651: ". . . it seems to me the best way, not to have anything of monarchical power in the Settlement of our Government." Carlyle: Cromwell's Letters and Speeches, Vol. III, p. 13.
See also the Clarke Papers. Edited by C. H. Firth, Four volumes. Volumes One and Two Printed for the Camden Society MDCCCXCI and MDCCCXCIV. Volumes Three and Four Printed for the Royal Historical Society and Published by Longmans, Green, London, 1899 and 1901. See the statement of Waldman, Vol. I, pp. 384-385. For the decision of Cromwell that the king should be brought to trial, see Vol. II, pp. 140-144. Cromwell

'seems to have questioned its expediency but not its justice. See Vol. II, p. 202.

102. Firth, C. H. and Rait, R. S.: Acts and Ordinances of the Interregnum, 1642-1660. 3 vols. London, H. M. Stationery Office, 1911, Vol. II, p. 122.

103. Journals of the Continental Congress, Vol. V, 1777, June 5-October 8, p. 500.

104. Journals of the Continental Congress—Declaration and Resolves, Vol. I, pp. 63-64: Jefferson to Henry Lee, May 8, 1825, in Works: Ford ed. Vol. X, pp. 342-343.

105. "But if a long train of abuses, Prevarications and Artifices, all tending the same way, make the design [of tyranny] visible to the People . . . 'tis not to be wonder'd that they should then rouse themselves, and endeavour to put the rule into such hands which may secure to them the ends for which Government was at first erected." Locke: Two Treatises of Government, London, 1698, Book II, Section 225, p. 341.

Compare with the Declaration of Independence: "But when a long train of abuses and usurpations, pursuing invariably the same object evinces a design to reduce them under absolute Despotism, it is their right, it is their duty, to throw off such Government and to provide New Guards for their future security."

Compare also with Locke: op. cit. Section 220, p. 336; Section 222, pp. 337-339; Section 230, pp. 344-346.

106. Jefferson's Writings, Ford edition, Vol. IX, pp. 71, 481; Vol. X, p. 376; Van Tyne: The War of Independence, p. 353.

107. James Sullivan: The Antecedents of The Declaration of Independence, in Annual Report of the American Historical Association for the Year 1902. In two volumes, Washington, Government Printing Office, 1903, Vol. I, pp. 67-81. See also R. W. and A. J. Carlyle: A History of the Mediaeval Political Theory in the West, Vol. V, pp. 457-476.

108. "When a King has Dethron'd himself and put himself in a state of War with his People, what shall hinder them from prosecuting him who is no King, as they would any other Man, who has put himself into a state of War with them..." Locke: op. cit. Book III, Section 239, p. 354.

109. Washington referred to "the sound doctrine and unanswerable reasoning contained in the pamphlet Common Sense . . . " Writings: Ford edition. Letter to Joseph Reed, 31, January, 1776, Vol. 3, p. 396; "Common Sense has a prodigious effect." Franklin to Le Veillard, April 15, 1787, Writings: Smyth ed. Vol. IX, p. 558; R. R.

Palmer: Tom Paine: Victim of the Rights of Man, in The Pennsylvania Magazine of History and Biography, April, 1942, Vol. LXVI, Number 2, pp. 161-166. "... *Common Sense* swept through the colonies, rolling up a reported total of half a million copies ... Never was a pamphlet more electrically effective. In half a year came the Declaration of Independence." Ibid, p. 166.

110. Moses Coit Tyler: The Literary History of the American Revolution, Two vols. G. P. Putnam's Sons, New York, 1897. Vol. 2, pp. 37-49; S. M. Berthold: Thomas Paine—America's First Liberal. Boston, Meador Publishing Company, 1938, p. 59. See also Cecelia M. Kenyon: Where Paine Went Wrong, in American Political Science Review, Vol. XLV, December, 1951, No. 4, p. 1097.

The fifth number of *The Crisis,* dated at Lancaster, Pennsylvania, March 21, 1778, has been said to have greatly stimulated the morale of the American troops at Valley Forge. See Philip S. Foner, Editor: The Complete Writings of Thomas Paine. Two vols. The Citadel Press, New York, 1945, Vol. I, p. 106.

111. See supra, note No. 105.

112. Jameson: op. cit. pp. 34-35. For an account of the Irish confiscations at the close of the Cromwellian revolution, see the "Act of Satisfaction" of Sept. 26, 1653, in R. Dunlop: Ireland From the Plantation of Ulster to the Cromwellian Settlement, 1611-59, Cambridge Modern History, New York, The MacMillan Company, 1934, Vol. V, pp. 536-537.

113. William MacDonald Sinclair: Memorials of St. Paul's Cathedral, Philadelphia, George W. Jacobs & Co. n.d. pp. 199-200; Henry Hart Milman: Annals of St. Paul's Cathedral, John Murray, London, 1868, pp. 351, 354; Sir William Dugdale: History of St. Paul's Cathedral, continued by Henry Ellis, London, Longmans, 1818, p. 115.

For a more brutal and senseless desecration of Lambeth Palace, see the account in Walter Thornbury and Edward Walford: Old and New London, Six vols. London, Cassel, Petter and Galpin, n.d. Vol. VI, p. 435.

114. Cross: The Anglican Episcopate and the American Colonies, pp. 259-260. For an excellent general summary of the decline of the state churches, see Miller: Triumph of Freedom, 1775-1783, pp. 354-356.

115. Jameson: op. cit. p. 86.

116. Everett W. Burdett: History of the Old South Meeting House, Boston, B. B. Russell, 1877, pp. 82-85. See also Justin Winsor: The Memorial History of Boston, Four vols. Ticknor and Company,

1881, Vol. III, p. 156. "The Old North Meeting-house was pulled down for fuel." Ibid.

117. "During the revolutionary contest, the British armies, in various places and in a most wanton manner, manifested their hostility to churches not Episcopalian. 'Of the nineteen places of worship in that city New York when the war began . . . there were but nine fit for use when the British troops left it . . . Boston, Newport, Philadelphia and Charleston all furnished melancholy instances of this prostitution and abuses of the houses of God.' " Benjamin B. Wisner: The History of the Old South Church in Boston . . . Boston, Crocker & Brewster. 1830, p. 108, note 47. See also Jameson: op. cit. pp. 91-92.

118. Allen Nevins: The American States During and After the Revolution, 1775-1789, New York, The MacMillan Company, 1924, p. 1.

119. Journals of the Continental Congress, Vol. I, p. 89.

120. "Of the twelve commonwealths which prior to 1787, had adopted constitutions, six had inserted . . . a general distributing clause . . ." William Bondy: The Separation of Governmental Powers, in Columbia University Studies in History, Government and Public Law, New York, 1896, Vol. V, No. 2, p. 19. See also The Federalist, No. 47, in Beard: The Enduring Federalist, pp. 209-216.

121. ". . . That the constitution ascertains and limits both Sovereignty and allegiance . . ." Massachusetts Circular Letter. February 11, 1768, Commager: No. 45, p. 66.

122. Massachusetts Bill of Rights, Commager: No. 70, p. 107.
    Thus, for example, the Massachusetts House of Representatives under date of April 6, 1742, in refusing a fixed salary grant to Governor William Shirley, declared that: "This House humbly conceive there ought not to be an Independency in either Branch of the Legislature, forasmuch as to be Independent and Arbitrary, are the same Things in civil Policy; and from thence doubtless it has ever been tho't that the Strength & Beauty of the British Constitution chiefly consists in that mutual Check which each Branch of the Legislature has on the others . . . we humbly apprehend to settle a Salary on His Majesty's Governour here, would greatly tend to lessen the just Weight of the other two Branches of the Government, which ought ever to be maintained and preserved . . ." Journals of the House of Representatives of Massachusetts, 1741-1742. The Massachusetts Historical Society. Boston, Wright & Potter Printing Co., 1943, p. 230.

123. Commager: op. cit. p. 107.

124. Ibid. p. 108.

125. Hockett: Vol. I, p. 117.

126. J. F. Jameson: Early Political Uses of the Word "Convention", in American Antiquarian Society Proceedings, Worcester, Massachusetts. Published by the Society, 1899. New Series. Vol. XII, pp. 183-196.

127. Holdsworth: op. cit. Vol. V, pp. 449-456, Vol. VI, p. 293.

128. Holdsworth: op. cit. Vol. IX, pp. 112-125; Willoughby: The Constitutional Law of the United States, Vol. 3, pp. 1681-1682; Rodney L. Mott: Due Process of Law. Indianapolis, The Bobbs-Merrill Company, 1926, pp. 141-142, 168-170.

129. Holdsworth: op. cit. Vol. IX, p. 201.

130. Even Jefferson proposed retaining a property qualification in Virginia. Years later he wrote that had he been in the state convention he "probably would have favored a general suffrage, because my opinion has always been in favor of it. Still, I find some very honest men who, thinking the possession of some property necessary to give due independence of mind, are for restraining the elective franchise to property." Jefferson to Jeremiah Moor. August 14, 1800. Works: Ford edition, Vol. IX, p. 142. See also Kirk H. Porter: A History of the Suffrage in the United States, The University of Chicago Press, Chicago, 1918, pp. 1-2.

131. Charles Edward Merriam: A History of American Political Theories, New York, The MacMillan Company, 1906, pp. 84-86; Nevins: The American States During and After The Revolution, p. 95.

132. Merriam: op. cit. p. 87.

133. Jefferson: Notes on the State of Virginia, in Writings: Ford ed. Vol. III, p. 223; Charles Henry Ambler: Sectionalism in Virginia From 1776 to 1861, Chicago, University of Chicago Press, 1910, pp. 29-30.

134. William Jay: Life of John Jay, 2 vols., New York. J. and J. Harper, 1833, Vol. I, pp. 70-71. "It was a favorite maxim with Mr. Jay," writes his son, "that those who own the country ought to govern it." Ibid. p. 70. See also Carl L. Becker: The History of Political Parties in the Province of New York, 1760-1776, Bulletin of the University of Wisconsin, No. 286, Madison, Wisconsin, 1909, pp. 275-276; Alexander C. Flick, Editor: History of the State of New York, Ten volumes. New York, Columbia University Press. 1933-1937, Vol. IV, Chapter X, The Results of the Revolution, by Frank Monaghan, p. 324.
"The franchise of the colonial period was extended . . . but of the estimated 14,000 male inhabitants of New York City as late as 1790 only 1,303 owned enough property to vote for governor. The

result was that a landed class governed the state through the closing years of the eighteenth, and well into the nineteenth century." Ibid.

135. Porter: op. cit. pp. 11-14.

136. James Curtis Ballagh: The Letters of Richard Henry Lee, 2 vols. New York. The Macmillan Company, 1912-1914. Vol. I. Letter to Edmund Pendleton, p. 191.

137. Quoted in Gaetano Salvemini: The Concepts of Democracy and Liberty in the Eighteenth Century, in Conyers Read: The Constitution Reconsidered, pp. 107-108. We have been unable to find the quotation in Paine's Collected Works, edited by Philip S. Foner.

138. See the statement of Governor Randolph in the opening days of the Federal Convention: "Our chief danger arises from the democratic parts of our constitutions . . . None of the constitutions have provided sufficient checks against the democracy." Max Farrand: Records of the Federal Convention, Vol. I, pp. 26, 27, May 29, 1787.

139. For defects of the Confederation, see those listed by Madison, in Farrand: op. cit. Vol. I, pp. 18-19, Tuesday, May, 29, 1787. See also those listed by Randolph, in Farrand: Vol. I, pp. 24-26. Tuesday, May 29, 1787.

140. Governor Randolph "observed that the Confederation fulfilled none of the objects for which it was framed." Farrand: Vol. I, p. 24, Tuesday, May 29, 1787.

141. McLaughlin: Constitutional History of the United States, p. 125; Jensen: The Articles of Confederation, p. 239.

142. See the statement of Madison in the federal convention that: "By the plan proposed a compleat power of taxation, the highest prerogative is proposed to be vested in the national government." Farrand: Vol. I, p. 447. See also McLaughlin: op. cit. p. 125.

For the opposition of the states, see Madison's analysis of each state, in Journals of the Continental Congress, 1774-1788, Vol. XXV, 1783, September 1-December 31, Wednesday, Feb. 26, 1783, pp. 913-915.

143. Journals of the Continental Congress, 1774-1789. Vol. XXX, 1783. September 1-December 31—Friday, February 21, 1783, p. 910.

144. At the opening of the federal convention Madison has pointed out "that the federal government could not check the quarrels between states . . ." Farrand: Vol. I, p. 19. See also Homer Cummings and Carl McFarland: Federal Justice, New York, 1937, p. 11.

145. Keith: Constitutional History of the First British Empire, pp. 305-

311. For a detailed account, see George A. Washburne: Imperial Control of the Administration of Justice in the Thirteen American Colonies, 1684-1776. New York, Columbia University Press, 1923, Chapters III-IV, pp. 78-120.

146. McLaughlin: Constitutional History of the United States, p. 129; Robert Granville Caldwell: The Settlement of Inter-State Disputes, in American Journal of International Law, Vol. 14, 1920, pp. 38-69. Note especially pp. 38-42.

147. Commager: Vol. I, p. 113.

148. J. C. Bancroft Davis: Appendix to the Reports of the Decisions of the Supreme Court of the United States. New York and Albany, Banks & Brothers 1889, in U. S. Reports, Vol. 131, pp. L, LIV, LVIII.

The case in which a settlement was reached was a dispute between Connecticut and Pennsylvania involving title to land in the Wyoming region in Pennsylvania. It was decided in favor of Pennsylvania. See the account of the case in Journals of the American Congress from 1774 to 1778—From April 1, 1782 to November 1, 1788, Washington. Printed and Published by Way and Gideon, 1823, pp. 129-140.

149. Washburne: op. cit. pp. 188-198; J. Franklin Jameson, Editor: Essays in the Constitutional History of the United States in the Formative Period, 1775-1789, Boston and New York, Houghton, Mifflin and Company, 1889— J. Franklin Jameson: The Predecessors of the Supreme Court, pp. 3-4.

Dr. Jameson also suggests that a precedent for this complex arrangement may have been found in Grenville's Act of 1770 for the settlement of disputed elections by the House of Commons. He explains that American lawyers were well acquainted with the nature of this act. Ibid. pp. 44-45.

150. Keith: op. cit. pp. 261-265.

151. Washburne: op. cit. pp. 163-177.

152. Journals of the Continental Congress, Vol. III, November 25, 1775, pp. 373-374, November 28, 1775, pp. 378-387; Jameson: op. cit. pp. 4-20. For a summary of the establishment of American national maritime jurisdiction, see the decision of the Supreme Court in the case of Penhallow et al versus Doane's Administrators, 3 Dallas, pp. 54-62, decided in 1795.

153. Journals of the Continental Congress, Vol. VII, p. 75, January 30, 1777.

154. Brightly N.P. 9 (Pa.); 13 C Courts. Sec. 1376.

155. For a final review of the case by Chief Justice Marshall, see U. S. v. Judge Peters, 5 Cranch 136, 141.

156. Journals of the Continental Congress, Vol. 16, pp. 61-64, January 15, 1780. For the election of personnel, see ibid. p. 79, January 22, 1780.

157. Journals of the Continental Congress, Vol. 16, pp. 402-409, May 2, 1780.

158. Jameson: op. cit. p. 34.

159. "The Court of Appeals in cases of capture may, therefore, be justly regarded not simply as the predecessor, but as one of the origins, of the Supreme Court of the United States." Ibid. p. 44. See, also, the excellent summary in Hockett: Vol. I, pp. 154-157.

160. Herbert B. Adams: Maryland's Influence upon Land Cessions to the United States, in Johns Hopkins University Studies in Historical and Political Science. Third Series, No. 1, Baltimore, Johns Hopkins University, 1885, pp. 22-40.

161. "Resolved *unanimously* that if it is the opinion of this convention, that the very extensive claim of the state of Virginia to the back lands hath no foundation in justice, and that if the same, or any like claim, is admitted, the freedom of the smaller states, and the liberties of America, may be thereby greatly endangered; this convention being firmly persuaded, that if the dominion over those lands should be established by the blood and treasure of the United States, such lands ought to be considered as a common stock, to be parcelled out at proper times into convenient, free and independent governments." Proceedings of the Maryland Convention, Wednesday, October 30, 1776, p. 8. Annapolis. Printed by Frederick Green, 1777.

See also Journals of the Continental Congress, Vol. XVIII, pp. 936-937; Wharton: Revolutionary Diplomatic Correspondence, Vol. V, pp. 88-89; Beverly W. Bond: State Government in Maryland, 1777-1781, Baltimore, The Johns Hopkins Press, March-April, 1905, p. 24.

162. For text of the Northwest Ordinance of 1787, see Thorpe: Vol. II, pp. 957-962.

163. Bond: op. cit. p. 20.

164. The Ordinance expressly states that one of its objects is to "provide also, for the establishment of States, and permanent government therein, and for their admission to a share in the Federal councils on an equal footing with the original States, at as early periods as may be consistent with the general interest." Thorpe: Vol. I, p. 960.

165. Frederick Jackson Turner: The Significance of Sections in American History, Chapter IV—Western State Making in the Revolutionary Era, pp. 86-138. Note especially, pp. 86-91, 136-138.

166. Louise B. Dunbar: A Study of Monarchical Tendencies in the United States from 1776-1801, Illinois Studies in the Social Sciences, Urbana, University of Illinois Press, 1922, Vol. X, No. 1, pp. 50, 52, 73-75, 95, 97. See also Richard Krauel: Prince Henry of Prussia and the Regency of the United States, 1786, in American Historical Review, Vol. XVII, October, 1911, No. 1, pp. 44-51.

167. "Certain military characters agreed in case of civil convulsion to rally the officers and soldiers of the late army, and with the help of supplies to be furnished by some rich merchants, to give a government to this country by force." Noah Webster: A Letter to General Hamilton, Occasioned by his Letter to President Adams, by a Federalist, New York [?], 1800, p. 7.

168. Mrs. Mercy Warren: History of the Rise, Progress and Termination of the American Revolution, Three volumes, Boston, E. Larkin, 1805, Vol. III, pp. 280-291, 359.

169. "...many of the younger class, particularly the students at law and the youth of fortune & pleasure are crying out for a monarchy & a standing army to support it . . ." Letter of Mrs. Mercy Warren to her husband, Jan. 4, 1787. Quoted in Alice Brown: Mercy Warren, Charles Scribner's Sons, New York, 1898, p. 296.

170. J. P. Brussot De Warville: New Travels in the United States of America, Performed in 1788. Berry and Rogers, New York, 1792, Letter XLIV, pp. 259-264.

171. "I have myself urged in Congress the propriety of uniting the influence of the public creditors and the army, as a part of them, to prevail upon the States to enter into their views." Hamilton to Washington, March 17, 1783, in Wharton: Diplomatic Correspondence of the Revolution, Vol. VI, p. 312. See also Edward S. Corwin: The Progress of Constitutional Theory Between the Declaration of Independence and the Meeting of the Philadelphia Convention, in American Historical Review, Vol. XXX, No. 3, April, 1925, pp. 517-521.

172. See the classic account in McMaster: Vol. I, pp. 298-355.

173. There are frequent references to Monk in the material dealing with Arnold. It has been said that Arnold was urged by Beverly Robinson, an American Loyalist, to emulate the example of Monk. See the discussion in Winsor: Narrative and Critical History, Vol. VI, p. 452; Oscar Sherwin: Benedict Arnold—Patriot and Traitor, The Century Company, New York, 1931, p. 271; Malcolm Decker:

Benedict Arnold—Son of the Havens, William Abbatt, Tarrytown, New York, 1932, p. 403.

Hamilton's approach to the problem was better timed and much more subtle. "The Tories, to a man, sided with Hamilton and his party, and it was the successful efforts of that gentleman to overcome the public animosities that enabled him to obtain his election to the Assembly of 1787, and to carry out his favorite measure—the repeal of the laws of exclusion under which the Loyalists were disfranchised. There he had the address and influence to procure the abrogation of the most important part of those laws, and by the accession of the great body of the enfranchised Tories to his party to frustrate at once his opponents in the city, and to secure his election to the general Convention of 1787, and afterwards that of his friends from the city in the convention of the state assembled in 1788." Isaac Q. Leake: Memoir of the Life and Times of General John Lamb. Albany, J. Munsell, 1850, Appendix, p. 389.

174. See the summary in Beard: An Economic Interpretation of the Constitution, pp. 149-151, 324-325.

CHAPTER V

1. Samuel Flagg Bemis: Diplomacy of the American Revolution, New York, Appleton-Century Company, 1935, p. 219, note II. Professor Bemis does not think that Clark's work played an important part in the negotiations. See, however, the summary of the evidence presented in James Alton James: The Life of George Rogers Clark. The University of Chicago Press, Chicago, Illinois, 1928, pp. 282-287. See also James Alton James: Oliver Pollock—The Life and Times of An Unknown Patriot. D. Appleton-Century Company, New York, 1937, Chapter XIV, pp. 222-249. It is the opinion of James that "Clark was really in military control of the greater part of the Northwest when negotiations for peace were begun." Ibid., p. 245.

2. John Adams: Works, edited by Charles Francis Adams, 10 vols. Boston, Little, Brown & Company, 1850-1856, Vol. III, pp. 333-334, November 29, 1782.

3. Franklin had exclaimed to the British delegation: "Your ministers require that we should receive again into our bosom those who have been our bitterest enemies, and restore their properties who have destroyed ours; and this while the wounds they have given us are still bleeding. It is many years since your nation expelled the Stuarts and their adherents and confiscated their estates. Much of your resentment against them may by this time be abated, yet, if we should propose it, and insist on it as an article of our treaty

with you, that this family should be recalled and the forfeited estates of its friends restored, would you think us serious in our professions of earnestly desiring peace?" Francis Wharton: The Revolutionary Diplomatic Correspondence of the United States, Vol. VI, p. 80. Franklin to Oswald, November 26, 1782.

4. "I am like to be as insignificant here as you can imagine." Adams to Jay, in Adams: Works, Vol. VII, p. 355, December 3, 1785.

5. Journals of the Continental Congress, Vol. XXVI, 1784, United States Government Printing Office, Washington, 1928, p. 319.

6. "Virginia certainly owed two millions sterling to Great Britain at the conclusion of the war. Some have conjectured the debt as high as three millions. I think that state owed near as much as all the rest put together . . . These debts had become hereditary from father to son for many generations, so that the planters were a species of property annexed to certain mercantile houses in London." Jefferson's Answers to Questions Propounded by M. De Meusnier, January 24, 1786, in Jefferson's Writings, Ford edition, Vol. IV, p. 155.

7. William Waller Hening: The Statutes at large; being a collection of all the laws of Virginia, from the first session of the legislature, in the year 1619. Published pursuant to an act of the General Assembly of Virginia, passed on the fifth day of February one thousand eight hundred and eight, Richmond, 1810-23. [Various printers.] Vol. IX, Richmond, J. & G. Cochran, Printers, 1821, p. 380.—Suits by British subjects suspended. See also the various obstacles listed in Vol. X, Richmond, George Cochran, 1822, pp. 67-71, 153-156, 201, 227; Vol. XI, Richmond, George Cochran, 1823, pp. 81, 101-102, 162, 195, 313.

For Jefferson's defense of American action, see his letter to William Jones, January 5, 1787. Writings: Ford edition, Vol. 4, pp. 351-357.

8. For the text of the treaty of peace with Great Britain, September 3, 1783, see Commager: No. 74, pp. 117-119.

For the problem of the western posts, see A. C. McLaughlin: The Western Posts and the British Debts, in Annual Report of the American Historical Association, Washington, Government Printing Office, No. 7, pp. 413-444.

9. The American-British treaty of 1783 had provided that the 31st parallel should be the northern boundary. See Commager: p. 118. When West Florida had been in British hands during the years 1763-1783, the northern boundary had been the Yazoo line at 32° 28'. After 1783 Spain claimed the area to the Ohio and Tennessee Rivers on the ground that she had driven the British from

that area during the war. See the diplomatic correspondence dealing with the problem in Wharton: Vol. 5, p. 657, Vol. 6, pp. 260, 261, 269. See the excellent summary in Samuel Flagg Bemis: A Diplomatic History of the United States, New York, Henry Holt, 1942, pp. 73-74. See also Thomas Jefferson's Correspondence. Printed from the Originals in the Collection of William K. Bixby with Notes by Worthington Chauncey Ford. Boston, The Plimpton Press, 1916, Jefferson to Hugh Williamson, Trenton, II December, 1784, p. 5. This letter contains a brief notice of the Spanish activities in the Mississippi Valley and West Florida.

10. Bemis: A Diplomatic History of the United States, Chap. V—The Diplomatic Efforts of the Confederation, pp. 65-84.

11. Journals of the Continental Congress, Vol. XXX, 1786. United States Government Printing Office. Washington, 1934, pp. 95, 97, 122.

For the requisitions of 27 and 28 of April, 1784 and the arrears of all the states as of October 6, 1786, see Journals, Vol. XXXI, p. 751.

12. "... a conspicuous defect in the Articles was the absence of congressional authority to obtain necessary funds; the old trouble of the taxing power in an imperial system remained." McLaughlin: Constitutional History of the United States, p. 142; Andrews: The Colonial Period of American History, Vol. IV, pp. 422, 423.

13. See the account of state enmity and particularism as presented in the letter of William Grayson to James Monroe, New York, May 29, 1787, in Farrand: Records of the Federal Convention, Vol. III, p. 30.

14. Thomas Jefferson Correspondence—Bixby Collection, Jefferson to De Chastellux, Paris, September 2, 1785, pp. 11-13.

15. Charles Warren: The Making of the Constitution, Boston, Little Brown & Company, 1928, p. 29.

16. "The commercial treaty with Spain is considered to be cruel, oppressive and unjust. The prohibition of the navigation of the Mississippi has astonished the whole western country. To sell us and make us vassals to the merciless Spaniards is a grievance not to be borne . . . The minds of the people here are very much exasperated against both the Spaniards and Congress." Thomas Green to the Hon. the Governour, the Council and Legislature of the State of Georgia, December 23, 1786, in Secret Journals of the Acts and Proceedings of Congress . . . Four volumes, Boston, Thomas B. Wait, 1821, Vol. IV, pp. 315-316.

See also Samuel Flagg Bemis: Pinckney's Treaty—A Study of

America's Advantage from Europe's Distress, 1783-1800, Baltimore, The John Hopkins Press, 1926, Chapters III-IV, pp. 91-123; Arthur Preston Whitaker: The Spanish-American Frontier, 1783-1795, Houghton Mifflin, Boston and New York, 1927, pp. 63-77.

17. The Writings of James Monroe. Edited by Stanislaus Murray Hamilton. Seven volumes, New York, G. P. Putnam's Sons, 1898-1903, Monroe to Jefferson, New York, August 19, 1786, Vol. I, p. 157.

18. Charles Pettit to Jeremiah Wadsworth, New York, 27th May, 1786, in Letters of Members of the Continental Congress, edited by Edmund C. Burnett. Eight volumes, Washington, D. C. Carnegie Institution of Washington, 1921-36, Vol. 8, pp. 369-370.

    See also Monroe to Governor Patrick Henry, New York, August 12, 1786, in which he says: "Certain it is that committees are held in this town of Eastern men and others of this State upon the subject of a dismemberment of the States east of the Hudson from the Union & the erection of them into a separate govt." Monroe: Works, Vol. I, p. 148.

19. James Madison to Edmund Pendleton, New York, Feb. 24, 1787, in Letters of Members of the Continental Congress: Vol. 8, pp. 547-548.

20. Elbridge Gerry of Massachusetts, in speaking of the neighboring state of Connecticut, declared that "The D [evi] l is in that state." Elbridge Gerry to Rufus King, May 27, 1785, in The Life and Correspondence of Rufus King, edited by Charles R. King, 6 vols., New York, G. P. Putnam's Sons, 1894-1900, Vol. I, p. 101.

21. Farrand: Records of the Federal Convention, Vol. III, Appendix A, CCCI, p. 542.

22. Calendar of Virginia State Papers, IV, 147, 240, 264; Laws of Maryland (1765-1784), Chap. 50, 1782; Chap. 84, 1784.

    For acts of retaliation, see Calendar of Virginia State Papers, IV, 60, 61; Madison: Works, Vol. I, p. 216; Laws of New York, March 15, 1785, Chap. 34; ibid., April 11, 1787, Chap. 81.

    For an excellent summary of the situation, see Albert Anthony Giesecke: American Commercial Legislation Before 1789, University of Pennsylvania, D. Appleton and Company, New York, 1910. Chap. VI, pp. 134-140.

23. Washington to Henry Knox, 26 December, 1786, Washington: Writings, Ford edition, Vol. XI, pp. 103-107; same to same, 3 February, 1787, ibid: pp. 108-112; John Marshall to James Wilkinson, Jan. 5, 1787, in American Historical Review, Vol. XII, Number 2, January, 1907, pp. 347-348; Washington to Madison, 5 November, 1786, in Washington: Writings, Ford edition, Vol. XI, pp. 80-82; Brant: James Madison: The Nationalist, p. 394.

24. See to this effect remarks of Madison in the Federal Convention, June 6, 1787, in Farrand: Records, Vol. I, pp. 134-136. See also the speech of Charles Pinckney, June 25, 1787, in Farrand: Records, Vol. I, pp. 397-404. After declaring that: "The people of the U. S. may be divided into three classes"—professional, commercial and landed—he adds: "The dependence of each on the other is mutual." Ibid, pp. 402-403.

Note also the effective summary by Irving Brant: "The great necessity in forming a system of government, therefore, was to make the sovereignty sufficiently neutral to prevent one faction from oppressing another, yet sufficiently controlled to be itself subject to the interest of the whole society." Brant: James Madison— The Nationalist, 1780-1787. The Bobbs-Merrill Company, Indianapolis, 1948, p. 414.

25. Beard: The Euduring Federalist, No. 10, p. 70.

26. John U. Nef: English and French Industrial History after 1540 in Relation to the Constitution, in Conyers Read: The Constitution Reconsidered, pp. 102-103; Joseph Dorfman: The Economic Mind in American Civilization, Three vols. New York, The Viking Press, 1946-1949, Vol. I, pp. 241-244.

27. Alexander Hamilton: Works, Comprising His Correspondence and His Political and Official Writings . . . Edited by John C. Hamilton, 7 vols. New York, Charles S. Francis & Company, 1851. Report on Manufactures Communicated to the House of Representatives, December 5, 1791, Vol. 3, pp. 192-284.

28. Keith: Constitutional History of the First British Empire, pp. 65-66. Thus the fact that foreign ships were excluded from the imperial carrying trade was an important element in the development of colonial shipbuilding, especially in New England. See Sir Josiah Child: A New Discourse of Trade, 2nd edition, London, 1694, p. 215; Hutchinson Papers, 2 vols. Prince Society Publications, Albany, 1865, Vol. II, p. 232; G. L. Beer: The Commercial Policy of England Toward the American Colonies, Columbia University Studies in History, Economics and Public Law, Vol. III, Number 2, New York, Columbia College, 1893, pp. 155-157.

29. "Had Julius or Napoleon committed these acts they would have been pronounced coup d'etat." John William Burgess: Political Science and Comparative Constitutional Law, 2 vols. Boston, Ginn & Company, 1890, Vol. I, p. 105.

"If it [the proposed system] should miscarry . . . the framers will have to encounter the disrepute of having brought about a revolution in government, without substituting anything that was worthy of the effort." Hamilton to Washington, September, 1788, in Alexander Hamilton: Works, edited by Henry Cabot Lodge, 12 vols. G. P. Putnam's Sons, 1904, Vol. IX, p. 446.

30. In 1783 he had sent a circular letter to the governors of the states in which he declared: "That it is indispensable to the happiness of the individual States that there should be lodged somewhere a supreme power to regulate and govern the general concerns of the confederated republic, without which the Union cannot be of long duration." Washington: Writings, Ford edition, Vol. X, p. 258.

31. Washington to Madison, in Writings: Ford edition, Vol. II, p. 82, 5 November, 1786; Brant: James Madison—The Nationalist, p. 392.

32. Madison's "Vices of the Political System of the United States," in Writings: Ford edition, Vol. II, pp. 361-369. See also Stanley Pargellis: The Theory of Balanced Government, in Read: The Constitution Reconsidered, p. 38.

33. See the royal answer to the nineteen demands of parliament written for the king by Sir John Colepepper and Lord Falkland, in John Rushworth: Historical Collections. Five volumes. London, MDCCXXI, Volume IV, pp. 731-735. See also the Life of Edward, Earl of Clarendon, Written by Himself, Three volumes, Oxford at the Clarendon Press. MDCCCXXVII, Vol. I, pp. 154-156.

Colepepper was also an important figure in the restoration so that in a sense his views tended ultimately to prevail. Note the references to Colepepper in The Nicholas Papers—Correspondence of Sir Edward Nicholas—Secretary of State. Edited by George F. Warner. Four volumes. Printed for the Camden Society. Vol. I, Nichols and Sons, Westminster, MDCCCLXXVI, Vol. II, MDCCCXCII, Vol. III, MDCCCXCVII, Vol. IV, London, Offices of the Society, 1920. See especially Vol. IV, pp. 1, 183, 186, 188.

34. Leopold von Ranke: A History of England Principally in the Seventeenth Century. Six volumes. Oxford. At the Clarendon Press, 1875. Vol. III, pp. 211-215.

35. See Chapter IV, note 68.

36. John Dickinson: Writings. Edited by Paul Leicester Ford, Philadelphia. The Historical Society of Pennsylvania, Letter IV, pp. 328-335.

37. McLaughlin: Constitutional History of the United States, p. 58, note 13.

38. John Adams: A Defence of the Constitutions of Government of the United States of America. Philadelphia. Printed for Hall and Sellers; J. Crukshane; and Young and McCulloch, MDCCLXXXVII. Note especially the reference to balance in Let-

ters LIV and LV, pp. 365-382. "All nations, under all governments, must have parties; the great secret is to controul them: there are but two ways, either by a monarchy and standing army, or by a balance in the constitution." Ibid. p. 382.

39. Beard: The Enduring Federalist, No. 14, p. 85. Publius (Madison); Charles A. Merriam: A History of Political Theories, New York, The MacMillan Company, 1906, pp. 103-105.

40. "How ungenerous is the human heart when under the Controul of tumultuous Passions." James Mitchell Vernum to Horatio Gates, 15th Feb., 1781, in Burnett: Letters of Members of the Continental Congress, Vol. V, p. 571.

Mr. Gerry: "The evils we experience flow from the excess of democracy. The people do not want virtue but are the dupes of pretended patriots." Farrand: Records, Vol. I, p. 48.

Mr. Randolph also referred to "the turbulence and follies of democracy." Ibid: Vol. I, p. 51.

Hamilton referred to "the amazing violence and turbulence of the democratic spirit." Ibid: Vol. I, p. 289.

Mr. G. Morris: "We must remember that the people never act from reason alone. The rich will take advantage of their passions and make these the instruments for oppressing them." Ibid: Vol. I, p. 514.

41. Roland Bainton: The Appeal to Reason, in Read: The Constitution Reconsidered, pp. 121-125, 128-129; Arthur O. Lovejoy: The Great Chain of Being, Cambridge, Mass. Harvard University Press, 1936, p. 122.

"The truth was that all men having power ought to be distrusted to a certain degree." Madison, in Farrand: Records, Vol. I, p. 584.

42. Andrew C. McLaughlin: The Background of American Federalism, in American Political Science Review, Vol. XII, May, 1918, pp. 215-240.

See also the argument of Mr. King in the federal convention, June 19, 1787, in Farrand: Records, Vol. I, pp. 331-332; Madison to N. P. Trist, December, 1831, in Farrand: op. cit. Vol. III, p. 516. In both cases it is argued that the federal convention developed and strengthened the idea of union.

43. McLaughlin: Constitutional History of the United States, pp. 14-15. "... in essentials American federalism was the child of the old empire." Ibid. p. 15.

44. McLaughlin: op. cit. p. 180.

45. "If the new Constitution be examined with accuracy and candor, it will be found that the change which it proposes consists much less in the addition of new powers to the Union than in the in-

vigoration of its original powers . . . The powers relating to war and peace, armies and fleets, treaties and finance, with the other more considerable powers, are all vested in the existing Congress by the Articles of Confederation." Beard: The Enduring Federalist. No. 45, p. 202.

For examples of identical language in the two documents, see Ford: The Federalist, No. 41, pp. 269-270.

46. For text of Franklin's plan see Documents Relative to the Colonial History of the State of New York, Vol. 6, pp. 889-891; Commager: Documents, pp. 43-45.

47. "In the several colonies the varied charters, compacts, and orders which defined the basis of government accustomed the colonists to the conception of a basic law or constitution laid out in a formal written statement." Carl Brent Swisher: American Constitutional Development, Houghton Mifflin, Boston, 1943, pp. 9-10. See also the excellent summary in Ford: The Federalist, Introduction, p. IX.

48. See the comprehensive account in Charles M. Andrews: Colonial Commerce, American Historical Review, Vol. XX, No. 1, October, 1914, pp. 43-63. Note especially pp. 50-52.

49. Mr. L. Martin in the federal convention, June 27, 1787, Farrand: Records, Vol. I, pp. 437-438; Jefferson's Writings, Ford ed. Vol. 4, Letter to William Stephens Smith, Nov. 13, 1787, pp. 465-468. This letter contains the statement that: "The tree of liberty must be refreshed from time to time with the blood of patriots and tyrants." Ibid. p. 467.

50. Charles Warren: The Making of the Constitution, p. 622. Under the Maryland state constitution of 1776, the qualified voters, voting by counties, elected county delegates, who, in turn, met at the state capital and elected fifteen senators. See Thorpe: Federal and State Constitutions: Vol. III, pp. 1693-1694.

51. "The interpretation of the Constitution of the United States," said Mr. Justice Gray, in U. S. vs Wong Kim Ark, "is necessarily influenced by the fact that its provisions are framed in the language of the English common law, and are to be read in the light of its history." U. S. vs Wong Kim Ark, 169 U. S. 649. Mr. Justice Gray was quoting the words of Mr. Justice Matthews in the case of Smith vs Alabama, 124 U. S. 478.

It is related that Professor Parsons of the Harvard Law School told his students that they must study English cases with great diligence. "Do you ask me," said he, "if we have not achieved our independence, if we are still governed by England? No, gentlemen, we have not achieved our independence. England governs us still, not by reason of force but by force of reason." Samuel F.

Batchelder: Bits of Harvard History. Cambridge, Harvard University Press, 1924, Chap. VI—Old Times at the Harvard Law School, p. 222.

52. Leonard D. White: Introduction to the Study of Public Administration, New York, The MacMillan Company, 1939, pp. 18-19.

53. Thus in No. 43 of the Federalist, Publius (Madison) defended the nine-state ratification by appealing "to the great principle of self-preservation, to the transcendent law of nature and nature's God, which declares that the safety and happiness of society are the objects at which all political institutions aim, and to which all such institutions must be sacrificed." Beard: The Enduring Federalist, p. 192.

In No. 78 of The Federalist, we even find Hamilton declaring: "I trust the friends of the proposed Constitution will never concur with its enemies in questioning that fundamental principle of republican government which admits the right of the people to alter or abolish the established Constitution whenever they find it inconsistent with their happiness . . ." Ford: The Federalist, No. 78, p. 523. He adds, however, that such a procedure must not be the result of "a momentary inclination" but of "some solemn and authoritative act." Ibid, pp. 523-524.

54. Note the discussion of this problem by Madison under the title, The General View of the Powers Supposed to Be Vested in the Union, Ford: The Federalist, No. 41, pp. 260-270.

55. The debates in the Federal Convention abounded with references to the idea of compact. See, for example, Farrand: Records, Vol. II, p. 93, where Madison refers to "alterations of the federal compact."

Note also the significant statement in Washington's letter submitting the proposed constitution to Congress: "It is obviously impracticable in the federal government of these States, to secure all rights of independent sovereignty to each, and yet provide for the interest and safety of all. Individuals entering into society, must give up a share of liberty to preserve the rest." Journals of the Continental Congress, Vol. XXXIII, 1787, July 21-December 19. United States Government Printing Office, Washington, 1936, p. 502.

56. See the numerous references to Locke in Chapter IV.

57. "It is by this mixture of monarchical, aristocratical and democratical power, blended together in one system, and by these three estates balancing one another, that our free constitution of government hath been preserved so long inviolate, or hath been brought back, after having suffered violations, to its original prin-

ciples and been renewed, and improved too, by frequent and salutary revolutions." Lord Bolingbroke: Works, Four volumes, Carey and Hart, Philadelphia, 1841. Vol. II, A Dissertation Upon Parties, p. 119.

58. Sir William Blackstone: Commentaries on the Laws of England, Two volumes, Philadelphia, J. B. Lippincott Company, 1893, Vol. I, pp. 111-112.

59. Edmund Burke: Select Works, Payne edition, Vol. I, Thoughts on the Causes of the Present Discontents, p. 32.

60. Turner: The Frontier in American History, pp. 3-4; William Seal Carpenter: The Development of American Political Thought, pp. 87-88.

61. "Mr. Govr. Morris . . . thought the rule of representation ought to be so fixed as to secure to the Atlantic States a prevalence in the National Councils" Farrand: Records, Vol. I, p. 533.

"I perceive now, that I mistook the drift of your inquiry, which is substantially whether the Congress can admit, as a new State, territory which did not belong to the United States when the Constitution was made. In my opinion they cannot.

"I always thought that, when we should acquire Canada and Louisiana, it would be proper to govern them as provinces, and allow them no voice in our councils. In wording the third section of the fourth article, I went as far as circumstances would permit to establish this exclusion. Candor obliges me to add my belief, that, had it been more pointedly expressed, a strong opposition would have been made." Gouverneur Morris to Henry W. Livingston, December 4th, 1803, in Jared Sparks: The Life of Gouverneur Morris with Selections from His Correspondence and Miscellaneous Papers, Three volumes, Boston, Gray & Bowen, 1832, Vol. 3, p. 192.

62. Constitution, Article IV, Section 3.

63. Max Farrand: Compromises of the Constitution, in American Historical Review, Vol. IX, Number 3, April, 1904, pp. 482-484; Warren: The Making of the Constitution, pp. 595-598.

64. Leonard D. White: The Federalists—A Study in Administrative History, New York, The MacMillan Company, 1948, p. 15.

65. "The direct and explicit enactment of such a rule [as removal by impeachment] was indeed of the highest importance, but it must not be thought that this was in principle an innovation. It is, I think, quite clear that this was constantly contemplated in medieval times, and was actually carried out in some famous cases. At

least two emperors and the king of England had been formally deposed." A. J. Carlyle: Political Liberty, Oxford, 1941, p. 161.

66. Beard: The Enduring Federalist, No. 48, pp. 217, 220.

67. Charles J. Stillé: The Life and Times of John Dickinson, 1732-1808. Philadelphia, J. B. Lippincott Company, 1891, pp. 205-209; Diary of James Allen, Esq. of Philadelphia, in Pennsylvania Magazine of History and Biography, Vol. IX, 1885, pp. 176-196. Note especially pp. 188-189, 196, under date of January 25, 1777. See also the excellent summary in Samuel B. Harding: Party Struggles over the First Pennsylvania Constitution, in Annual Report of the American Historical Association for the year 1894, Washington, Government Printing Office, 1895, pp. 371-402. Note especially the "radical" legislation passed in 1785. Ibid. pp. 389-391.

68. Madison: Writings, edited by Hunt, Vol. II, 1783-1787—Notes of Speech on Proposed Amendment to the Constitution of Virginia, Note 1, pp. 54-55.

69. Carlyle: Political Liberty, p. 160.

70. 8 Coke Reports 118a (1610) "In short the American Revolution was a lawyer's revolution to enforce Lord Coke's theory of the invalidity of acts of Parliament in derogation of common right and the rights of Englishmen". Report of a Special Committee of the New York State Bar Association, New York, 1915, p. 11. Quoted in Boudin: Government by Judiciary, Vol. I, p. 10.

71. John Adams: Works, edited by C. F. Adams, Vol. II, Appendix, p. 522; Commager, No. 32, p. 45.

72. Journal of the House of Representatives of Massachusetts Bay in New England. Boston. Printed by Green and Russell, 1765, p. 134.
   "Instead of a certain constitutional Law, adapted to the nature of the Governments, established by the Sovereign or Imperial State, and recognized by the Dependent or subordinate state, America has been hitherto, governed by temporary expedients . . ." Governor [Francis] Bernard: Select Letters on the Trade and Government of America and the Principles of Law and Polity Applied to the American Colonies, London, W. Bowyer and J. Nichols MDCCLXXIV, p. 111.

73. Virginia Gazette, March 21, 1776. Quoted by McLaughlin: Constitutional History of the United States, pp. 47-48. Professor McLaughlin adds: "This decision, the first probably of any court in America, and probably in the world, to declare an act void because of unconstitutionality, was given by a court held for Northampton County, February 11, 1766." McLaughlin: Ibid, p. 48, note 28.

74. Austin Scott: Holmes vs Walton, the New Jersey Precedent, in American Historical Review, Vol. IV, No. 3, pp. 456-469, April, 1899.

75. Trevett v Weeden (1786). Records of State of Rhode Island, Vol. X, p. 213.

76. Bayard and Wife v Singleton, 1 Martin (N.C.) 5, 1787.

77. "Mr. Randolph said that there were features so odious in the Constitution as it now stands that he doubted whether he should be able to agree to it." Farrand: Records, Vol. II, p. 452, August 29, 1787. On September 10, 1787, he had suggested the calling of "another general Convention." Farrand: Records, Vol. II, p. 564. A month later, on October 10, 1787, he wrote to the Speaker of the Virginia House of Delegates announcing that he was in favor of ratification. See Jonathan Elliot: The Debates in the Several State Conventions on the Adoption of the Federal Constitution . . . Five volumes, Philadelphia, J. B. Lippincott, 1876, Vol. I, pp. 482-491.

Speaking in the Virginia State Ratifying Convention on June 24, 1788, Randolph declared: "If . . . we reject the Constitution, the Union will be dissolved, the dogs of war will break loose, and anarchy and discord will complete the ruin of this country." Elliot: Debates, Vol. III, p. 603.

For Randolph's defense and an explanation of his willingness to consider an office under the new government, see his letter to Madison, 19, July 1789, in Moncure Daniel Conway: Omitted Chapters of History Disclosed in the Life and Papers of Edmund Randolph. Second edition, New York and London, G. P. Putnam's Sons, 1889, pp. 126-128.

78. Life and Correspondence of Rufus King. Edited by His Grandson, Charles R. King. Six vols. New York, G. P. Putnam's Sons, 1894-1900, Vol. I, pp. 317-319, 360. The letters here reproduced are most revealing. See also Samuel Bannister Harding: The Contest Over the Ratification of the Federal Constitution in the State of Massachusetts, New York, Longmans, Green, 1896, pp. 84-89. For Hancock's remarks in favor of ratification see Elliot: Debates, Vol. 2, pp. 174-176.

79. Diary and Correspondence of Samuel Pepys, 6 vols., London, Bickers and Sons, 1875, Vol. I, pp. 134, 498, Vol. 2, pp. 69, 93, 221, Vol. III, pp. 128, 135, 508.

80. Madison to Randolph, January 10, 1788, Writings: Hunt, editor, Vol. V, p. 81. See also R. King to Madison, January 27, 1788, in which King refers to "the superiority of talent in favor of the Constitution" in Massachusetts. Rufus King: Life and Correspondence, Vol. I, p. 317.

81. [Richard Henry Lee]: Observations Leading to a Fair Examination of the System of Government Proposed by the Late Convention; and to Several Essential and Necessary Alterations in It. In a Number of Letters from the Federal Farmer to the Republican. Printed in the year MDCCLXXXVII. Letter V. October 15th 1787, p. 36.

82. Alexander Graydon: Memoirs of His Own Times with Reminiscences of the Men and Events of the Revolution. Edited by John Stockton Littel, Philadelphia, Lindsay & Blakiston, 1846, p. 333.

83. Ibid., p. 332.

84. See the remarks of Hon. Mr. Singletary, in Massachusetts Constitutional Convention, January 24, 1788: "These lawyers, and men of learning, and moneyed men, that talk so finely, and gloss over matters so smoothly, to make us poor illiterate people swallow down the pill, expect to get into Congress themselves; they expect to be the managers of this Constitution, and get all the power and all the money into their own hands, and then they will swallow up all us little folks, like the great Leviathan, Mr. President, yes, just as the whale swallowed up Jonah." Elliot. Debates, Vol. 2, p. 102.

85. The Revolutionary Records of the State of Georgia, compiled and published by Allen D. Chandler. Three vols. Atlanta, The Franklin-Turner Company, 1908, pp. 90, 103, 266, 431, 670; Randolph C. Downes: Creek-American Relations, 1782-1790, in The Georgia Historical Quarterly. Published by the Georgia Historical Society, Vol. XXI, No. 2, June, 1937, pp. 142-184; Ulrich B. Phillips: Georgia and State Rights—A Study of the Political History of Georgia from the Revolution to the Civil War, With Particular Regard to Federal Relations, in Annual Report of the American Historical Association for the year 1901. In two vols. Washington, Government Printing Office, 1902, pp. 16-18, 66-67.

For a summary of Georgia commerce and trade during the confederation period, see Amanda Johnson: Georgia as Colony and State. Walter W. Brown Publishing Company, Atlanta, Georgia, 1938, pp. 158-159.

86. John Bach McMaster and Frederick D. Stone: Pennsylvania and the Federal Constitution, Historical Society of Pennsylvania, Lancaster, 1888, p. 458.

87. Ibid., pp. 459-460.

88. Elliot: Debates, Vol. 3, p. 226.

89. Beveridge: Marshall, Vol. I, p. 420; McLaughlin: Constitutional History of the United States, p. 142, footnote.

90. "The passions of men stimulate them to avail themselves of the weakness of others." Elliot: Debates, Vol. 3, p. 227.

91. Hugh Blair Grigsby: The History of the Virginia Federal Convention of 1788 . . . Edited by R. A. Brock, Two vols., Virginia Historical Society, Richmond, Virginia, MDCCCXC-MDCCCXCI, Vol I, pp. 29, 35-36.

92. Grigsby: op. cit. Vol. I, p. 339. "I think," said Grayson, "that were it not for one great character in America, so many men would not be for this government." Elliot: Debates, Vol. 3, p. 616. See the same account in Grigsby: op. cit. Vol. I, p. 314.

93. Mason seems to have had these former Tories in mind when he remarked: "But when I look around the number of my acquaintance in Virginia, the country wherein I was born, and have lived so many years, and observe *who* are the warmest and most zealous friends to this new government, it makes me think of the story of the cat transformed into a fine lady—forgetting her transformation, and happening to see a rat, she could not restrain herself, but sprung upon it out of the chair." Grigsby: Vol. I, p. 193. See also Elliot: Debates, Vol. III, p. 269; Kate Mason Rowland: Life of George Mason, 2 vols. G. P. Putnam's Sons, New York, 1892, Vol. II, p. 240; Patrick Henry: Life, Correspondence and Speeches. Edited by William Wirt Henry, 3 vols. New York, C. Scribner's Sons, 1891, Vol. II, pp. 357-358.

94. Beveridge: Marshall, Vol. I, pp. 285, 371-372.

95. Elliot: Debates, Vol. III, p. 410.

96. [Richard Henry Lee]: Observation leading to a fair examination of the system of government proposed by the late Convention; and to several essential and necessary alterations in it. In a number of Letters from the Federal Farmer to the Republican [New York] Printed [by Thomas Greenleaf] in the Year MDCCLXXXVII, p. 21.

97. Elliot: Debates, Vol. III, p. 319.

98. Ibid., Vol. III, p. 322.

99. Ibid., Vol. III, p. 322.

100. Turner: The Frontier in American History, pp. 110-111. In the Virginia Convention Grayson and Henry stressed the plea that the western people had been betrayed by the Jay-Gardoqui transaction. Elliot: Vol. III, pp. 349-356; Orin Grant Libby: The Geographical

Distribution of the Vote of the Thirteen States on the Federal Constitution, 1787-88, Madison, Wisconsin, 1894, p. 69.

101. Grigsby: Vol. I, p. 110, footnote; Virginia Calendar of State Papers, Vol. 4, 1785-89, pp. 20, 30, 164. See also note 85 of this chapter for the Indian problem in Georgia.

102. Beveridge: Marshall, Vol. I, p. 432.

103. "a distrust of men of property or education has a more powerful effect upon the minds of our opponents than any specific objections against the Constitution." Rufus King: Life and Correspondence, King to Madison, Jan. 20, 1788, Vol. I, p. 314.
    See, however, the "specific objection" raised by John Holmes in the Massachusetts convention, who feared the federal judicial power as a threat to the bill of rights. Elliot: Debates, Vol. 2, pp. 109-112.

104. Harding: The Contest Over the Ratification of the Federal Constitution in the State of Massachusetts, p. 48.

105. Elliot: Vol. II, p. 111.

106. Ibid., Vol. II, p. 148.

107. Locke based his idea that property was a natural right by reasoning that men are naturally inclined to respect the property as well as the person of another and that property when mixed with one's own labor and personally used, is really an extension of one's own person. Locke: Two Treatises of Government, London, 1698, Book II, Chapter V, pp. 198-199.

108. Ibid., Book II, Sects. 123-124.

109. Locke was a strong advocate of religious liberty. In his Letter Concerning Toleration, he had declared: "No man by nature is bound unto any particular church or sect, but every one joins himself voluntarily to that society in which he believes he has found that profession and worship which is truly acceptable to God." Locke: Works, Ten vols. The Eleventh edition. London, 1812. Printed for W. Otridge and Son, Leigh and Sotheby [etc.], Vol. 6—A Letter Concerning Toleration, p. 13.

110. William Warren Sweet: Religion in Colonial America, New York, Charles Scribner's Sons, 1942, Chap. X—America and Religious Liberty, pp. 319-339. "The embodiment of these great principles [of religious freedom and the separation of church and state] in the new state constitutions and finally in the Federal constitution itself was simply writing colonial experience into the fundamental law of the land." Ibid., p. 339; Sanford H. Cobb: The Rise of

Religious Liberty in America, New York, The Macmillan Company, 1902 pp. 507-509; See also the thoughtful evolutionary presentation in Hall: The Religious Background of American Culture, Chap. XIV, pp. 177-190.

111. Holdsworth: Vol. VI, pp. 140, 167, 240-241.

112. Joseph Needham: Human Law and the Laws of Nature in China and the West, L. T. Hobhouse Memorial Trust Lecture, No. 20, Geoffrey Cumberlege, Oxford University Press, London, 1951, pp. 13, 15-16; Edward S. Corwin: The "Higher Law" Background of American Constitutional Law, in Harvard Law Review, Vol. XLII, December, 1928, No. 2, pp. 163-165; Huntington Cairns: Philosophy as Jurisprudence, in Paul Sayre, Editor: Interpretations of Modern Legal Philosophers, New York, Oxford University Press, 1947, p. 62.

113. Jerome Frank: A Sketch of an Influence, in Paul Sayre, Editor: Interpretation of Modern Legal Philosophers, pp. 222-223, 253-254; Corwin: The "Higher Law" Background of American Constitutional Law, Vol. XLII, Number 2, Harvard Law Review, December, 1928, pp. 173-174; H. M. Robertson: Aspects of the Rise of Economic Individualism—A Criticism of Max Weber and His School. Cambridge University Press, Cambridge, England, 1933, p. 85.

114. Hall: Religious Background of American Culture, Chap. IV, pp. 40-48.

115. See John Adams: A Defence of the Constitutions of Government of the United States of America, London, Printed. New York Reprinted H. Gaines, 1787. Letter XXX, pp. 156-167. In these pages Adams summarizes and quotes the views of Harrington with approval. He is especially interested in Harrington's theory of the balance of property and political power.

116. Perry: Puritanism and Democracy, pp. 126, 127, 148, 185-187; Malone: Jefferson The Virginian, pp. 175, 275.

117. James Otis: The Rights of the British Colonies Asserted and Proved, Boston, Edes and Gill, 1764, pp. 5, 25-27.

118. "They [the leaders of the federal convention] kept the same ground as the Revolution had taken, and which was seen in all the State Governments. They took their principles from that set of political economists and philosophers now generally denominated in the English language Whigs, and consecrated them as a Constitution for the government of the Country." Abraham Baldwin in the

House of Representatives, January 11, 1799. Annals of Congress. Fifth Congress, III, pp. 2630-2631.

119. Hockett: Vol. I, Preface, p. VII.

CHAPTER VI

1. The republican members of Congress objected to thanking the President for his *most gracious* speech on the ground that the same words were used to describe the speech of the English king. They succeeded in having the words erased. See the Journal of William Maclay, Introduction by Charles A. Beard. New York, A. & C. Boni, 1927, pp. 10-11. For other alleged signs of royalty see ibid., pp. 66, 111, 119, 141, 151, 162-163, 171, 172, 340, 341, 346.

2. John Quincy Adams was present at Newburyport when the delegates from that town returned with the news that Massachusetts had ratified the new constitution and wrote in his diary that: "The mob huzza'd, and one would have thought that every man from the adoption of the Constitution had acquired a sure expectancy of an independent fortune." Diary of John Quincy Adams, February 8, 1788, in Proceedings of the Massachusetts Historical Society. Second Series, Vol. XVI, 1902, Boston. Published by the Society, 1903, p. 379.

   For an account of the celebration in the leading cities, see Rufus Wilmot Griswold: The Republican Court, or American Society in the Days of Washington, New York, D. Appleton and Company, 1855, pp. 105-112.

3. "Before we got to Bedloe's Island a large sloop came, with full sail, on our starboard bow, when there stood up about twenty gentlemen and ladies, who, with the most excellent voices, sung an elegant ode, prepared for the purpose, to the tune of 'God Save the King,' welcoming their great chief to the seat of government." Griswold: op. cit. p. 13.

   After Washington had taken the oath of office Chancellor Livingston had proclaimed: "Long live George Washington, President of the United States." Annals of Congress, Vol. I, p. 28, April 30, 1789.

4. Jefferson: Works, Washington edition, Vol. IX, pp. 95, 96.

5. John Adams: Old Family Letters, copied by Alexander Biddle, Philadelphia, 1892, Series A, p. 60.

6. Henry Jones Ford: The Rise and Growth of American Politics, New York, The Macmillan Company, 1898, note 2, pp. 79-80;

Henry B. Learned: The President's Cabinet, New Haven, Yale University Press, 1912, pp. 127-128; Leonard D. White: The Federalists—A Study in Administrative History, New York, The Mac-Millan Company, 1948, pp. 28-29.

7. Washington begged Jefferson not to resign because he "thought it important to preserve the check of my opinion in the administration in order to keep things in their proper channel and prevent them from going too far." Jefferson's Works: Federal edition, October 1, 1792, Vol. I, pp. 233-237.

8. John Adams: Works, edited by Charles Francis Adams, Vol. VIII, p. 491.

9. Hamilton: Works, edited by J. C. Hamilton, Vol. IV, pp. 1-3.

10. "The Worcester Spy . . . refers to the President as 'His Highness.' " Griswold: p. 185.

11. Ibid., p. 217.

12. "Yet that we may not appear to be defective even in earthly honors let a day be solemnly set apart for proclaiming the charter; let it be brought forth placed on the divine law, the Word of God; let a crown be placed thereon by which the world may know, that so far as we approve of monarchy, that in America the law is king." Philip S. Foner: The Complete Writings of Thomas Paine, Vol. I, p. 29.

13. Commager: pp. 171, 172.

14. Frank I. Schechter: The Early History of the Tradition of the Constitution, in American Political Science Review, Vol. IX, November, 1915, pp. 707-734.

15. Farrand: Records, Vol. I, pp. 288-289. See also the remarks of "Mr. Dickenson" in the Federal Convention, August 13, 1787: "It was not Reason that discovered the singular & admirable mechanism of the English Constitution. It was not Reason that discovered or ever could have discovered the odd & in the eye of those who are governed by reason, the absurd mode of trial by Jury. Accidents probably produced these discoveries, and experience has given a sanction to them." Farrand: Records, Vol. II, p. 278.

16. James Wilson: Works, edited by James DeWitt Andrews. Two volumes, Chicago, Callaghan and Company, 1896, Vol. I, p. 18.
    See also Jefferson to John Dickinson, March 6, 1801: ". . . I join with you in the hope and belief that . . . the inquiry which has been excited among the mass of mankind by our revolution and its consequences, will ameliorate the condition of man over a great portion of the globe." Works: Ford edition, Vol. VIII, p. 8.

17. See his eloquent defense of "the tillers of the soil" in his *Notes on the State of Virginia,* in Writings: Ford edition, Vol. III, pp. 268-269.

18. "The situation was similar to that in England after the Revolution of 1688." Ford: The Rise and Growth of American Politics, p. 103.

19. Jefferson's *Notes on the State of Virginia,* in Writings: Ford edition, Vol. III, pp. 278-279; Ford: op. cit. pp. 103-105; Charles A. Beard: The Economic Origins of Jeffersonian Democracy, New York, The MacMillan Company, 1915, Chap. XIV, pp. 415-467. Note especially pp. 427-428.

20. "I consider the pure federalist as a republican who would prefer a somewhat stronger executive; and the republican as one more willing to trust the legislature as a broader representation of the people and a safer deposit of power for many reasons. But both sects are republican, entitled to the confidence of their fellow citizens. Not so their quondam leaders, covering under the mark of federalism hearts devoted to monarchy. The Hamiltonians, the Essex-men, the revolutionary tories." Jefferson to John Dickinson, July 23, 1801, Works, Ford edition, Vol. VIII, pp. 76-77.

See also Jefferson's letter to Dupont de Nemours, January 18, 1802, in which he said: "It was my destiny to come to the government when it had for several years been committed to a particular political sect, to the absolute and entire exclusion of those who were in sentiment with the body of the nation . . . When this government was first established, it was possible to have kept it going on true principles, but the contracted, English, half-lettered ideas of Hamilton destroyed that hope in the bud." Works: Ford edition, Vol. VIII, pp. 126-127.

21. Charles F. Dunbar: Some Precedents Followed by Alexander Hamilton, in The Quarterly Journal of Economics, Vol. III, October, 1888, pp. 32-59.

Other federalists were also under the influence of the British administration of its public debt. See the reference to Grenville and his payment of the national creditors in George Gibbs: Memoirs of the Administrations of Washington and John Adams. Two vols. New York. William Van Norden, 1846, Vol. I, p. 34. Letter from Oliver Wolcott senior to Oliver Wolcott junior, Dec. 23, 1789.

"For in point of fact, the history of the Bank of England during its first years is in no slight degree the history of the settlement of 1689, and of the new departure which that great event makes in the politics of the civilised world." James E. Thorold Rogers: The First Nine Years of the Bank of England, Oxford, Clarendon Press, 1887, Preface, p. XII.

22. Sir William Blackstone: Commentaries on the Law of England,

edited by Thomas M. Cooley. Second edition—Revised. Two vols., Chicago, Callaghan and Company, 1872, Vol. I, p. 327.

23. Hamilton's First Report on the Public Credit, in Works: Lodge edition, 1904, Vol. II, pp. 227-289. See also Hamilton to Washington, August 18, 1792, in which Hamilton defends his funding system under the title Objectives and Answers Respecting the Administration of the Government, Works: Lodge edition, Vol. II, pp. 426-472.

See also Hamilton's financial reports as given in The Debates and Proceedings of the Congress of the United States, Washington, Gales and Seaton, 1834, Vol. II, pp. 2042-2141.

24. "The Secretary . . . entertains a full conviction that an assumption of the debts of the particular States by the Union . . . will be a measure of sound policy and substantial justice." Hamilton: Works, Lodge edition, Vol. II, p. 244.

25. Charles A. Beard: Some Economic Origins of Jeffersonian Democracy, in American Historical Review, Vol. XIX, January, 1914, Number 2, pp. 282-298. "It was a clear case of a collision of economic interests: fluid capital versus agrarianism." Ibid., p. 298.

"The funding system, they [Southern members of Congress] say, is in favor of the moneyed interest—oppressive to the land . . . They pay tribute, they say, and the middle and eastern people . . . receive it." Fisher Ames to Minott, Nov. 30, 1791, in Ames: Works, from his Speeches and Correspondence, edited by his Son, Seth Ames, 2 vols. Boston, 1854, Vol. I, p. 104. See also Gore to King, July 25, 1790, in King: Vol. I, p. 392.

26. "The establishment . . . was opposed by the tories on the grounds that such an institution was more suited to a republic than to a monarchy, and that the terms of the loan would be disastrous to borrowers upon landed security." Richard Lodge: The History of England From the Restoration to the Death of William III (1660-1702). Longmans, Green, London, 1919, p. 386. See also Rogers: The First Nine Years of the Bank of England, pp. 11-12.

27. William and Mary C. XX.

28. Dunbar: Quarterly Journal of Economics, Vol. III, pp. 46-50.

29. Gibbs: Memoirs, Vol. I, pp. 39, 59; Virginia Calendar of State Papers, Vol. 5, 1790-92, pp. 46-47; Jefferson's Writings: Ford edition, Vol. I, p. 164; Stuart to Washington, June 2, 1790, in Washington's Writings: Ford edition, Vol. XI, p. 482, footnote; Washington to Stuart, June 15, 1790, ibid. Vol. XI, pp. 481-482, Beard: Economic Origins of Jeffersonian Democracy, in American Historical Review, Vol. XIX, pp. 293-294; Beveridge: Marshall, Vol. II, p. 62.

30. Hening: Statutes at Large of Virginia, Vol. XIII, pp. 237-238; Henry: Life, Vol. II, pp. 453-455; American State Papers—Finance, Vol. I, pp. 90-91; Commager: No. 92, pp. 155-156.

31. Hamilton: Works, edited by J. C. Hamilton, Vol. IV, pp. 104-138; Hamilton to Washington, Aug. 18, 1792, in Works: Lodge edition, Vol. II, pp. 426-472; Commager: No. 93, pp. 156-158.

32. Annals of Congress, Vol. II, p. 1948, Feb. 2, 1791.

33. "The State debts have begun already to travel towards the central parts of the Union, and to such an amount as to make it probable that if they are provided for by us, nearly the whole will follow." Madison in the House of Representatives, April 22, 1790, Annals: Vol. II, p. 1590.

"... such a system may benefit large cities, like Philadelphia and New York, but the remote parts of the continent will not feel the invigorating warmth of the American treasury ..." Mr. Jackson of Georgia, in Annals: Vol. I, p. 1142, Feb. 9, 1790.

C. Gore to R. King, July 25, 1790, in King: Life and Correspondence, Vol. I, p. 392. See also the summary of the debate in McMaster: Vol. I, pp. 570-578, 580-584.

34. Fisher Ames: Works, Vol. I, p. 110, Ames to Dwight, January 23, 1792.

35. Letters of Hamilton to R. King, September 17, 1794, September 22, 1794, and Oct. 30, 1794, in King: Vol. I, pp. 573-575; McMaster, Vol. II, pp. 189-203.

36. H. M. Brackenridge: History of the Western Insurrection in Western Pennsylvania. Pittsburgh, W. S. Haven, 1859, pp. 17-20; Maclay: Journal, p. 376.

37. Brackenridge points out that some of the resolutions adopted by the western men "were modeled after those passed before the Revolutionary war in relation to the stamp act and other excises." Ibid., p. 22.

38. Commager: No. 102, pp. 178-183.

39. Frank M. Anderson: Contemporary Opinion of the Kentucky and Virginia Resolutions, in American Historical Review, Vol. V, October, 1899, No. 1, pp. 45-63, Vol. V, December, 1899, No. 2, pp. 225-252.

40. Maclay: Journal, pp. 9-10-11, 13-14. See the account of his first address, in Annals: Vol. I, pp. 25-29, April 30, 1789.

41. White: The Federalists, p. 27.

42. Claude G. Bowers: Jefferson and Hamilton—The Struggle for

Democracy in America, Boston and New York, Houghton Mifflin Company, 1926, p. 69.

43. Hamilton: Works, J. C. Hamilton edition, Vol. IV, p. 545, Hamilton to Randolph, April 27th, 1794.

44. Hamilton to Washington, July 22nd, 1792, in Hamilton: Works, J. C. Hamilton edition, Vol. IV, p. 226; same to same, August 10, 1792, ibid., Vol. IV, pp. 242-244.

45. Hamilton to Jefferson, March, 1792, in Hamilton: Works, Lodge edition, Vol. IV, pp. 359-362.

46. Jefferson to Hamilton, March 5, 1792, in Hamilton: Works, Lodge edition, Vol. IV, p. 358.

47. Jefferson to Washington, September 9, 1792, in Jefferson: Works, Federal edition, Vol. VII, p. 140; Hamilton to Jay, May 6, 1794, in Hamilton: Works, J. C. Hamilton edition, Vol. IV, pp. 551-555.
    See also the summary of the situation in White: The Federalists, pp. 212-214.

48. Hamilton: Works, Lodge edition, Vol. VII, pp. 284-286.

49. White: The Federalists, pp. 28-29.

50. I Stat. 65 Sept. 2, 1789.

51. Note the remarks of Mr. Findley in the House, March 8, 1792, Annals, Vol. III, pp. 447-452. "I wholly object to a Minister's dictating or propounding revenue systems, and still more to his supporting them with arguments, as it is carrying the influence of the Executive administration to a still greater extent." Ibid., p. 450. See also his condemnation of the Secretary of the Treasury on March 1, 1793: "His reports spoke the language of a Frederick of Prussia, or some other despotic Prince, who had all the political power vested in himself—not the language of a dependent Secretary, under a free and well ordered Government." Annals: Vol. III, p. 923.

52. "Hamilton, literally speaking, is moving heaven and earth in favor of his [funding] system." Maclay: Journal, p. 189. "Mr. Hamilton is all-powerful and fails in nothing he attempts." Ibid., p. 376; Ralph Volney Harlow: The History of Legislative Methods in the period Before 1825, New Haven, Yale University Press, 1917, p. 145; McLaughlin: Constitutional History of the United States, p. 240.

53. Annals: Vol. I, pp. 1043-45, Jan. 9, 1790.

54. Annals: Vol. IV, p. 531; Madison to Jefferson, March 31, 1794, in Madison: Letters, Congressional edition, Vol. II, pp. 9-10.

55. Richardson: Messages and Papers of the President, Vol. I, p. 125; Bennett Milton Rich: The Presidents and Civil Disorder, Washington, D. C. The Brookings Institution, 1941, pp. 2-6.

56. Leland D. Baldwin: Whiskey Rebels, Pittsburgh, University of Pittsburgh Press, 1939, pp. 110-112; Rich: op. cit. pp. 6-7.

57. Pennsylvania Archives, 2nd series, Harrisburg, 1874-1926, Vol. IV, pp. 139, 358; Rich: op. cit. pp. 9-10.

58. Hamilton to Washington, August 2d, 1794, in Hamilton: Works, J. C. Hamilton edition, Vol. IV, p. 577.

59. Rich: p. 8.

60. Brackenridge: p. 265; Rich: p. 9.

61. Baldwin: pp. 262-263; Solon J. Buck and Elizabeth Hawthorn Buck: The Planting of Civilization in Western Pennsylvania, University of Pittsburgh Press, 1939, p. 472; Rich: pp. 18-20.

62. Rich: p. 20.

63. Adams: Works, C. F. Adams edition, Vol. IX, pp. 20-23, 60; Richardson: Messages and Papers, Vol. I, p. 303.

64. "You express a wish in your letter to be generally advised as to the tenor of your conduct, in consequence of the late revolution in France .. We certainly cannot deny to the other nations that principle whereon our government is founded, that every nation has a right to govern itself internally under what forms it pleases, and to transact business with other nations through whatever organ it chooses, whether that be a King, Convention, Assembly, Committee, President, or whatever it be. The only thing essential is, the will of the nation." Jefferson to Thomas Pinckney, December 30, 1792, in Jefferson: Works, Monticello edition, Vol. IX, pp. 7-8.

65. "You may, on every occasion, give assurances which cannot go beyond the real desires of this country, to preserve a fair neutrality in the present war, on condition that the rights of neutral nations are respected in us, as they have been settled in modern times ..." Jefferson to Thomas Pinckney, April 20, 1793, in Jefferson: Works, Monticello edition, Vol. IX, p. 67. See also Jefferson to Monroe, May 5, 1793, ibid., Vol. IX, pp. 75-76.

For text of Washington's proclamation of neutrality see Richardson: Vol. I, p. 156; Commager: No. 96, pp. 162-163.

66. "Mr. Jefferson likes us because he detests England; he seeks to draw near to us because he fears us less than Great Britain; but tomorrow he might change his opinions about us if Great Britain should cease to inspire his fear ... Jefferson, I repeat, is an Ameri-

can and therefore, he can never sincerely be our friend." French Minister Adet to French Minister of Foreign Relations, in American Historical Association Annual Report for 1903. Two vols. Washington, Government Printing Office, 1904, Vol. II, p. 983.

67. McLaughlin: Constitutional History of the United States, p. 255; Schachner: Hamilton, p. 316.

68. For Hamilton's defense see his Pacificus, June 29, 1793, in Works: Lodge edition, Vol. IV, pp. 432-489. "The general doctrine of our Constitution, then is, that the executive power of the nation is vested in the President; subject only to the exceptions and qualifications which are expressed in the instrument." Ibid., p. 439.

69. Madison's Letters of Helvidius, in Madison: Works, Hunt edition, Vol. VI, pp. 144-145.

70. "It has been asked also whether the authority of the Executive extended by any part of the Constitution to a declaration of the *Disposition* of the U. S. on the subject of war and peace? . . . On the last point I must own my surprise that such a prerogative should have been exercised . . . The right to decide the question whether the duty and interest of the U. S. require war or peace under any given circumstances, and whether their disposition be towards the one or the other seems to be essentially and exclusively involved in the right vested in the Legislature of declaring war in time of peace . . ." Madison to Jefferson, June 13, 1793, in Madison: Works, Hunt edition, Vol. VI, p. 131.

71. Madison to Jefferson, June 13, 1793, in Madison: Works, Hunt edition, Vol. VI, p. 132.

72. Madison: Works, Hunt edition, Vol. VI, pp. 138-188.

73. Madison: Works, Hunt edition, Vol. VI, p. 150.

74. Madison: Works, Hunt edition, Vol. VI, p. 180.

75. For text see Hunter Miller, Editor: Treaties and Other International Acts of the United States, 1783-1855, Washington, Government Printing Office, 1931-1942, 6 vols., Vol. II, pp. 245-267.

76. Samuel Flagg Bemis: Jay's Treaty—A Study in Commerce and Diplomacy, New York, The MacMillan Company, 1923, Chap. XIII, pp. 252-271. "The elixir of national credit which energized the Government depended . . . almost wholly on imports, which a war or even commercial hostility with Great Britain would have destroyed." Ibid., p. 270. See also Octavius Pickering and Charles W. Upham: The Life of Timothy Pickering, Four volumes, Boston, Little, Brown and Company, 1867-1873, Vol. III, pp. 343, 410.

77. For the report of the XYZ affair, see Walter Lowrie and Matthew St. Clair Clarke: American State Papers—Foreign Relations, 6 vols. 1789-1828, Washington, Gales and Seaton, 1833-1859, Vol. II, pp. 157-168.

78. "Colonel Pickering states that 'every Federalist was astonished [at Adams' plan for a second mission to France]. Among others, Harrison Gray Otis (then a member of the House of Representatives) came over to my office and asked, 'How is all this? the nomination of Mr. Murray to treat with the French republic?' 'I know nothing of it,' said I, 'but the fact I hear that the President has so nominated him.' 'Why, is the man mad?' said Mr. Otis." "Colonel Pickering states: 'I was informed at the time, by some members of the Senate, that the nomination would have been at once negatived, but for some of the President's Federal friends, who engaged to see him, in the hope of inducing him to abandon the project. This he would not do." Pickering and Upham: Life of Pickering, Vol. III, p. 439.

   On July 18th, 1798, Jay in a letter to Pickering, had referred to himself as: "Being of the number of those who expect a severe war with France . . ." Ibid: Vol. III, p. 423.

   "The Federalist leaders really wanted war with France, most of them as a matter of patriotism; some, undoubtedly, because war would insure party success in the approaching presidential election." Beveridge: Marshall, Vol. II, p. 424.

79. ". . . it [Adams' second mission] silences all arguments against the sincerity of France, and renders desperate every further effort towards war." Jefferson to Madison, Feb. 19, 1799, in Jefferson: Works, Monticello edition, Vol. X, p. 113. See also Gilbert Chinard: Thomas Jefferson, Second edition, revised, Boston, Little, Brown and Company, 1939, p. 355.

   Note the guarded statement in Pickering and Upham: Life of Pickering: "The subsidence of the national spirit, on the renewal of negotiations with the Directory, was a vital blow to the strength of the Federal administration." Ibid., Vol. III, p. 447.

80. Maclay: Journal, pp. 125-129; J. Q. Adams: Memoirs, Vol. VI, p. 427.

81. Farrand: Records, Vol. I, pp. 104, 288, 513.

82. "Mr. Wilson moved to add, after the word 'Senate' the words, 'and House of Representatives.' As treaties he said are to have the operation of laws, they ought to have the sanction of laws also." Farrand: Records, Vol. II, p. 538.

   Note also the objection of Mr. Mason of Virginia: "By declaring all treaties supreme laws of the land, the Executive and Senate have, in many cases, an exclusive power of legislation; which might have been avoided by . . . requiring the assent of the House of Representatives, where it could be done with safety." Farrand: Records, Vol. II, p. 639.

83. John Locke: Two Treatises of Government, Seventh edition. J. Whiston, W. Strahan [etc.], London, 1772. Book II, Chap. XII, pp. 293-296. Locke's presentation is obscure and difficult to follow. In Book II, Chap. XIII—Of the Subordination of the Powers of the Commonwealth, pp. 296-306, he seems to say that the administration of this federative power should be in the hands of persons ultimately subject to the legislature. One wonders if he foresaw the evolution of the foreign office "bureaucracy" that has developed in modern states.

That the executive and the Senate were to share in the treaty making power had also been Hamilton's view in No. 75 of The Federalist. See Beard: The Enduring Federalist, pp. 317-321.

84. R. Earl McClendon: Origin of the Two-Thirds Rule in the Senate Action Upon Treaties, in American Historical Review, Vol. XXXVI, July, 1931, pp. 768-772.

85. Maclay: Journal, pp. 125-129; J. Q. Adams: Memoirs, Vol. VI, p. 427; J. Ralston Hayden: The Senate and Treaties, 1789-1817, The MacMillan Company, New York, 1920, p. 104.

86. Lindsay Rogers: The American Senate, New York, Alfred Knopf, 1926, pp. 62-63; Hayden: op. cit., pp. 79-80.

87. Madison: Writings, Hunt edition, Vol. VI, p. 161.

88. Annals: Vol. V, pp. 759-60, March 24, 1796; Richardson: Messages, Vol. I, pp. 194-196; Washington: Writings, Fitzpatrick edition, Vol. XXXV, p. 6.

89. Annals: Vol. V, p. 771, April 6, 1796; ibid., Vol. V, p. 782, April 7, 1796.

90. John Maybry Mathews: The Conduct of American Foreign Relations, The Century Company, New York, 1922, pp. 149-150.

91. U. S. Statutes at Large. Vols. 1-64 [Various publishers], Vol. I, Boston, Charles C. Little and James Brown, 1845, Chap. XX, Secs. 1-35, pp. 73-93, Sept. 24, 1789.

92. Charles A. and Mary R. Beard: The Rise of American Civilization, One volume edition, New York, The MacMillan Company, 1930, Part I, p. 340.

93. I Cranch, 137 (1803).

94. See the cases listed in Charles Warren: The Supreme Court in

United States History, revised edition, 2 vols., Little Brown and
Company, Boston, 1935, Vol. I, pp. 65-69.

95. Warren: op. cit. Vol. I, pp. 70-71; Max Farrand: The First Hayburn Case, in American Historical Review, Vol. XIII, Number 2,
January, 1908, pp. 281-285.

96. Warren: pp. 72-76.

97. "It was a perversion of democratic principles in that it [the situation in South Carolina] made one-fifth of the population the rulers
of the other four-fifths. The result was that South Carolina had an
aristocratic government instead of a democratic one. According to
the census of 1790, the three lower districts had a white population
of 28,644, the upper districts one of 111,534. Yet the former
elected 20 senators and 70 members of the assembly, while the latter was allowed only 17 senators and 54 assembly men." William
A. Schaper: Sectionalism in South Carolina, in Annual Report of
the American Historical Association for the Year 1900, Two vols.,
Washington, Government Printing Office, 1901, Vol. I, p. 408.

"In Virginia, twenty counties in the western portion of the
State, with 31,000 white men of military age, sent 40 delegates to
the assembly or one to 775 fighting men; on the other hand, 18
counties in the eastern part of the State, with 13,000 fighting men,
sent 36 delegates, or one to every 361. Stating the matter in terms
of taxation, the upper counties sent one delegate for every one
thousand dollars contributed, the seaboard one for every hundred
and twenty-six dollars paid in taxes." Edward Channing: A History of the United States, Vol. IV, p. 244 note.

98. Kirk H. Porter: A History of the Suffrage in the U. S. p. 10;
Charles H. Lincoln: The Revolutionary Movement in Pennsylvania, Philadelphia, 1901, pp. 94-96, 279.

99. Thorpe: Federal and State Constitutions, Vol. VI, p. 3779.

100. Ibid: Vol. IV, Art. XI, p. 2472.

101. Ibid: Vol. I, Art. IV, Section I, p. 574.

102. Ibid: Vol. III, Art. III, Section I, p. 1269.

103. Ibid: Vol. VI, Art. III, Section I, p. 3418. A person to be eligible
for a seat in the general assembly had to possess "not less than
two hundred acres of land." Ibid: Vol. VI, Article I, Section 7,
p. 3415; while the governor shall "possess a freehold estate of five
hundred acres of land." Ibid: Vol. VI, Art. II, Section 3, p. 3417.

104. Frederick J. Turner: Social Forces in American History, in American Historical Review, Vol. XVI, Number 2, January, 1911, p. 251,

105. Philip S. Foner, editor: The Complete Writings of Thomas Paine, Vol. I, p. 251.

106. Beveridge: Marshall, Vol. II, pp. 12-14.

107. Charles Downer Hazen: Contemporary American Opinion of the French Revolution, Baltimore, Johns Hopkins Press, 1897, pp. 203-207; Beveridge: Vol. II, pp. 38-42. See also the famous account in McMaster: Vol. II, pp. 89-95.

108. John Quincy Adams: Writings, Ford edition, John Quincy Adams to John Adams, October 19, 1790, Vol. I, p. 64.

109. Madison: Writings, Hunt edition, Vol. VI, p. 55 note, p. 81 note; Beard: Economic Origins of Jeffersonian Democracy, pp. 51-52. See also Sydney Howard Gay: James Madison, Boston, Houghton Mifflin and Company, 1884, pp. 183-186. These pages refer to the New England tour in which Jefferson is supposed to have converted Madison.

110. Brackenridge: pp. 24-26; McMaster, Vol. II, pp. 204-206.

CHAPTER VII

1. "Many times I had spoken about 'mental bipolarity' and proved that our affects are bipolar. Desire and disgust, love and hate, will-to-power and will-to-submission, are composed of negative and positive parts like the current of electricity. My contention was that any human affect has its own counterpart. Later Bleuler described this fact as 'ambivalence,' a term that was accepted by everybody, whereas previously they had laughed at my discovery, and given me the nickname 'Stekel with his Bipolarity.' " The Autobiography of Wilhelm Stekel: Liveright Publishing Corporation, New York, 1950, p. 132.

2. See supra, p. 6.

3. "To take away all such mutual grievances, injuries and wrongs, there was no way but only by growing into composition and agreement among themselves, by ordaining some kind of government public, and by yielding themselves subject thereunto . . ." Richard Hooker: Of the Lawes of Ecclesiastical Politie, Printed by William Standbye, London, 1638-39, Book I, Section X, p. 26.

4. See supra, pp. 6-8.

5. Hall: The Religious Background of American Culture, pp. 89-90.

6. John Winthrop: History of New England, 1630-1649, edited by James Kendall Hosmer, 2 vols., New York, C. Scribner's Sons, 1908, Vol. II, pp. 279-292.

7. The Complete Works of Benjamin Franklin, edited by John Bigelow, 10 vols., New York. G. P. Putnam's Sons, 1887-1889, Vol. II, p. 323.

8. Hall: op. cit., pp. 118-119.

9. Ibid: pp. 185, 188.

10. Edward S. Corwin: The "Higher Law" Background of American Constitutional Law, in Harvard Law Review, Vol. 42, No. 2, December, 1928, pp. 149-185; Vol. 42, No. 3, January, 1929, pp. 365-409. See also Louis B. Boudin: The Anarchic Element in the Notion of a Higher Law, in New York University Law Quarterly Review, September, 1930, pp. 32-33.

11. The Federalist, edited by Paul Leicester Ford, New York, Henry Holt and Company, 1898, Number 10, pp. 54-63.

12. John G. Nicolay and John Hay: Abraham Lincoln — Complete Works. Twelve volumes, New York; 1905, Vol. VI, pp. 169-185.

It is a curious fact that Lincoln in this paragraph seems to be a forerunner of Freud and his theory of the mass psyche. This theory has been described as follows: "Freud expressed one of his most interesting speculations in his assumption of a psyche of the mass in which psychic processes occur just as in the psychic life of the individual . . . The individual inherits certain psychic dispositions which, however, usually need incentives in his own life to become effective. Furthermore, every person, in his unconscious psychic activity has 'an apparatus' which enables him to interpret the reactions of others. This unconscious understanding of all customs, ceremonies and laws left behind from the initial relation to the primal father, Freud surmises, may also have enabled later generations to acquire the legacy of feelings of past generations." Patrick Mullahy: Oedipus Myth and Complex, Hermitage Press, New York, 1948, pp. 69-70. See also Sigmund Freud: Totem and Taboo. Translated by A. A. Brill. New Republic, Inc. New York, 1927, p. 276.

The value of Lincoln's idea rested in its poetic artistry of expression rather than in its newness in American constitutional history. Madison, in Number 43 of The Federalist, after discussing the problem of "assenting and dissenting states", adds: "The claims of justice, both on one side and on the other, will be in force and must be fulfilled; the rights of humanity must in all cases be duly and mutually respected; whilst considerations of a common interest, and, above all, the remembrance of the endearing scenes which are past, and the anticipation of a speedy triumph over the obstacles to reunion, will, it is hoped, not urge in vain Moderation on one side, and Prudence on the other." The Federalist: Ford edition, No. 43, pp. 293-294.

The first draft of the last paragraph of Lincoln's first inaugural was written by Seward and given its stylistic revision by Lincoln. See Allen Nevins: The Emergence of Lincoln. Two vols. New York, Charles Scribner's Sons, 1950, Vol. II, p. 460. Did either Seward or Lincoln recall the passage from The Federalist cited above and did it influence their thoughts?

BIBLIOGRAPHY

I. CASES

American Insurance Company et al vs. Cantor, I Peters, 511-546.

Bayard and Wife vs. Singleton, I Martin (N. C.), 5, 1787.

Bonham's Case, 8 Coke Reports, 118a (1610); 77 English Reports, 638 (1609).

Calvin's Case, 7 Coke's Reports, I, 4b (1610); 2 State Trials, 559.

Hampden's Case (1637), 3 State Trials, 825.

First Hayburn Case. See Max Farrand: American Historical Review, Vol. XIII, No. 2, Jan., 1908, pp. 281-285.

Holmes vs. Walton (1780), New Jersey Supreme Court, Opinion unrecorded. See Austin Scott: Holmes vs. Walton: The New Jersey Precedent, in American Historical Review, Vol. IV, Number 3, April, 1899, pp. 456-469.

Marbury vs. Madison, I Cranch, 137 (1803).

Olmstead Case, Brightly N. P. 9 (Pa.); 13 C. Courts, Sec. 1376.

Penhallow et al. vs. Doane's Administrators, 3 Dallas 54.

Smith vs. Alabama, 124 U. S. 478.

Trevett vs. Weeden (1786). Records of the State of Rhode Island, Vol. X, p. 213.

U. S. vs. Judge Peters, 5 Cranch, 136.

U. S. vs. Wong Kim Ark, 169 U. S. 649.

Ware vs. Hylton, 3 Dallas, 199 (1796).

II. DOCUMENTARY SOURCES, PUBLIC DOCUMENTS AND COLLECTIONS

Acts of the Privy Council, Colonial Series, 1613-1783, London, 1908-12.

American State Papers—Foreign Relations. Edited by Walter Lowrie and Matthew St. Clair Clarke, 6 vols., 1789-1828, Washington, Gales and Seaton, 1833-1859.

British Calendars of State Papers, Colonial Series, America and West Indies, 1574-, London, 1862-.

Brodhead, John Romeyn: Documents Relative to Colonial History of the State of New York. 15 volumes. Albany, New York, Weed, Parsons and Company, 1853-1857.

207

Burnett: Edmund Cody: Letters of Members of the Continental Congress, edited by Edmund Cody Burnett. 8 vols., The Carnegie Institution of Washington, Washington, D. C. 1931.

Calendar of Virginia State Papers and Other Manuscripts, Vols. I-IX, 1652-1807, Richmond, Virginia [Various editors and printers], 1875-1890.

Commager, Henry Steele, Editor: Documents of American History, Two vols., F. S. Crofts & Company, 1935; Second edition in one volume, New York, 1940.

Davis, J. C. Bancroft: Appendix to the Reports of the Decisions of the Supreme Court of the United States, New York and Albany. Banks & Brothers, 1889, in U. S. Report, Vol. 131.

Elliot, Jonathan: The Debates in the Several State Conventions on the Adoption of the Federal Constitution . . . Five volumes, Philadelphia, J. B. Lippincott, 1876.

Farrand, Max, Editor: The Records of the Federal Convention of 1787. Revised edition in four volumes, New Haven, Yale University Press, 1937.

Federalist, The: The Enduring Federalist, edited by Charles A. Beard, Doubleday & Company, Garden City, New York, 1948.

Federalist, The: Edited by Paul Leicester Ford, New York, Henry Holt and Company, 1898.

Firth, C. H. and Rait, R. S.: Acts and Ordinances of the Interregnum, 1642-1660, 3 vols., London, H. M. Stationery Office, 1911.

Gray, Horace, Editor: Quincy Reports on Constitutional Law with notes, 1761-1772. Two vols., Cambridge, 1894-1895.

Great Britain. House of Commons Journals, 1547-1784 reprinted.

Hening, William Waller: The Statutes at large; being a collection of all the laws of Virginia from the first session of the legislature, in the year 1619. Published pursuant to an act of the General Assembly of Virginia, passed on the fifth day of February one thousand eight hundred and eight, Richmond, 1810-23 [Various printers].

Howell, T. B.: A complete collection of state trials and proceedings . . . from the earliest period to the year 1783 . . . In twenty-one volumes. London: Printed by T. C. Hansard for Longman, Hurst, Rees, Orme and Brown, 1816-26.

Journals of the American Congress from 1774 to 1788. Washington. Printed and published by Way and Gideon, 1823.

Journals of the Continental Congress, 1774-1789. Edited by Worthington C. Ford and Gaillard Hunt. 34 volumes, Washington, Government Printing Office, 1904-1937.

Journal of the Commissioners for Trade and Plantations, 1704. London. Published by His Majesty's Stationery Office, 1920.

Journal of the House of Representatives of Massachusetts Bay in New England. Boston. Printed by Green and Russell, 1765.

Journals of the House of Representatives of Massachusetts, 1741-1742. The Massachusetts Historical Society, Boston, Wright & Potter Printing Co., 1943.

MacDonald, William: Documentary Source Book of American History, 1606-1913, New York, The MacMillan Company, 1916; Third edition, New York, The MacMillan Company, 1928.

MacDonald, William: Select Charters, New York, The MacMillan Company, 1899.

MacDonald, William: Select Documents Illustrative of the History of the United States, 1776-1861, The MacMillan Company, New York, 1924.

Maryland Laws . . . made since 1763 consisting of acts of Assembly under the proprietary government, resolves of conventions . . . and acts of Assembly since the Revolution. Annapolis: Printed by F. Green, 1787.

Massachusetts State Papers: Speeches of the Governors of Massachusetts from 1765 to 1775 and The Answers of the House of Representatives of the Same . . . Boston. Printed by Russell and Gardner, 1818.

Miller, Hunter, Editor: Treaties and Other International Acts of the United States, 1783-1855, 6 vols., Washington, Government Printing Office, 1931-1942.

Moore, John Bassett: Digest of International Law, 6 vols., Washington, Government Printing Office, 1906.

Morrison, S. E., Editor: Sources and Documents Illustrating the American Revolution, 1764-1788 and the Formation of the Federal Constitution, Oxford, Clarendon Press, 1923.

New York State. Statutes 1785. Laws of the state of New York. Passed at the First Meeting of the Eight Sessions of the Legislature of said State. Beginning the Fourth Day of October, 1784 and Ending the Twenty-ninth Day of November following. New York. Printed by Elizabeth Holt, 1784 & 1785.

Old South Leaflets. 8 vols. Nos. 1-200, Boston, Directors of the Old South Work, n.d.

Proceedings and Debates of the British Parliament Respecting North America. Five volumes. Edited by Leo Francis Stock. Washington, D. C. Published by the Carnegie Institution of Washington, 1924-1941.

Proceedings of the Maryland Convention. Annapolis. Printed by Frederick Green, 1777.

Report of the President's Committee on Administrative Management, Washington, Government Printing Office, 1937.

Reports of Sir Edward Coke, Knt (1572-1617). In thirteen parts. A new ed., with additional notes and references, and with abstracts of the principal points . . . by John Henry Thomas, esq. The rest of the fourth and the remaining nine parts by John Farquhar Fraser . . . London, J. Butterworth and Son. 1826.

Revolutionary Records of the State of Georgia, compiled and published by Allen D. Chandler. Three vols., Atlanta. The Franklin-Turner Company, 1908.

Richardson, J. D. Editor: Messages and Papers of the Presidents, 1789-1897. 10 vols. Washington. Published by the authority of Congress, 1898-1899.

Rushworth, John: Historical Collections of private passages of State, weighty matters of law . . . Beginning the sixteenth year of King James, anno 1618 . . . to the death of King Charles the First, 1648. 8 vols., London, D. Browne, 1721.

Thorpe, Francis Newton: The Federal and State Constitutions, Colonial Charters and Other Organic Laws . . . Seven volumes. Washington, Government Printing Office, 1909.

United States Congress. American State Papers. Documents, legislative and executive of the Congress of the United States . . . Selected and edited under the authority of Congress, by Walter Lowrie . . . Mathew St. Clair Clarke . . . [and others], 38 vols., Washington, Gales and Seaton, 1833-61.

United States Congress. The Debates and Proceedings in the Congress of the United States . . . comprising the period from March 3, 1789 to May 27, 1824, inclusive. Comp. from authentic materials. Washington, Gales and Seaton, 1834-56.

United States Continental Congress. Secret Journals of the Acts and Proceedings of Congress—From the First Meeting Thereof to the Dissolution of the Confederation by the Adoption of the Constitution of the United States. Four volumes. Boston. Printed and published by Thomas B. Wait, 1821.

United States Statutes at Large, Vols. 1-64.

Wharton, Francis: Revolutionary Diplomatic Correspondence of the United States, 6 vols., Washington. Government Printing Office, 1889.

III. *AUTOBIOGRAPHIES AND BIOGRAPHIES*

Adams, Henry: The Education of Henry Adams, Boston and New York, Houghton Mifflin Company, 1918.

Bemis, Samuel Flagg: John Quincy Adams and the Foundations of American Foreign Policy, New York, Alfred A. Knopf, 1950.

Berthold, S. M.: Thomas Paine. America's First Liberal, Boston, Meador Publishing Company, 1938.

Beveridge, Albert J.: Life of John Marshall. 4 volumes. Boston and New York, Houghton Mifflin Company, 1916-1919.

Brant, Irving: James Madison. The Nationalist, 1780-1787. The Bobbs-Merrill Company, Indianapolis, 1948.

Brown, Alice: Mercy Warren, Charles Scribner's Sons, New York, 1898.

Casanova. The Memoirs of Casanova De Seingalt. Twelve volumes. The Venetian Society, London and New York, 1929.

Chinard, Gilbert: Thomas Jefferson, Second edition, revised, Boston, Little Brown and Company, 1939.

Clarendon, Earl of: Life of Edward, Earl of Clarendon. Written by himself. Three vols., Oxford at the Clarendon Press, MDCCCXXVII.

Conway, Moncure Daniel: Omitted Chapters of History Disclosed in the Life and Papers of Edmund Randolph. Second edition, New York and London, G. P. Putnam's Sons, 1899.

Gay, Sydney Howard: James Madison, Boston, Houghton Mifflin and Company, 1884.

Henry, Patrick: Life, Correspondence and Speeches, edited by William Wirt Henry, 3 vols., New York, Charles Scribner's Sons, New York, 1891.

Herben, Jan: Huss and His Followers, Geoffrey Bles, London, 1926.

Horry, Brigadier General P. and Weems, M. L.: The Life of General Francis Marion, New York, John W. Lovell Company, n.d.

James, James Alton: The Life of George Rogers Clark. The University of Chicago Press, Chicago, Illinois, 1928.

James, James Alton: Oliver Pollock: The Life and Times of an Unknown Patriot. D. Appleton-Century Company, New York, 1937.

Jay, William: Life of John Jay, 2 vols., New York, J. and J. Harper, 1833.

Johnson, Samuel: Lives of the Poets, edited by George Birbeck Hill, 3 vols., Oxford, Clarendon Press, 1905.

Knollenberg, Bernhard: Washington and the Revolution: A Reappraisal, New York, The MacMillan Company, 1940.

Lockmiller, David A.: Sir William Blackstone, University of North Carolina Press, Chapel Hill, 1938.

Loseith, Johann: Wiclif and Hus. Translated by the Rev. M. J. Evans, London, Hodder and Stoughton, 1884.

Malone, Dumas: Jefferson the Virginian, Boston, Little Brown and Company, 1948.

Nevins, Allen: The Emergence of Lincoln, Two vols., New York, Charles Scribner's Sons, 1950.

Patterson, Samuel White: Horatio Gates: Defender of American Liberties, New York, Columbia University Press, 1941.

Pickering, Octavius and Upham, Charles W.: The Life of Timothy Pickering, Four volumes, Boston, Little Brown and Company, 1867-1873.

Rowland, Kate Mason: Life of George Mason, 2 vols., G. P. Putnam's Sons, New York, 1892.

Schachner, Nathan: Alexander Hamilton, New York, D. Appleton-Century Company, 1946.

Sparks, Jared: The Life of Gouverneur Morris with Selections from His Correspondence and Miscellaneous Papers. Three volumes, Boston, Gray & Bowen, 1832.

Stekel, Wilhelm: The Autobiography of Wilhelm Stekel. Liveright Publishing Corporation, New York, 1950.

Stillé, Charles J.: The Life and Times of John Dickinson, 1732-1808. Philadelphia. J. B. Lippincott Company, 1891.

Van Doren, Carl: Benjamin Franklin, New York, The Viking Press, 1938.

Venables, General, The Narrative of: edited by C. H. Firth, Longmans, Green, New York, 1900.

Waller, Sir William: Vindication of the Character and Conduct of Sir William Waller . . . (Written by Himself), London. Printed for J. Debrett, 1793.

Winthrop, Robert Charles: Life and Letters of John Winthrop, Second edition, 2 vols., Boston, Little Brown and Company, 1869.

Wittels, Fritz: Freud and His Times, Liveright Publishing Corporation, New York, 1931.

IV. COLLECTED WORKS, DIARIES, JOURNALS, LETTERS AND MEMOIRS

Adams, John: Old Family Letters, copied by Alexander Biddle, Philadelphia, 1892.

Adams, John: Works: edited by Charles Francis Adams, 10 vols., Boston, Little Brown and Company, 1850-1856.

Adams, John Quincy: Diary of John Quincy Adams, in Proceedings of the Massachusetts Historical Society, Second Series, Vol. XVI, 1902, Boston. Published by the Society, 1903.

Adams, Samuel: The Writings of Samuel Adams, edited by Harry Alonzo Cushing. Four volumes, New York. G. P. Putnam's Sons, 1904-1908.

Allen, James: Diary of James Allen, Esq., of Philadelphia, in Pennsylvania Magazine of History and Biography, Vol. IX, 1885, pp. 176-196.

Ames, Fisher: Works, from his Speeches and Correspondence, edited by his son, Seth Ames, 2 vols., Boston, Little Brown and Company, 1854.

Ballagh, James Curtis: The Letters of Richard Henry Lee, 2 vols., New York, The MacMillan Company, 1912-14.

Bernard, Governor [Francis]: Select Letters on the Trade and the Principles of Law and Polity Applied to the American Colonies, London, W. Bowyer and J. Nichols, MDCCLXXIV.

Bolingbroke, Lord: Works, Four volumes, Carey and Hart, Philadelphia, 1841.

Burke, Edmund: Select Works, Three volumes, edited by E. J. Payne, Oxford, The Clarendon Press, 1872.

Burke, Edmund: Works and Correspondence. A new edition. Eight volumes. Francis and John Rivington, London, 1852.

Carlyle, Thomas: Oliver Cromwell's Letters and Speeches. Four volumes, New York, Charles Scribner's Sons, 1899-1900.

Clarke Papers. Edited by C. H. Firth. Four volumes. Volumes one and two printed for the Camden Society. MDCCCXCI and MDCCCXCIV. Volumes three and four printed for the Royal Historical Society and published by Longmans, Green, London, 1899 and 1901.

Correspondence of the French Ministers to the United States, 1791-1797. Edited by Prof. Frederick J. Turner, in Annual Report of the American Historical Association for the Year 1903. In two vols., Vol. II, Washington. Government Printing Office, 1904.

Dearborn, Henry: Journals, 1776-1783. Reprinted from the Proceedings of the Massachusetts Historical Society, 1886, Cambridge, John Wilson and Son, University Press, 1887.

Dickinson, John: Writings, edited by Paul Leicester Ford, in Pennsylvania Historical Society Memoirs, Vol. XIV, Philadelphia, The Historical Society of Pennsylvania, 1895.

Franklin, Benjamin: The Complete Works of Benjamin Franklin, edited by John Bigelow, 10 vols., New York, G. P. Putnam's Sons, 1887-1889.

Gibbs, George: Memoirs of the Administrations of Washington and John Adams, two vols., New York, William Van Norden, 1846.

Gray, Colonel Robert: Observations on the War in Carolina, in South Carolina Historical and Genealogical Magazine, Vol. XI, July, 1910, No. 3, pp. 139-159.

Graydon, Alexander: Memoirs of His Own Times with Reminiscences of the Men and Events of the Revolution, edited by John Stockton Littel, Philadelphia, Lindsay & Blakiston, 1846.

Hamilton, Alexander: Works, edited by Henry Cabot Lodge, 12 vols., New York, G. P. Putnam's Sons, 1904.

Hamilton, Alexander: Works, Comprising His Correspondence and His Political and Official Writings . . . Edited by John C. Hamilton, 7 vols., New York, Charles S. Francis & Company, 1851.

Higginson Letters, 1783-1804. In Annual Report of the American Historical Association for the year 1896. Two vols., Washington, Government Printing Office, Vol. I, pp. 704-841.

Hutchinson [Thomas], 1711-1780: The Hutchinson Papers, Albany, New York, The [Prince] Society, Two volumes in one, 1865.

Jefferson, Thomas: Correspondence. Printed from the Originals in the Collection of William K. Bixby, with notes by Worthington Chauncey Ford, Boston, The Plimpton Press, 1916.

Jefferson, Thomas: Papers edited by Julian P. Boyd. Four volumes to date. Princeton, New Jersey, Princeton University Press, 1950-1951.

Jefferson, Thomas: Works, Monticello edition, 20 vols., The Thomas Jefferson Memorial Association, 1904.

Jefferson, Thomas: Writings, edited by Paul Leicester Ford, 10 vols., New York, G. P. Putnam's Sons, 1892-1899.

King, Rufus: The Life and Correspondence of Rufus King, edited by Charles R. King, 6 vols., New York, G. P. Putnam's Sons, 1894-1900.

Leake, Isaac Q.: Memoir of the Life and Times of General John Lamb. Albany, J. Munsell, 1850.

Letter from John Marshall to James Wilkinson, January 5, 1787, in American Historical Review, Vol. XII, Number 2, January, 1907, pp. 347-348.

Locke, John: Works: Ten volumes. The eleventh edition. Printed for W. Otridge and Son, Leigh and Sotheby [etc.], London, 1812.

Maclay, William: Journal of William Maclay, Introduction by Charles A. Beard, New York, A. & C. Boni, 1927.

Madison, James: Writings, edited by Gaillard Hunt, 9 vols., New York, G. P. Putnam's Sons, 1900-1910.

Memoirs of the Life of Colonel Hutchinson, Governor of Nottingham, by his wife, Lucy, edited by C. H. Firth, two vols., London, 1885.

Monroe, James: The Writings of James Monroe. Edited by Stanislaus Murray Hamilton. Seven volumes, New York, G. P. Putnam's Sons, 1898-1903.

Nicholas Papers: Correspondence of Sir Edward Nicholas, Secretary of State, edited by George F. Warner. Four volumes. Printed for the Camden Society, Vol. I, Nichols and Sons, Westminster, MDCCC-LXXVI, Vol. II, MDCCCXCII, Vol. III, MDCCCXCVII, Vol. IV, London, Offices of the Society, 1920.

Nicolay, John G. and Hay, John: Abraham Lincoln: Complete Works. Twelve volumes, New York, Francis D. Tandy Co., 1905.

Paine, Thomas: Complete Writings, edited by Philip S. Foner. Two volumes, The Citadel Press, New York, 1945.

Pepys, Samuel: Diary and Correspondence of Samuel Pepys, 6 vols., London, Bickers and Sons, 1875.

Price Papers, in Massachusetts Historical Society Proceedings, 2d Series 1903, Vol. XVII, Boston. Published by the Society, MXCCCCIII.

Warwick, Sir Philip: Memoirs of King Charles the First. Edinburgh. James Ballantyne, 1813.

Washington, George: The Writings of George Washington, collected and edited by W. C. Ford, 14 vols., New York, G. P. Putnam's Sons, 1891-93.

Washington, George: The Writings of George Washington from the original manuscript sources, 1745-1799; prepared under the direction of the United States George Washington Bicentennial Commission and published by authority of Congress. John C. Fitzpatrick, editor, 39 vols., Washington. United States Government Printing Office, 1931-1944.

Webster, Noah: A Letter to General Hamilton Occasioned by His Letter to President Adams, by a Federalist, New York [?] 1800.

Whitelock, Sir Bulstrode: Memorials of the English Affairs, London, Printed for Nathaniel Ponder, MDCLXXXII.

Wilson, James: Works, edited by James DeWitt Andrews. Two volumes, Chicago, Callaghan and Company, 1896.

V. MONOGRAPHS AND SPECIAL STUDIES

Adams, Herbert B.: Maryland's Influence upon Land Cessions to the United States, in Johns Hopkins University Studies in Historical and Political Science. Third Series No. 1, Baltimore, Johns Hopkins University, 1885.

Adams, James Truslow: The Adams Family. The Literary Guild, New York, 1930.

Adams, John: A Defence of the Constitution of Government of the United States of America. Philadelphia. Printed for Hall and Sellers; J. Crukshane; and Young and M'Culloch, MDCCLXXXVII.

Albion, Robert Greenhalgh: Forests and Sea Power: The Timber Problem of the Royal Navy, 1652-1862, Cambridge, Harvard University Press, 1926.

Alvord, Clarence W.: The Mississippi Valley in British Politics, Two volumes, Cleveland, The A. H. Clark Co., 1917.

Ambler, Charles Henry: Sectionalism in Virginia from 1776 to 1861, Chicago, University of Chicago Press, 1910.

Andrews, Charles M.: The Acts of Trade, in Cambridge History of the British Empire. Eight volumes. Cambridge. At the University Press, 1929-1936, Vol. I, Chap. IX, pp. 268-299.

Andrews, Charles M.: British Committees, Commissioners and Councils of Trade and Plantations, 1622-1675, Baltimore, Johns Hopkins Press, 1908.

Andrews, Charles M.: The Colonial Period of American History, New Haven. Yale University Press, 4 vols., 1934.

Bainton, Roland: The Appeal to Reason, in Conyers Read: The Constitution Reconsidered, New York, Columbia University Press, 1938.

Baldwin, Leland D.: Whiskey Rebels, Pittsburgh, University of Pittsburgh Press, 1939.

Baxter, James P.: Sir Ferdinando Gorges. Three volumes, Boston, Prince Society, 1890.

Beard, Charles A.: The Economic Origins of Jeffersonian Democracy, New York, The MacMillan Company, 1915.

Becker, Carl: The Declaration of Independence, New York, Alfred A. Knopf, 1942.

Becker, Carl L.: The History of Political Parties in the Province of New York, 1760-1776. Bulletin of the University of Wisconsin, No. 286, Madison, Wisconsin, 1909.

Beer, George Louis: The Commercial Policy of England Toward the American Colonies, Columbia University Studies in History, Economics and Public Law, Vol. III, Number 2, New York, Columbia College, 1893.

Beer, George Louis: The Old Colonial System, 1660-1754. Two vols., New York. The MacMillan Company, 1912.

Beer, George Louis: The Origins of the British Colonial System, 1578-1660, New York, The MacMillan Company, 1908.

Bemis, Samuel Flagg: Diplomacy of the American Revolution, New York, Appleton-Century Company, 1935.

Bemis, Samuel Flagg: Jay's Treaty: A Study in Commerce and Diplomacy, New York, The MacMillan Company, 1923.

Bemis, Samuel Flagg: Pinckney's Treaty: A Study of America's Advantage from Europe's Distress, 1783-1800, Baltimore. The Johns Hopkins Press, 1926.

Bond, Beverly W.: State Government in Maryland, 1777-1781, Baltimore, The Johns Hopkins Press, 1905.

Bondy, William: The Separation of Governmental Powers, in Columbia University Studies in History and Public Law, Vol. V, No. 2, New York, 1896, pp. 135-318.

Boudin, Louis B.: Government by Judiciary, 2 vols., W. Godwin, Inc., New York, 1932.

Bowle, John: Western Political Thought. London, Jonathan Cape. Second impression, 1948.

Brackenridge, H. M.: History of the Western Insurrection in Western Pennsylvania, Pittsburgh, W. S. Haven, 1859.

Buck, Solon J. and Buck, Elizabeth Hawthorn: The Planting of Civilization in Western Pennsylvania, University of Pittsburgh Press, 1939.

Cairns, Huntington: Philosophy as Jurisprudence, in Paul Sayre, Editor: Interpretations of Modern Legal Philosophers, New York, Oxford University Press, 1947.

Callcott, W. H.: The Caribbean Policy of the United States, 1890-1920. Baltimore, Johns Hopkins University Press, 1942.

Cannon, H. L.: The Poor Priests: A Study in the Rise of English Lollardry, in Annual Report of the American Historical Association for the Year 1899. Two vols., Washington, Government Printing Office, 1900, Vol. I, pp. 451-482.

Carlyle, R. W. and A. J.: A History of Mediaeval Political Theories in the West, Six volumes. William Blackwood and Sons, Edinburgh and London, 1927-1936.

Chalmers, George: Opinions of Eminent Lawyers in Various Points of English Jurisprudence, Chiefly concerning the Colonies, Fisheries and Commerce of Great Britain. Two volumes, Reed and Hunter, London, 1814.

Chalmers, George: Opinions on Interesting Subjects of Public Law and Commercial Policy Arising From American Independence, a new edition. Corrected, London, J. Debrett, 1785.

Child, Sir Josiah: A New Discourse of Trade, 2nd edition, London, 1694.

Cobb, Sanford H.: The Rise of Religious Liberty in America, New York, The MacMillan Company, 1902.

Corwin, Edward S.: Court Over Constitution, Princeton University Press, 1938.

Craven, Wesley Frank: The Southern Colonies in the Seventeenth Century, 1607-1689. Louisiana State University Press, 1949.

Cross, Arthur Lyon: The Anglican Episcopate and the American Colonies. Longmans, Green and Company, New York, 1902.

Cummings, Homer and McFarland, Carl: Federal Justice, New York, The MacMillan Company, 1937.

Del Vecchio, Giorgio: The Formal Bases of Law, New York, The MacMillan Company, 1921.

Dickerson, Oliver Morton: American Colonial Government, Cleveland, Ohio. The Arthur H. Clark Company, 1912.

Dimock, Marshall E.: The Meaning and Scope of Public Administration, in John M. Gaus, Leonard D. White and Marshall E. Dimock: The Frontiers of Public Administration, The University of Chicago Press, Chicago, 1936.

Dunbar, Louise B.: A Study of Monarchical Tendencies in the United States from 1776-1801, Illinois Studies in the Social Sciences, Urbana, University of Illinois Press, 1922.

Dunlop, R.: Ireland From the Plantation of Ulster to the Cromwellian Settlement, 1611-59, in Cambridge Modern History, New York, The MacMillan Company, 1934, Vol. V, pp. 536-537.

Dunning, William Archibald: A History of Political Theories from Luther to Montesquieu. New York, The MacMillan Company, 1938.

Edward, Earl of Clarendon: The History of the Rebellion and Civil Wars in England. Edited by W. Dunn Macray. Six volumes, Oxford, At the Clarendon Press, MDCCCLXXXVIII.

Edwards, Thomas: The Third Part of Gangraena, or, A New and Higher Discovery of the Errors . . . of the Sectaries. London. Printed for R. Smith, 1646.

Ellis, Havelock: Studies in the Psychology of Sex. Six volumes. F. A. Davis Company, Philadelphia, 1926-1927.

Figgis, J. N.: Studies in Political Thought from Gerson to Grotius, 1414-1625. Second edition, Cambridge University Press, 1916.

Fish, Carl Russell: The Civil Service and the Patronage, New York, Longmans, Green, 1905.

Ford, Henry Jones: The Rise and Growth of American Politics. The MacMillan Company, 1911.

Fortesque, Sir John William: A History of the British Army, 13 vols., London, MacMillan and Company, 1899-1930.

Frank, Jerome: A Sketch of An Influence, in Paul Sayre, Editor: Interpretation of Modern Legal Philosophers, New York, Oxford University Press, 1947.

Freud, Sigmund: Totem and Taboo. Translated by A. A. Brill. New York, New Republic, Inc., 1927.

Gairdner, James: Lollardy and the Reformation in England. Four volumes. London. MacMillan and Company, 1908-1913.

Gardiner, Samuel Rawson: A History of the Great Civil War. Four vols., London, Longmans, Green, 1888-1901.

Gardiner, Samuel Rawson: The First Two Stuarts and the Puritan Revolution, 1603-1660, Second edition, London, Longmans, Green, 1877.

Gaus, John M., White, Leonard D., and Dimock, Marshall E.: The Frontiers of Public Administration. The University of Chicago Press, 1936.

German, Christopher Saint: The Doctor and Student, or Dialogues Between a Doctor of Divinity and a Student in the Laws of England ... Revised and corrected by William Muchall, Gent., Cincinnati, Robert Clarke & Co., 1874.

Giesecke, Albert Anthony: American Commercial Legislation Before 1789. University of Pennsylvania, D. Appleton and Company, New York, 1910.

Grigsby, Hugh Blair: The History of the Virginia Federal Convention of 1788 . . . Edited by R. A. Brock, Two vols., Virginia Historical Society, Richmond, Virginia, MDCCCXC-MDCCCXCI.

Griswold, Rufus Wilmot: The Republican Court, or American Society in the Days of Washington, New York, D. Appleton and Company, 1867.

Hall, Thomas Cuming: The Religious Background of American Culture, Boston, Little Brown and Company, 1930.

Harding, Samuel Bannister: The Contest Over the Ratification of the Federal Constitution in the State of Massachusetts, New York, Longmans, Green, 1896.

Harding, Samuel B.: Party Struggles Over the First Pennsylvania Constitution, in Annual Report of the American Historical Association for the Year 1894, Washington, Government Printing Office, 1895.

Harlow, Ralph: The History of Legislative Methods in the Period Before 1825, New Haven, Yale University Press, 1917.

Hatch, Louis Clinton: The Administration of the American Revolutionary Army, New York, Longmans, Green, 1904.

Hayden, J. Ralston: The Senate and Treaties, 1789-1817, The MacMillan Company, New York, 1920.

Hazen, Charles Downer: Contemporary American Opinion of the French Revolution, Baltimore, Johns Hopkins Press, 1897.

Hearnshaw, F. J. C., Editor: The Social and Political Ideas of Some Great Mediaeval Thinkers, George G. Harrap, London, 1921.

Hearnshaw, F. J. C., Editor: The Social and Political Ideas of Some Great Thinkers of the Sixteenth and Seventeenth Centuries. George G. Harrap, London, 1926.

Hockett, Homer C.: The Constitutional History of the United States, 1776-1826. Two vols., The MacMillan Company, 1939.

Holdsworth, W. S.: A History of English Law. Third edition. Twelve volumes, Methuen & Co., London, 1922-1938.

Hutchinson, Thomas: History of Massachusetts Bay, 3 vols., Thomas and John Fleet, Boston, 1764.

Innis, Harold A.: The Cod Fisheries—The History of An International Economy, New Haven, Yale University Press, 1940.

Jameson, J. Franklin: The American Revolution Considered as a Social Movement. Princeton University Press, 1940.

Jameson, J. Franklin, Editor: Essays in the Constitutional History of the United States in the Formative Period, 1775-1789, Boston and New York, Houghton Mifflin and Company, 1889.

Jensen, Merrill: The Articles of Confederation, Madison, Wisconsin, The University of Wisconsin Press, 1940.

Johnson, Amanda: Georgia as Colony and State. Walter W. Brown Publishing Company, Atlanta, Georgia, 1938.

Jolliffe, J. E. A.: The Constitutional History of Mediaeval England, London, A. & C. Beach, 1937.

Keith, A. Berriedale: Constitutional History of the First British Empire, Oxford, The Clarendon Press, 1930.

Keith, Arthur Berriedale: The Dominions as Sovereign States, London. MacMillan and Co., 1938.

Kellogg, Louise P.: The American Colonial Charter—A Study of English Administration in Relation Thereto, Chiefly After 1688, in Annual Report of the American Historical Association for the Year 1903. In two volumes, Washington, Government Printing Office, 1904.

Labaree, Leonard Woods: Royal Government in America, New Haven, Yale University Press, 1930.

Lamprecht, Sterling Power: The Moral and Political Philosophy of John Locke, New York, Columbia University Press, 1918.

Lapsley, Gaillard Thomas: The County Palatine of Durham, A Study in Constitutional History. Harvard Historical Studies, Vol. VIII, Longmans, Green and Company, New York, 1900.

Larkin, Paschal: Property in the Eighteenth Century with Special Reference to England and Locke, Longmans, Green, London, 1930.

Laski, Harold: The Foundations of Sovereignty, New York, Harcourt, Brace & Company, 1921.

Learned, Henry B.: The President's Cabinet, New Haven, Yale University Press, 1912.

Lee, Henry: Memoirs of the War in the Southern Department of the United States, New York, University Publishing Company, 1869.

[Lee, Richard Henry]: Observations leading to a fair examination of the system of government proposed by the late Convention; and to several essential and necessary alterations in it. In a number of Letters from the Federal Farmer to the Republican. New York [Printed by Thomas Greenleaf] in the year MDCCLXXXVII.

Libby, Orin Grant: The Geographical Distribution of the Vote of the Thirteen States on the Federal Convention, 1787. Madison, Wisconsin, 1894.

Lincoln, Charles H.: The Revolutionary Movement in Pennsylvania, Philadelphia, University of Pennsylvania, 1901.

Lovejoy, Arthur O.: The Great Chain of Being, Cambridge, Mass., Harvard University Press, 1936.

Lucas, Sir Charles P.: The Beginnings of Overseas Enterprise, Oxford, Clarendon Press, 1917.

MacIver, R. M.: European Doctrines and the Constitution, in M. Conyers Read, Editor: The Constitution Reconsidered, New York, The Columbia University Press, 1938.

Maine, Sir Sumner: Ancient Law. Fourth American Edition, New York, Henry Holt, 1906.

Mathews, John Maybry: The Conduct of American Foreign Relations, The Century Company, New York, 1922.

McIlwain, C. H.: The High Court of Parliament and Its Supremacy, New Haven, Yale University Press, 1911.

McKechnie, W. S.: A Commentary on the Great Charter of King John, Glasgow, Scotland, James MacLehose and Sons, 1914.

McKinley, A. E.: The Suffrage Franchise in the Nineteen English Colonies in America, Ginn and Company, Philadelphia, 1905.

McLaughlin, Andrew C.: The Foundations of American Constitutionalism, New York University Press, New York, 1932.

McLaughlin, A. C.: The Western Posts and the British Debts, in Annual Report of the American Historical Association, 1894, Washington, Government Printing Office, 1895, No. 7, pp. 413-444.

McMaster, John Bach and Stone, Frederick D.: Pennsylvania and the Federal Constitution, Historical Society of Pennsylvania, Lancaster, Pa., 1888.

Merriam, Charles E.: A History of American Political Theories, New York, The MacMillan Company, 1906.

Miller, John C.: Origins of the American Revolution, Little Brown and Company, Boston, 1943.

Morris, Richard B.: Government and Labor in Early America, Columbia University Press, New York, 1946.

Mott, Rodney L.: Due Process of Law, Indianapolis, The Bobbs-Merrill Company, 1926.

Mullahy, Patrick: Oedipus Myth and Complex, Hermitage Press, New York, 1948.

Needham, Joseph: Human Law and the Laws of Nature in China and the West, L. T. Hobhose Memorial Trust Lecture, No. 20, Geoffrey Cumberlege, Oxford University Press, London, 1951.

Nef, John U.: English and French Industrial History After 1540 in Relation to the Constitution, in M. Conyers Read: The Constitution Reconsidered, Columbia University Press, 1938.

Nevins, Allen: The American States During and After the Revolution, 1775-1789, New York, The MacMillan Company, 1924.

Osgood, Herbert L.: The American Colonies in the Seventeenth Century, Two vols., Columbia University Press, 1930.

Osgood, Herbert L.: The American Colonies in the 18th Century, Four volumes, New York, The Columbia University Press, 1924.

Otis, James: The Rights of the British Colonies Asserted and Proved, Boston, Edes and Gill, 1764.

Pargellis, Stanley: The Theory of Balanced Government, in Read: The Constitution Reconsidered, Columbia University Press, New York, 1938.

Perry, Ralph Barton: Puritanism and Democracy, New York, The Vanguard Press, 1944.

Phillips, Ulrich B.: Georgia and State Rights—A Study of the Political History of Georgia from the Revolution to the Civil War, with Particular Regard to Federal Relations, in Annual Report of the American Historical Association for the Year 1901. In two vols., Washington, Government Printing Office, 1902.

Porter, Kirk H.: A History of the Suffrage in the United States, The University of Chicago Press, Chicago, 1918.

Pound, Roscoe: Interpretations of Legal History, Cambridge University Press, Cambridge, England, 1930.

Pound, Roscoe: Organization of Courts, Boston, Little Brown and Company, 1940.

Read, M. Conyers, Editor: The Constitution Reconsidered. Columbia University Press, New York, 1938.

Reddaway, W. F.: Rivalry for Colonial Power, 1660-1713, in The Cambridge History of the British Empire, eight volumes, Cambridge. At the University Press, 1929-1936. Vol. I, Chap. X, pp. 300-329.

Rees, J. F.: Mercantilism and the Colonies, in Cambridge History of the British Empire. Eight volumes, Cambridge. At the University Press, 1929-1936, Vol. I, Chap. XVIII, pp. 507-560.

Rich, Bennett Milton: The Presidents and Civil Disorder, Washington, D. C. The Brookings Institution, 1941.

Robertson, H. M.: Aspects of the Rise of Economic Individualism—A Criticism of Max Weber and His School, Cambridge University Press, Cambridge, England, 1922.

Robinson, Henry: Certain proposalls in order to the peoples freedome and accomodation in some particulars. With the advancement of trade and navigation of this commonwealth in generall . . . London. Printed by M. Simmons, 1652.

Rogers, James E. Thorold: The First Nine Years of the Bank of England, Oxford, Clarendon Press, 1887.

Rogers, Lindsay: The American Senate, New York, Alfred Knopf, 1926.

Rose, J. Holland: Sea Power and Expansion, 1660-1763, in Cambridge History of the British Empire. Eight volumes, Cambridge. At the University Press, 1929-1936, Vol. I, Chapter XVIII, pp. 507-537.

Russell, E. B.: The Review of Colonial Legislation by the King in Council, in Columbia University Studies in History, Economics and Public Law, Vol. LXIV, No. 2, New York, 1915.

Salvemini, Gaetano: The Concepts of Democracy and Liberty in the Eighteenth Century, in M. Conyers Read: The Constitution Reconsidered, Columbia University Press, New York, 1938.

Schaper, William A.: Sectionalism in South Carolina, in Annual Report of the American Historical Association for the Year 1900. Two vols., Washington, Government Printing Office, 1901.

Schuyler, Robert L.: Parliament and the British Empire, Columbia University Press, New York, 1929.

Smith, T. V.: The American Philosophy of Equality. University of Chicago Press, 1927.

Strong, Frank: A Forgotten Danger to the New England Colonies, in American Historical Association Reports, 1898. Washington, Government Printing Office, 1899, pp. 77-94.

Sullivan, James: The Antecedents of the Declaration of Independence, in Annual Report of the American Historical Association for the

Year 1902. In two volumes, Washington, Government Printing Office, 1903, Vol. I, pp. 67-81.

Sweet, William Warren: Religion in Colonial America, Charles Scribner's Sons, New York, 1942.

Turner, Frederick J.: The Frontier in American History, Henry Holt and Company, New York, 1928.

Turner, Frederick Jackson: The Significance of Sections in American History, New York, Henry Holt, 1932.

Tyler, Moses Coit: The Literary History of the American Revolution, Two vols., G. P. Putnam's Sons, New York, 1897.

Van Doren, Carl: Secret History of the American Revolution. Garden City Publishing Company, Garden City, New York, 1941.

Van Tyne, Claude H.: The Causes of the War of Independence, Houghton Mifflin Company, Boston and New York, 1922.

Von Ranke, Leopold: A History of England Principally in the Seventeenth Century. Six volumes. Oxford. At the Clarendon Press, 1875.

Warren, Charles: A History of the American Bar, Boston, Little Brown and Company, 1911.

Warren, Charles: The Making of the Constitution, Little Brown and Company, Boston, 1928.

Warren, Charles: The Supreme Court in United States History, revised edition, 2 vols., Little Brown and Company, Boston, 1935.

Warren, Mrs. Mercy: History of the Rise, Progress and Termination of the American Revolution, Three volumes, E. Larkin, Boston, 1805.

Washburne, George A.: Imperial Control of the Administration of Justice in the Thirteen American Colonies, 1684-1776. Columbia University Press, New York, 1923.

Whitaker, Arthur Preston: The Spanish-American Frontier, 1783-1795, Houghton Mifflin Company, Boston and New York, 1927.

White, Leonard D.: The Federalists—A Study in Administrative History, The MacMillan Company, New York, 1948.

White, Leonard D.: The Jeffersonians—A Study in Administrative History, 1801-1928, The MacMillan Company, 1951.

Willis, Hugh Evander: Introduction to Anglo-American Law, in Indiana University Studies, Bloomington, Indiana, No. XIII, 1926.

Willoughby, W. F.: Principles of Judicial Administration, The Brookings Institution, Washington, 1929.

Winsor, Justin: The Memorial History of Boston, Four vols., Ticknor and Company, Boston, 1881.

Winthrop, John: History of New England, 1630-1649, edited by James Kendall Hosmer, Two vols., Charles Scribner's Sons, New York, 1908.

Wise, John: A Vindication of the Government of the New England Churches, Printed by J. Allen for N. Boone, Boston, 1717.

VI. SPECIAL ARTICLES, MAGAZINES, PERIODICALS

Anderson, Frank M.: Contemporary Opinion of the Kentucky and Virginia Resolutions, in American Historical Review, Vol. V, October, 1899, No. 1, pp. 45-63, Vol. V, December, 1899, No. 2, pp. 225-252.

Andrews, Charles M.: Colonial Commerce, in American Historical Review, Vol. XX, No. 1, October, 1914, pp. 43-63.

Andrews, Charles M.: The Royal Disallowance, in Proceedings American Antiquarian Society, April, 1914-October, 1914, Worcester Massachusetts. Published by the Society, New Series, Vol. XXIV, 1914.

Beard, Charles A.: Some Economic Origins of Jeffersonian Democracy, in American Historical Review, Vol. XIX, January, 1914, No. 2, pp. 282-298.

Boudin, Louis B.: The Anarchic Element in the Notion of a Higher Law, in New York University Law Quarterly Review, Vol. VIII, Number 1, September, 1930, pp. 1-40.

Caldwell, Robert Granville: The Settlement of Inter-State Disputes, in American Journal of International Law, Vol. 14, 1920, pp. 38-69.

Carpenter, William Seal: The Separation of Powers in the Eighteenth Century, in American Political Science Review, February, 1928, Vol. XXII, pp. 32-44.

Corwin, Edward S.: The "Higher Law" Background of American Constitutional Law, in Harvard Law Review, Vol. XLII, No. 2, December, 1928, pp. 149-185; Vol. XLII, No. 3, January, 1929, pp. 365-409.

Corwin, Edward S.: The Progress of Constitutional Theory Between the Declaration of Independence and the Meeting of the Philadelphia Convention, in American Historical Review, Vol. XXX, No. 3, April, 1925, pp. 511-536.

Crouse, Nellis M.: Causes of the Great Migration, 1630-1640, in New England Quarterly, Vol. V, January, 1932, pp. 3-36.

Downes, Randolph C.: Creek-American Relations, 1782-1790, in The Georgia Historical Quarterly. Published by the Georgia Historical Society, Vol. XXI, No. 2, June, 1937, pp. 142-184.

Dunbar, Charles F.: Some Precedents Followed by Alexander Hamilton, in The Quarterly Journal of Economics, Vol. III, October, 1888, pp. 32-59.

Dwight, T. W.: Harrington and His Influence Upon American Political Institutions and Political Thought, in Political Science Quarterly, Vol. II, 1887, pp. 1-44.

Farrand, Max: Compromises of the Constitution, in American Historical Review, Vol. IX, Number 3, April, 1904, pp. 479-489.

Farrand, Max: The First Hayburn Case, in American Historical Review, Vol. XIII, Number 2, January, 1908, pp. 281-285.

Foster, H. D.: International Calvinism through Locke and the Revolution of 1688, in American Historical Review, Vol. XXXII, April, 1927, pp. 475-499.

Hazeltine, H. D.: The Influence of Magna Carta on American Constitutional Development, in Columbia Law Review, Vol. XVII, No. 1, January, 1917.

Jameson, J. F.: Early Political Uses of the Word "Convention", in American Antiquarian Society Proceedings, Worcester, Massachusetts. Published by the Society, 1899. New Series, Vol. XII, pp. 183-196.

Kelsey, Rayner: The Originator of the Federal Idea, in The Nation, Vol. XCIV, June 6, 1912, pp. 562-563.

Kenyon, Cecelia M.: Where Paine Went Wrong, in American Political Science Review, Vol. XLV, December, 1951.

Krauel, Richard: Prince Henry of Prussia and the Regency of the United States, 1786, in American Historical Review, Vol. XVII, October, 1911, No. 1, pp. 44-51.

Mathews, Lois K.: Benjamin Franklin's Plan for a Colonial Union, 1750-1775, in American Political Science Review, Vol. VIII, pp. 393-412, August, 1914.

McClendon, R. Earl: Origin of the two-thirds rule in the Senate Action Upon Treaties, in American Historical Review, Vol. XXXVI, July, 1931, pp. 768-772.

McLaughlin, Andrew C.: The Background of American Federalism, in American Political Science Review, Vol. XII, May, 1918, pp. 215-240.

Mullins, Claud: The Law and Poor Persons, in The Quarterly Review, No. 563, London, January, 1945.

Palmer, R. R.: Tom Paine: Victim of the Rights of Man, in the Pennsylvania Magazine of History and Biography, April, 1942, Vol. LXVI, Number 2, pp. 161-175.

Plucknett, Theodore F. T.: Bonham's Case and Judicial Review, in Harvard Law Review, Vol. XL, 1926-1927, pp. 30-70.

Robinson, J. H.: The Original and Derived Features of the Constitution, in Annals of the American Academy of Political and Social Science, October, 1890, Vol. I, pp. 202-243.

Sapir, Edward: Article on Custom, in Encyclopaedia of the Social

Sciences: The MacMillan Company, New York, 1942, Vols. III-IV, pp. 659-662.

Schechter, Frank I.: The Early History of the Tradition of the Constitution, in American Political Science Review, Vol. IX, November, 1915, pp. 707-734.

Schlesinger, A. M.: Colonial Appeals to the Privy Council, in Political Science Quarterly, Vol. XXVIII, September, 1913, pp. 433-450.

Scott, Austin: Holmes vs. Walton: The New Jersey Precedent, in American Historical Review, Vol. IV, No. 3, April, 1899, pp. 456-469.

Sparling, H. Halliday: John Lilburne as a Pamphleteer, in The Bookworm, Vol. six, New York, A. C. Armstrong and Son, and London, Elliot Stock, n.d. pp. 315-318.

Turner, Frederick J.: Social Forces in American History, in American Historical Review, Vol. XVI, Number 2, January, 1911, pp. 217-233.

Van Tyne, C. H.: The Influence of the Clergy and of Religious and Sectarian Forces on the American Revolution, in American Historical Review, Vol. XLX, Number 1, October, 1913, pp. 48-52.

VII. GENERAL AND MISCELLANEOUS WORKS

Acton, John Emerich Edward: Lectures on Modern History, MacMillan Company, London, 1912.

Bailey, Thomas A.: A Diplomatic History of The American People, Third edition, F. S. Crofts & Company, New York, 1946.

Batchelder, Samuel F.: Bits of Harvard History. Cambridge. Harvard University Press, 1924.

Beard, Charles A. and Beard, Mary R.: The Rise of American Civilization. One volume edition, The MacMillan Company, New York, 1930.

Bemis, Samuel Flagg: A Diplomatic History of the United States, Henry Holt, New York, 1942.

Binkley, Wilfred E. and Moos, Malcolm C.: A Grammar of American Politics, Alfred A. Knopf, New York, 1949.

Blackstone, Sir William: Commentaries on the Laws of England, edited by Thomas Cooley. Second edition. Two volumes, Callaghan and Company, Chicago, 1872.

Blackstone, Sir William: Commentaries on the Laws of England. Two volumes, J. B. Lippincott Company, Philadelphia, 1893.

Bowers, Claude G.: Jefferson and Hamilton—The Struggle for Democracy in America, Houghton Mifflin Company, Boston and New York, 1926.

Bryce, James: The American Commonwealth. Two volumes, The MacMillan Company, New York, 1910.

Burdett, Everett W.: History of the Old South Meeting House, B. B. Russell, Boston, 1877.

Burgess, John William: Political Science and Comparative Constitutional Law, Two volumes, Ginn & Company, Boston, 1890.

Cambridge History of the British Empire. Eight volumes. At the University Press, Cambridge, 1929-1936.

Carlyle, A. J.: Political Liberty, Oxford, 1941.

Carpenter, William Seal: The Development of American Political Thought, Princeton University Press, 1930.

Catlin, George: The Story of the Political Philosophers, Whittlesey House, New York, 1939.

Channing, Edward: A History of the United States, 6 volumes, New York, The Macmillan Company, 1921-1926.

De Warville, J. P. Brussot: New Travels in the United States of America Performed in 1788. Berry and Rogers, New York, 1792.

Dugdale, Sir William: History of St. Paul's Cathedral, continued by Henry Ellis, Longmans, London, 1818.

Dunning, William Archibald: A History of Political Theories—Ancient and Modern, The MacMillan Company, New York, 1935.

Flick, Alexander C., Editor: History of the State of New York, Ten volumes. Columbia University Press, New York, 1933-1937.

Friedrich, Carl J.: Constitutional Government and Democracy, Little Brown and Company, Boston, 1941.

Gettell, Raymond G.: History of American Political Thought, The Century Company, New York, 1928.

Harrington, James: The Commonwealth of Oceana With an Introduction by Henry Morley, George Routledge and Sons, London, 1887.

Hogarth, David George: Accidents of An Antiquary's Life, MacMillan & Company, London, 1910.

Hooker, Richard: Of the Lawes of Ecclesiastical Politie. Printed by William Standbye, London, 1638-39.

Jacobson, J. Mark: The Development of American Political Thought—A Documentary History, D. Appleton-Century Company, New York, 1932.

James, William: Psychology. Henry Holt and Company, New York, 1915.

Keir, D. L.: The Constitutional History of Modern England, A. and C. Black, 1938.

Locke, John: Two Treatises of Government. Printed for Awansham and John Churchill, London, 1698.

Locke, John: Two Treatises of Government. Seventh edition, J. Whiston, W. Strahan [etc.], London, 1772.

Lodge, Richard: The History of England from the Restoration to the Death of William III (1660-1702), Longmans, Green, London, 1919.

Lossing, Benson J.: The American Revolution and the War of 1812. Three volumes, New York Book Concern, New York, 1875.

McMaster, John Bach: History of the People of the United States, from the Revolution to the Civil War, Five volumes, D. Appleton & Company, New York, 1885.

Miller, John C.: Triumph of Freedom, 1775-1783, Little Brown and Company, Boston, 1948.

Milman, Henry Hart: Annals of St. Paul's Cathedral, John Murray, London, 1868.

Milton, John: The Tenure of Kings and Magistrates. Printed by M. Simmons, London, 1649.

Milton, John: Doctrine and Discipline of Divorce. Printed by T. P. and M. S. London, 1643.

Montaigne: Essays. Translated by Charles Cotton. Edited by William Carew Hazlitt. Five volumes. Privately printed for the Navarre Society. London, 1923.

Mumford, Lewis: The Golden Day, Boni and Liveright, New York, 1926.

Munro, William Bennett: The Governments of Europe. Third edition. The MacMillan Company, New York, 1939.

Nettels, Curtis P.: The Roots of American Civilization—A History of American Colonial Life. F. S. Crofts and Company, New York, 1938.

Nietzsche, Friedrich Wilhelm: Human, All too Human. In two parts. Translated by Helen Zimmern. T. N. Foulis. Edinburgh and London, 1910.

Pater, Walter: Plato and Platonism. MacMillan and Company, London, 1922.

Plato, The Dialogues of. Translated by B. Jowett. Five volumes, Second edition. Oxford. The Clarendon Press, 1875.

Pollock, Sir Frederick and Maitland, Frederick W.: History of English Law. Two volumes. Second edition, Cambridge University Press, Cambridge, England, 1923.

Savelle, Max: Seeds of Liberty—The Genesis of the American Mind. Alfred Knopf, New York, 1948.

Sidney, Algernon: Discourses Concerning Government. Printed by the Booksellers of London and Westminster, London, 1698.

Sinclair, William MacDonald: Memorials of St. Paul's Cathedral, George W. Jacobs & Company, Philadelphia, n.d.

Smith, J. Allen:: The Spirit of American Government, The MacMillan Company, New York, 1907.

Stephen, Sir Leslie: History of English Thought in the Eighteenth Century. Two volumes. G. P. Putnam's Sons, New York, 1927.

Swisher, Carl Brent: American Constitutional Development, Houghton Mifflin, Boston, 1943.

Tawney, Richard Henry: The Sickness of An Acquisitive Society, Fabian Society, Westminster, 1920.

Thornbury, Walter and Walford, Edward: Old and New London. Six volumes, Cassel, Petter and Galpin, London, n.d.

Walford, Edward: Greater London. Two volumes, Cassell & Company, London, n.d.

White, Leonard D.: Introduction to the Study of Public Administration, The MacMillan Company, New York, 1939.

Willoughby, Westel Woodbury: The Constitutional Law of the United States, Three volumes, Baker, Voorhis and Company, New York, 1929.

Wisner, Benjamin B.: The History of the Old South Church in Boston . . . Crocker & Brewster, Boston, 1830.

INDEX

INDEX

INDEX

Abuse of political power, 128, 129-130

Acquisitive drives, 126, 127, 128, 135, 137-138

Acquisitive society, 124

Acton, Lord, 129

Adams, Henry, 124

Adams, John, 3, 10, 30, 32, 34, 36, 41, 44, 71, 72, 84, 100, 103, 114, 116, 131, 135

Adams, John Quincy, 122

Adams, Samuel, 40, 43

"Address to the People of Great Britain", 46

Admission of new states, 89

Africa, 24

African negroes, 135

Age of chivalry, 138

"Age of reason", 126

Agrarians, 68, 80, 82, 94, 96, 105, 107-108, 109, 110, 111, 117, 123, 129-130, 131, 136

Agricultural laborers, 130

Albany plan of union, 22, 77, 85

Alien and Sedition Acts of 1798, 110, 123

Alleghenies, The, 30, 61, 66, 78, 101, 122

American administrative functions, 111

American administrative tradition, 24-32

American admiralty courts, 64, 70

American anti-Jacobins, 123

American Attorney General, 112

American bankers, 68

American bill of rights, 17, 40, 55, 58-59, 69, 98-101, 106, 110

American cabinet, 20, 103, 112

American central powers, 70

American Civil War, 13, 23, 31, 107, 138, 140

American clergy, 135

American colonial charter, 19

American colonial frontier, 4, 27

American colonial governors, 13, 25, 89-90, 112, 117

American colonial legislatures, 58

American colonial-state system, 29

American Commissioners of Appeals in Admiralty, 64

American Congress, 14-15, 23, 29, 89, 90, 95, 111, 115, 116-118, 119-120

American constitutional consciousness, 121

American counter revolution, 82

American country gentry, 80

American Court of Appeals in Cases of Capture, 64

American creditors, 123

American debtors, 96-97, 123

American democratic societies, 122

American democratic theory, 7

American department heads, 111

American doctrine of popular sovereignty, 14

American election of 1800, 116, 131, 139

American electoral college, 86

American electorate, 121-123

American environment, 35, 42

American Episcopal church, 56

American executive power, 20, 21, 89-90, 103, 111, 115, 118-119

American federal courts, 21

American federalism, 21-22, 69, 77, 83-86

American Federalists, The, 30, 31, 92-101, 103, 105, 106, 107, 109, 115-116, 123, 131, 135-136

233